BLOODLINES

ALSO BY VAMIK VOLKAN

Richard Nixon: A Psychobiography (with Norman Itzkowitz and Andrew Dod)

Siblings in the Unconscious and Psychopathology (with Gabriele Ast)

The Infantile Psychotic Self and Its Fates: Understanding and Treating Schizophrenics and Other Difficult Patients

Turks and Greeks: Neighbours in Conflict (with Norman Itzkowitz)

Life after Loss: The Lessons of Grief (with Elizabeth Zintl)

The Need to Have Enemies and Allies: From Clinical Practice to International Relationships

Six Steps in the Treatment of Borderline Personality Organization

The Immortal Atatürk: A Psychobiography (with Norman Itzkowitz)

What Do You Get When You Cross a Dandelion with a Rose? The True Story of Psychoanalysis

Linking Objects and Linking Phenomena

Cyprus—War and Adaptation: A Psychoanalytic History of Two Ethnic Groups in Conflict

Primitive Internalized Object Relations: A Clinical Study of Schizophrenic, Borderline, and Narcissistic Patients

EDITED BY VAMIK VOLKAN

The Seed of Madness (with Salman Akhtar)

Depressive States and Their Treatment

The Psychodynamics of International Relationships, Vols. I and II (with Joseph Montville and Demetrios Julius)

BLOOD

FROM ETHNIC PRIDE TO ETHNIC TERRORISM

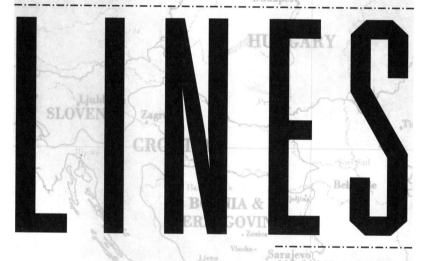

LINES

VAMIK VOLKAN

FARRAR, STRAUS AND GIROUX / NEW YORK

Farrar, Straus and Giroux
19 Union Square West, New York 10003

Copyright © 1997 by Vamık Volkan
All rights reserved
Distributed in Canada by Douglas & McIntyre Ltd.
Printed in the United States of America
Designed by Abby Kagan
First edition, 1997

LIBRARY OF CONGRESS CATALOGING-IN-PUBLICATION DATA
Volkan, Vamik D., 1932–
    Bloodlines : from ethnic pride to ethnic terrorism / Vamik Volkan.
        p.   cm.
    Includes bibliographical references and index.
    ISBN 0-374-11447-1 (alk. paper)
    1. Ethnicity.   2. Ethnic relations.   3. Psychoanalysis.   4. War.
    5. International relations and culture.   I. Title.
GN495.6.V65   1997
305.8—dc21   97-17747

TO STANLEY L. OLINICK, M.D.,

*who taught me how to listen to myself
and to others*

CONTENTS

BLOODLINES

Preface

DEADLY DISTINCTIONS:
THE RISE OF ETHNIC VIOLENCE

The Berlin Wall did not fall. It was disman-
tled, jubilantly, piece by piece, brick by stone, beginning on November 9, 1989. Parts of the wall were taken as souvenirs by those who
were tearing it down—some appeared in Western stores as mementos
of a presumably dead cold war. Other rubble was probably ground
into the dirt, trampled to dust by those who were frenetically tearing
apart this symbol of separation or perhaps later by people who simply
walked that way, day after day, and thought nothing of it.

The wall was not only a physical divider, but also a concrete symbol of a psychological border between Western democracies and the
Soviet-dominated communist world. Just as that wall was not a single,
smooth piece of concrete, but built of many bricks and stones, the
world it represented was in reality an amalgam of many pieces, a
substantial number of individual nations and ethnic groups with histories and heritages all their own.

No matter what happened to the cement of communist ideology
and bureaucratic power that had kept them together for the better part
of the twentieth century, these separate and distinct nations and ethnic
groups would remain intact. The Soviet Union was not, after all, the
first empire to subsume many of these entities and later cease to exist.
Around the world, in previous periods of great change and the dis-

integration of empires, many large groups redefined themselves and their distinctions from others under newly found freedom. Often, such changes were accompanied by much bloodletting.

Unlike the rapid demolition of the Berlin Wall, the dismantling of the Soviet Union was more gradual. First came perestroika and glasnost and increasing evidence of the waning of communism as a legitimate governmental force in Eastern Europe. A new sense of world peace was perceived; the Evil Empire was fading into cold war history.

The cover of the April 1990 issue of the Soviet political humor magazine *Krokodyl* (Crocodile) carried a cartoon remarkable in Soviet history. In it a man wearing a low-brimmed hat and an overcoat with the collar turned up to hide his face was warily attempting to write "Long live the Communist Party" on a wall in the middle of the night. Only a few years before this cartoon was published, anyone perusing *Krokodyl* would have seen drawings of fearsome American eagles devouring helpless populations—communist propaganda masquerading as humor.

Other signs of change were evident. On Arbat Street in Moscow, artists displayed paintings of well-known landscapes and buildings alongside paintings that made political statements. One showed President Mikhail Gorbachev attempting to dock a broken-down Soviet vessel. Another showed a toilet bowl afloat and aimlessly drifting in the sea, with the Soviet flag for a sail. One huge oil painting depicting the Stalin era showed chained men and mountains of skulls under the shadow of the dictator. There were also poets on Arbat Street reading verses on freedom and orators on street corners giving political speeches. Such activities in Moscow made Arbat Street seem like Moscow's version of Hyde Park, where freedom of speech was exemplified by soapbox orators voicing their beliefs to anyone who cared to listen.

Alongside these tangible, positive results of glasnost and perestroika, there were in Moscow in 1990 negative and uncertain ramifications of social change. There were palpable signs of economic collapse and whispers of *smuta,* or Smutnoye Vremya, a reference to the period between 1584 and 1613 when there was chaos and violence in Russia due to a vacuum of power.[1] There were grave concerns about the efficacy of the military and skepticism about the future of the

Soviet empire. The most frightening controversy involved mushrooming issues of independence for various Soviet republics and accompanying ethnonationalistic sentiments. These sentiments were evident in surprising contexts.

For example, after the massive earthquake in Soviet Armenia in 1988, the Soviets collected blood for Armenian victims. Blood was also collected from Armenia's neighbors, the Azerbaijanis, but the Armenians refused to accept it, even as casualties rose to more than twenty-five thousand. The long-standing enmity between Armenia and Azerbaijan had been mostly suppressed during the Soviet period, as had other tensions in Transcaucasia. After Gorbachev introduced perestroika and glasnost, however, fighting erupted between Armenians and Azerbaijanis in the autonomous region of Nagorno-Karabakh, a disputed territory of forty-four hundred square kilometers within Azerbaijan whose population of 188,000 was 88 percent Armenian.[2] By the time of the earthquake, tensions had risen to the point where Armenians would rather physically suffer or even die than accept Azerbaijani blood into their veins. Receiving Azerbaijani blood was a symbolic contamination of the Armenian identity.

The Soviets wanted to understand why the brotherly love of communism was not enough to keep Armenians and Azerbaijanis together. Why had the Soviet Man never truly materialized? Despite the Russification of the Soviet system, why had ethnic groups remained so distinct and separate that the idea of sharing blood was unthinkable? What did the blood represent? Was there a psychological explanation for the Armenians' refusal of life-giving blood? And if so, were psychological issues involved in the ethnic conflicts as well?

In order to answer such questions, Soviet leadership turned to psychologists. For decades, however, Soviet psychologists had been practically told what to study, and their thinking had been confined to prescribed areas. These new questions fell outside the boundaries of their centrally dictated training, making it difficult for them to analyze the "bloodlines" of ethnicity that made Armenians refuse Azerbaijani blood.

Meanwhile, the University of Virginia's Center for the Study of Mind and Human Interaction (CSMHI), an interdisciplinary think tank that I founded in 1987 and have directed since then, had signed

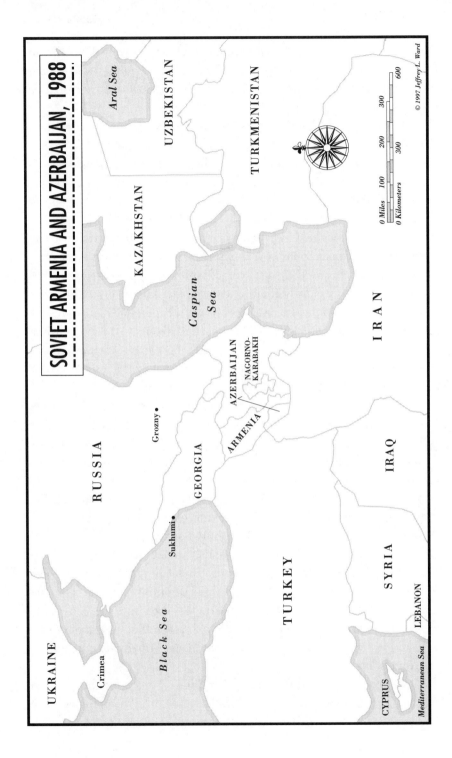

SOVIET ARMENIA AND AZERBAIJAN, 1988

UKRAINE

Crimea

Black Sea

Sukhumi•

Grozny•

RUSSIA

GEORGIA

ARMENIA

AZERBAIJAN

NAGORNO-
KARABAKH

Caspian
Sea

KAZAKHSTAN

Aral Sea

UZBEKISTAN

TURKMENISTAN

TURKEY

ARMENIA

IRAN

CYPRUS

LEBANON

SYRIA

IRAQ

Mediterranean Sea

0 Miles   100   200   300   600
0 Kilometers   300   300

© 1997 Jeffrey L. Ward

a contract with the Soviet government in 1989. This allowed us to work with Soviet psychologists and political scientists to study the nature of the Soviet-American relationship as well as the influence of glasnost and perestroika on this relationship. CSMHI faculty comprises psychoanalysts, former diplomats, historians, and other social scientists. When a group of us visited Moscow in April 1990, we were confronted with the Soviets' preoccupation with ethnic issues, such as the conflict between Armenians and Azerbaijanis. As one Soviet historian at the meeting put it, if the Soviets did not quickly fathom the power of psychologized forces that lay behind ethnic and nationalistic movements, the gigantic power that was the Soviet Union could crumble as easily as a cookie.

His comment proved prophetic. When CSMHI revisited Moscow just a year later, obvious cracks were apparent in the USSR. The Baltic republics had declared their independence, and the Armenian-Azerbaijani conflict had escalated to the point of a state of emergency. In January 1990, seventeen thousand Soviet troops were deployed to Nagorno-Karabakh and along the border between Armenia and Azerbaijan. Ethnic problems were also surfacing elsewhere in the Soviet Union, such as in the Republic of Moldova.

Moldova, with a population of four and a half million, has several ethnic groups: 65 percent are Moldovans; 14 percent are Ukrainians; and 13 percent are Russians. It also has a small minority, numbering fewer than two hundred thousand, of a unique people called Gagauses, who are Christian, but Turkic. As the power of the Soviet Union's center in Moscow was weakened, Moldovans, Ukrainians, Russians, and Gagauses began to experience their identity differences more keenly. In spite of their relatively small numbers, Gagauses wanted autonomy; Moldovans wanted less Russian influence.

Under Gorbachev, the Soviet government considered forcing a peaceful solution for the tensions in Moldova. But negotiating within the Soviet Union was an unfamiliar function in internal affairs, having been the exclusive domain of international politicians, diplomats, and foreign trade officials. In fact, the term *negotiation* was not a common word in Russian (the 1979 *Soviet Encyclopedic Vocabulary*, the most authoritative source on the Russian language, contains no entry for *negotiation*). The Soviet government decided to send a team of negotiators to Moldova, but the negotiators made a tactical error, perhaps because of a lack of familiarity with the issues involved. Bendery, a neutral town, was chosen as the site of negotiations after the Gagauses rejected Kishinev, the capital city, which is dominated by Moldovans. The nearest direct flight from Moscow flew to Kishinev, and the Moscow delegates took it. At the airport they met the Moldovan delegation, and the two groups decided to travel to Bendery together by car. Unfortunately, the Gagaus delegates immediately assumed the Moscow negotiators were not neutral, and the perception compromised their role as mediators. The mediation efforts failed.[3]

There was an acute need for Gorbachev's administration to understand and find solutions to ethnic problems in the Soviet Union. Soviet officials invited me to Moscow in the early summer of 1991 to conduct seminars on ethnic issues and the techniques of negotiation. The invitation came from Oleg Peressypkin, a former Soviet ambassador to Libya and Yemen and then rector of the Diplomatic Academy of the Soviet Foreign Ministry. Soon after I accepted it, the August coup (putsch) took place in the Soviet Union. The coup apparently took no one except Gorbachev by surprise—the army had gone unrebuked for a series of bloody suppressions of hostility, leading Soviets to think that the union was "governed not by constitutional civil bodies, but by the army and other law enforcing bodies."[4] Gorbachev did not rein in the KGB, which essentially had merged with the Communist Party, and in August found himself under house arrest, later to be "saved" by Boris Yeltsin. The downfall of the Soviet empire had finally become a reality.

Three months after the putsch, the political changes in Moscow had left evidence as hard as the collapse of the Berlin Wall. Passing by broken statues of Stalin and Lenin in parks and other public places, I arrived at the Diplomatic Academy, an old, run-down building on Ostozhenka Street near the Moscow River, where Soviet diplomats were trained. The long corridor in front of the rector's office leading to the main conference room had previously contained glass cases displaying pictures and statues of Lenin along with documents exalting the communist way of life. Now these items were gone, except for one lone handmade rug depicting Lenin. Pictures of Gorbachev, Yeltsin, George Bush, François Mitterrand, Margaret Thatcher, and even Dan Quayle had replaced the Soviet heroes and ideological declarations. This dramatic shift in icons gave the impression that a new and different identity for Soviets had been established and adopted; but beneath the surface, issues of identity were not so clear-cut.

Delegates from the Soviet republics, including the Baltics, which had already declared (or reestablished) their independence,[5] as well as General Vladimir Illarionov, Moscow's chief of police, had gathered at the Diplomatic Academy for the four-day workshop. As the meeting got under way, representatives began giving long, prepared speeches filled with statistics about the ethnic composition of their respective republics. While the Azerbaijanis presented their view of the Nagorno-Karabakh conflict, the Armenian representatives listened attentively and protested noisily. Then when a Moldovan official described problems in his republic, the Armenians carried on their own conversation in low voices, ignoring him. The Tartars wanted to stake a claim to the Crimea as their original territory, refuting the claims of Ukrainians and Russians, whom the Tartars considered latecomers.[6] Meanwhile, delegates from the Republic of Georgia, fearing that Abkhazians and South Ossetians in Georgia would wreak havoc in trying to obtain their own sovereignty, sought to downplay ethnic differences within their republic. Abkhazians and South Ossetians rejected this inclusive definition and stressed their identity as separate groups— separate bloodlines that deserved sovereign status.

A fundamental problem had resurfaced. As Norman Itzkowitz, a professor of history at Princeton University, explains: "Nationalism is based on the assumption that the basic cleavage in society is the vertical one that divides people into ethnonational groups. Marxism, on the other hand, says that the basic cleavage in society is the horizontal one of class division which cuts across national lines."[7] During the heyday of communism, there was so much confidence in ideology and the brotherhood of peoples in the Soviet Union that there seemed little harm in including a person's ethnicity or nationality on the internal passports required for travel within the Soviet Union. While one was a Soviet first, one was still classified as a Latvian, Uzbek, Chechen, Ingush, and so on. No one imagined that preserving these secondary distinctions would later come back to haunt the Soviet Union when many of these same groups sought separation.

Armenians, Azerbaijanis, Dagestanis, Kazakhs, Tartars, Lithuanians, and others began to carve vertical cleavages in the Soviet Union. They spoke in terms of Armenian history, Azerbaijani identity, the differentness of Dagestanis, Kazakhs, Tartars, Lithuanians; these were issues of group identity that had long been suppressed under communism. Doubts and anxieties pertaining to the dramatic transformations that had taken place boiled down to one overriding question: Who are we now?

The wars that broke out in some parts of the Soviet Union, such as the one between Armenia and Azerbaijan, escalated to the point of defying the four Geneva Conventions of 1949 and the First Protocol of 1977, which the international war-crime tribunals use to assess the conduct of warfare. In 1993, the International Committee of the Red Cross described the Armenian-Azerbaijani war as follows:

> There has been a complete lack of the knowledge of international humanitarian law among the combatants. The conflict has included violations of the law of war of the most gruesome kind; these have included mass killings of unarmed civilians, hostage-taking, and bargaining in dead bodies, attacks on populated areas where there are no military targets, orders to execute captured prisoners, de facto "ethnic cleansing," and restrictions imposed on the civilian population's freedom of movement to preclude any loss of ground, to name but a few.[8]

When Republic of Georgia troops entered Abkhazia in August 1992 and "captured" its major city, Sukhumi, "a pattern of vicious, ethnically-based pillaging, looting, assault, and murder emerged."[9] In turn, when Abkhazian forces and their allies took Sukhumi in September 1993, they "committed widespread atrocities against the Georgian civilian population, killing many women, children, and elderly, capturing some as hostages and torturing others . . . they also killed large numbers of Georgian civilians who remained in Abkhaz-seized territory."[10] Soldiers on both sides reportedly committed rape. In Tajikistan, fifty thousand people have perished since the collapse of the Soviet Union, and we have all watched on television the violent chaos in Chechnya in which well over thirty thousand people have been killed in Grozny alone.

— · —

Once the cohesion provided by the Soviet Union began to fray, divisiveness emerged and quickly escalated into full-blown conflicts and violence. Turmoil within the USSR spilled over into the communist countries of Eastern Europe. The division of Czechoslovakia into the Czech Republic and Slovakia was rather peaceful, mostly because of the influence of a "velvet underground" dating back to the 1960s and leaders such as Václav Havel. But in the Socialist Federal Republic of Yugoslavia, the situation was different.

In Yugoslavia, the communist system itself had created the legal conditions for the country's collapse. Communist Yugoslavia comprised six republics, two autonomous regions, and several different ethnic groups. Seven years before his death, Marshal Josip Broz Tito, then the head of communist Yugoslavia, developed a constitution that assured no single ethnic group could dominate all of Yugoslavia. Power was to be shared by representatives of the six republics and two autonomous provinces; the country would be governed collectively as the presidency rotated among representatives of the republics. Even though the Serbs held the numerical majority in the former Yugoslavia, under this constitution they would share power with other groups. This collective leadership never really worked. The breakdown of internal structures was accompanied by the emergence of new leaders who, unlike Havel, inflamed ethnonationalistic sentiments and brought on ethnic conflicts of the most vicious kind.

After the horrors of the Holocaust, it was generally thought that systematized atrocities could never again occur in Europe. Yet between the summer of 1991, the beginning of the Serbian-Croatian War, and the winter of 1995, the end of Bosnia's war, concentration camps were erected and mass graves were dug in the heart of Europe, in the former Yugoslavia. The world heard of beatings, forced relocations, mass killings, organized rapes of both women and men, and male prisoners who were forced to bite off the testicles of their fellow inmates. In 1992, at the detention camp Karaterm, near the city of Prijedor, the prisoners were starved: their daily food ration consisted of "a piece of bread and a spoonful of cabbage or beans."[11] The images of these starving, half-naked men with skins like shrouds over protruding bones flashed across television screens around the globe. *Ethnic cleansing* became a familiar term.

Though many of us envisioned a new era of peace and stability, the effects of the breakup of the Soviet Union and the communist world were more similar to the tumultuous periods following the breakup of empires such as the Ottoman Empire after World War I and the British, French, Belgian, and Portuguese colonial empires after World War II. The legacy of those events is still evident today.

— · —

Understanding tribalism, a concept popularized by colonial anthropologists, helps explain this turmoil in Africa. Okwudiba Nnoli, a Nigerian political scientist, writes that in the colonials' minds tribalism occupied an important place in racist ideology: "It was represented as a primitive and barbarous mystique peculiar to the African, the major link between the assumed ahistorical, primitive and barbarous African past in which no system of ethics and no human principle of conduct were developed on the one hand, and the 'civilizing mission' and 'white man's burden' of the colonial order on the other."[12]

The Europeans called every language group in Africa a tribe regardless of the nature of its social development. Nnoli suggests that "what the colonialists referred to as tribalism in Africa is empirically observable elsewhere in the world as ethnicity."[13] Divisions among large groups, whether they were called tribes or ethnic groups, were encouraged and kept alive by the colonial powers who also impressed on the masses the idea that their chiefs were effective leaders—as long as they administered to their people to the satisfaction of the colonial masters. This encouragement of distinction and division among groups, and the creation of a dichotomy between tribes whom the colonial powers considered "backward" and those they judged "advanced," was essentially an effort to divide and conquer, and it helped the colonial system to survive for as long as it did. In general, "backward" groups were economically worse off than "advanced" groups; the dichotomy reflected not only tribal (ethnic) distinctions, but economic and class divisions as well.[14]

Many African groups reached back to their precolonial kinship ties and loyalties in the process of establishing "tribal" identities.[15]

When the colonial powers began to leave Africa, efforts to solve the problem of divisions among ethnic groups, who were often thrown together within in a newly formed state, were largely unsuccessful. Most of these remedies involved what became known as "ethnic arithmetic," "ethnic balancing," or an "ethnic proportionality principle." For example, the Zambian cabinet was carefully balanced in the 1960s to include representation of both the Bemba in the north and the Lozi in the south. Quotas have been used to maintain or restore ethno-regional balance in Burundi, Kenya, and Uganda. The first Nigerian republic (1960–1966) consisted of three main regions. Each region was in turn controlled by a single ethnic majority. When this arrangement failed, many states were created as sub-federal governmental authorities in Nigeria, and attempts were made to use quotas in admissions to schools and appointment of public officers. In addition, manipulation of standards and requirements in favor of the less socioeconomically advanced ethnic groups was implemented.[16] Such arithmetic could not stop the eruption of massive ethnic violence, fueled with emotion, in Uganda, Equatorial Guinea, Angola, Kenya, Togo, and elsewhere. None matched the degree of human tragedy in Rwanda and Burundi.[17]

In 1962, Rwanda and Burundi were created as independent states in the Great Lakes region of Africa, out of a territory previously known as Ruanda-Urundi. This area had come under German control in 1899 and had fallen to Belgium in 1916. From then until Rwanda's and Burundi's independence, Belgium administered the territory under a League of Nations mandate and later a United Nations (UN) trusteeship. The region was mostly populated by two groups of people, known as Tutsi (Watusi) and Hutu, sharing the same religion and language (Kirundi).

While it is difficult to reconstruct much of the precolonial history of the Tutsi people since there are very few written records, it is generally accepted that they came to the region as conquerors from the north (probably from Ethiopia). Prior to the arrival of the Tutsi, Hutu were known as the Bantu people—in Kirundi, simply "human beings." The name Hutu, which means "slave" or "servant," was imported by the Tutsi. In the collective memories of these two groups, designation as a Tutsi or Hutu denotes a specific, contextualized political and economic relationship somewhat like landlord and tenant or master and servant.[18]

In both Burundi and Rwanda, the number of Tutsi is far lower than that of Hutu. In 1992, Burundi had a population of just over six million, of which 85 percent were Hutu, 14 percent Tutsi, and 1 percent Twa (pygmy). Rwanda's population was just over eight million, with 90 percent Hutu, 9 percent Tutsi, and 1 percent Twa. Under Belgian administration of the territory, the political power of the minority Tutsi was preserved because they were considered a more "advanced" tribe. The conscious and unconscious racist attitudes of the colonial powers, both German and Belgian, helped maintain distinctions between Hutu and Tutsi.

Tutsi typically are tall, with long, thin noses—hence more European-looking than Hutu, who are often shorter, with flat, broad noses. A preference toward Tutsi was institutionalized in the Belgian colonial administration and reinforced through a municipal registry that included a citizen's photo and ethnic affiliation. Every citizen over seventeen years old was required to carry an identification card that specified the bearer's ethnicity.[19] But because of more than four centuries of living in the same region and intermarrying, the physical distinction between many Tutsi and Hutu has gradually lessened, to the degree that most foreigners cannot distinguish between members of the two groups on the basis of physical characteristics alone. Hutu and Tutsi themselves, however, still know who is who. During the colonial period, as the differentness of each group was magnified, bonds were also strengthened, and the image of the other came to resemble that of an enemy. Ethnicity would be a focus of deadly distinction.

Prior to independence, ethnic dissension in Rwanda led in 1959 to a bloody Hutu rebellion, civil war, and abolishment of the UN-sponsored Tutsi monarchy. After independence, an unsuccessful Tutsi coup against the Hutu government took place in 1963. Another coup in 1973 brought the Tutsi back to power. A democratic constitution was drafted in 1978, and the first elected legislature was established in 1981 in an attempt to share power, yet tribal and regional divisions remained problematic. After Rwandan president Juvenal Habyarimana and Burundi president Cyprien Ntaryamira died in an unexplained plane crash near the capital city in April 1994, Rwanda's Hutu-led army and allied forces conducted systematic genocidal massacres of Tutsi and moderate Hutu for the next two months, killing an estimated five hundred thousand people. But when the capital fell to Tutsi rebels later that year, tens of thousands of fleeing Hutu were slaughtered, and the rage of polarized ethnic turmoil continued.

The situation in neighboring Burundi was equally horrifying. There, Hutu rebelled against a Tutsi monarchy in 1965, which dissolved in 1966. But a succession of Tutsi-dominated military governments continued to rule the country. The worst bloodshed was in 1972–1973 during an unsuccessful Hutu rebellion when an estimated hundred thousand deaths occurred, mostly Hutu, resulting in a flood of Hutu refugees to Tanzania and Zaire. The first Hutu president, Melchior Ndadye, was elected in 1993, but Tutsi troops assassinated him the same year. In the succeeding weeks, thousands of Hutu and Tutsi died, and more migrations to neighboring countries took place. In the summer of 1996, the then-president of Burundi, Sylvestre Ntibantunganya, took refuge in the U.S. ambassador's residence and was replaced by Pierre Buyoya, a Tutsi.

In October 1996, continual Hutu-Tutsi conflict began to inflame the tensions between Zaire and the Tutsi. Zaire was host to about 1.5 million Hutu refugees, mostly Rwandan, who had fled in the aftermath of Rwanda's ethnic massacres in the spring and summer of 1994. It seemed that the Zairian government, aided by Hutu who belonged to the former Rwandan army that had carried out the 1994 genocide, was trying to sweep the Banyamulenge Tutsi out of eastern Zaire. The Banyamulenge immigrated to Zaire from Rwanda decades ago and were now being accused by the Zairian government of inciting unrest. As an intense battle began between Zaire's military and Zairian Tutsi, about 225,000 Hutu refugees were forced to flee from their camps.

Beginning in November 1996, the situation in eastern Zaire became more complicated when longtime insurgent Laurent Kabila's rebel forces sought to control the region (an area roughly the size of the U.S. eastern seaboard from New York to Atlanta). This led to the dislocation of 4 million Zairians and of 450,000 mostly Hutu refugees from Rwanda and Burundi who had been sheltering in the region.

The Zairian government of President Mobutu Sese Seko helped arm Hutu refugees—even forcibly loading crates of guns onto UN planes bound for Tingi-Tingi, a massive UN camp outside Lubutu—to oppose the anti-Mobutu alliance. Nevertheless, after a seven-month civil war resulted in Mobutu's departure and the fall of the capital, Kinshasa, Kabila renamed Zaire the Democratic Republic of Congo in May 1997.

— · —

As these examples illustrate, ethnic conflict is becoming ever more dangerous, claiming a staggering number of victims each year. According to the statistics of the Stockholm International Peace Research Institute (SIPRI) in Sweden and the Conflict Resolution Program of The Carter Center in Atlanta, since 1986 the number of major armed conflicts has remained steady: between thirty and forty are occurring at any given moment. The term *major armed conflict* is defined as "prolonged combat between the military forces of two or more governments, or of one government and at least one organized armed group, and incurring the battle-related deaths of at least 1,000 people during the entire conflict."[20] In 1987 and 1988, the number of major armed conflicts peaked at thirty-nine. Then, in 1991, the number dipped to thirty, only to increase again in 1994 to thirty-three (per Carter Center) or thirty-four (per SIPRI). These took place in twenty-seven or twenty-eight separate locations. Statistics for 1995 identified thirty major armed conflicts in twenty-five locations. But while the number of such conflicts has gone down, their intensity and death toll have increased.

Ethnic terrorism is also on the rise. More terrorist attacks are now carried out by ethnically and religiously inspired groups than by secular groups or individuals. "Patterns of Global Terrorism," an annual report by the U.S. State Department, in 1996 reported another trend: attacks carried out by individuals and groups have overshadowed state-sponsored terrorism supported by nations such as Cuba, Iran, Iraq, Libya, North Korea, Sudan, and Syria.

Hundreds of thousands of lives have been lost in ethnic and related large-group conflicts during this decade. A SIPRI report published in 1996 shows that sixty-five thousand died in the former Yugoslavia alone—fifty-five thousand in Bosnia-Herzegovina and ten thousand in Croatia—since the beginning of the armed conflicts there in 1991. Afghanistan, Algeria, Angola, Azerbaijan, Bangladesh, Burundi, Cambodia, Colombia, Georgia, Guatemala, India, Indonesia, Iran, Iraq, Israel, Liberia, Myanmar (Burma), Peru, Philippines, Rwanda,

Somalia, Sri Lanka, Sudan, Tajikistan, Turkey, the United Kingdom, and Zaire have claimed hundreds of thousands more. But what is important is that many of these conflicts have taken place within the boundaries of a single country; they are considered ethnic, religious, and cultural large-group identity-related conflicts, not national conflicts between sovereign countries. This global phenomenon of ethnic, religious, and cultural large-group identity-related conflicts led Hugh D. S. Greenway to write in the *Boston Globe* in 1992, "The customs, laws and civility that allowed people of different cultures to live in peace together are going down all over Europe and beyond . . . the beast of ethnic hatred is loose."[21]

Given the pervasiveness of ethnic, religious, and cultural conflict, there is an urgent need to understand why, beyond their individualized motivations, people kill for the sake of protecting and maintaining their large-group identities. Why are they compelled to take revenge for the wrongs inflicted on their ancestors or others belonging to their bloodline? What happens to a group's "we-ness," its distinction from others, to become so deadly? Such questions are the subject of this book.

— · —

Despite the resurgence of ethnic and related large-group conflict, and evidence of complex and intertwined psychological issues in many cases, the tools and practices of foreign policy and intergroup relations have responded slowly to the changing international environment. Diplomacy as a concept can be traced back to the ancient Greeks. The word itself derives from *diplomata* (folded documents), which suggests that early diplomats may have been messengers offering proposals for negotiations. Eventually, diplomacy evolved further to meet the needs of advancing civilization, technology, and knowledge.[22] The concept of realpolitik, introduced by Ludwig von Rochau in 1853, continues to be the main foundation of the modern diplomatic world. Von Rochau advised politicians shrewdly to estimate what the opposition really wanted, rather than what they said they wanted, and to be prepared to exert force when necessary. Eventually the term came to mean the application of rational evaluation and realistic assessment of the options available to one's own group and to an opposing one.[23]

This perspective is certainly valuable. Nevertheless, in analyzing

the international milieu *only* through alliances, opportunities, economics, military strength, or other real-world factors, the rational and
traditional are overemphasized. This is not to say that politicians and
statesmen do not consider the emotional or psychological implications
of actions and statements, but their focus typically does not extend
beyond the realm of spin doctors who seek to manipulate or modify
outcomes to gain concrete and calculated results.

The rise of ethnic and other large-group conflicts based on issues
of identity, however, has begun to influence the practice of traditional
diplomacy and the activities of the United Nations. Diplomats have
started to see that complex new conflicts in the world cannot be mea-
sured by methods of realpolitik, nor can they easily be negotiated by
traditional diplomacy. Because many ethnic conflicts and hostilities
are not between sovereign states but within them, foreign policy and
traditional diplomacy have been less effective. Furthermore, Article
2.7 of the UN charter expressly forbids the United Nations from intervening in matters "essentially within the domestic jurisdiction of
any state." But even when two sovereign states are involved, sometimes the parties ignore the precepts of the Geneva Conventions and
the basic tenets of bilateral or multilateral relations.

Richard T. Arndt, a twenty-four-year veteran in cultural diplomacy,
has observed that "many of the world's cultures, for years crushed and
all but invisible beneath foreign domination, have only recently risen to
the surface of international consciousness, as they initiate their search,
sometimes through violent means, for political and social identity."[24]
Arndt suggests that rethinking the approach to diplomacy for the next
decade is necessary given increasing cultural diversification, interaction, conflict, and cooperation. Political scientist Donald Horowitz
notes that the amount of passion expressed in ethnic conflicts "calls out
for [an] explanation that does justice to the realm of feelings" and that "a
bloody phenomenon cannot be explained by a bloodless theory."[25]

Bloodlines seeks to fill this gap in the literature of diplomacy by
using the principles of psychoanalysis to search for the meaning of
cultural identity, ethnic attachment, and the passions related to such
relationships. But first, emotionally bonded large groups must be precisely defined in order to identify the awakened beast in international
relationships.

Chapter 1

ETHNIC TENTS: DESCRIPTIONS OF LARGE-GROUP IDENTITIES

We have traditionally wished to believe that what separates mankind from the rest of the animal kingdom is our rationality, our ability to reason and evaluate based on conscious consideration of alternatives. We like to think that we usually operate on a rational level; only a small minority of us, such as those we believe to have psychological disorders, are considered irrational or unreasonable.

This stress on individual rationality is then extended, sometimes to an exaggerated level, to our leaders, our institutions and organizations, and our governments. While we recognize that the individual is prone to irrational acts, to having his or her reason clouded by emotion, we tend to believe that larger social and political units are far more immune to this natural human tendency. Yet when we consider the interaction of people organized into collective entities, both recently and throughout history, the idea that these bodies are less susceptible to the same psychological frailties of the individuals they comprise comes into question. In the violent and brutal devastation of the former Yugoslavia, the vicious intertribal warfare in Rwanda, and countless other acts carried out between nations or ethnic groups, the lines between the rational and irrational, the behavior of the individual and of the group, seem to overlap.

Paradoxically, at the root of many group conflicts are bloodlines that establish a kind of border in times of crisis that cannot be crossed. Two groups who have been neighbors for generations may suddenly be transformed into merciless enemies, and the unthinkable may become a gruesome reality. Individual values can give way to a collective will and the monstrous vision of a charismatic leader. It is difficult for us to assimilate the horror of such acts or understand the wounds suffered by both victims and survivors. Sometimes, we can only ask, "How could this happen?"

There are various means by which we attempt to limit, deter, and restrain conflicts both within nations or ethnic groups and between them. Entities such as the United Nations, the North Atlantic Treaty Organization (NATO), the Organization of Petroleum Exporting Countries (OPEC), the General Agreement on Tariffs and Trade (GATT), and countless other supranational, governmental, and nongovernmental organizations attempt to manage or contain hostilities through negotiations, sanctions, and other forms of influence. Yet the primary focus of these institutions does not address the question "How can this happen?" or why bloody wars between neighbors not only persist, but proliferate.

There is a long tradition of attempting to understand the complex relationship of the individual and his or her tribal, ethnic, religious, and national group. From the earliest poets and prophets, through philosophers, anthropologists, and political theorists, to pioneers in psychology such as Sigmund Freud, many have sought to understand both the conscious and unconscious motivations of human beings and their behavior in social units. Modern statesmen have also noted the role that psychological processes play in internal and international relationships.

While there are many dissimilarities between the workings of the individual and the group mind, the tools of psychology, and especially of psychoanalysis, can shed light on group identity and behavior, not because they concern our unconscious drives or paths of psychosexual development, but because of the tacit assumption that each individual or group has complex and idiosyncratic ways of dealing with the demands of the inner and outer worlds.

—·—

What then are these bloodlines of ethnicity that so strongly link together the members of a group?

The word *ethnic* comes from the Greek word *ethnos*, meaning company, people, or tribe. Anthropologist George De Vos describes an ethnic group as those "who hold in common a set of traditions not shared by the others with whom they are in contact."[1] De Vos's list of traditions includes folk religious beliefs and practices, language, a sense of historical continuity, a common ancestry, place of origin, and shared history. According to him, there is a mythological beginning for the group "which includes some concept of an unbroken biological-genetic generational continuity, sometimes regarded as giving special characteristics to the group."[2] For De Vos, being unique and special is accompanied by a sense of being distinct from others. One group maintains its ethnic self-esteem, vanity, and superiority in comparison with another ethnic group, usually a neighbor.

Anthropologist Howard Stein focuses on subjective criteria in defining ethnicity as a marker of personal and social identity; ethnicity is a mode of thought, not a category in nature.[3] But there are those who are more concerned with objective criteria—physical characteristics, cultural and social community.[4] The categorization of physical features, however, does not conform to the popular usage of the term *ethnicity*. The conflict among Orthodox Serbs, Catholic Croats, and Muslim Bosnians in the former Yugoslavia is referred to as an ethnic conflict, yet individuals from all three groups share the same blood (gene pools)—all are southern Slavs. Their separate histories, cultures, and religions give them their different ethnic identities. So it would be inaccurate to call the problem in the former Yugoslavia an "ethnic" conflict based on the precepts of those anthropologists who consider ethnicity a function of physical characteristics.

Given the range of its usage, the concept of ethnicity should be flexible, for the bloodlines that separate large groups go beyond a simple consideration of gene pools. It seems that without considering subjective criteria it would be impossible to understand why a large group of people feels unique. Some scholars have wanted to take objective criteria still further and even attempted to categorize ethnic groups by cranial dimensions, nasal profiles, and the like.[5] But this confuses race with ethnicity.

Despite their frequent overlap in common parlance, *race* and *eth-*

nicity are not synonymous. Racial distinctions are based on the assumption that human beings can be divided into different subspecies according to their respective biological characteristics. Variations in physique, skin color, hair texture, or facial features, for example, are thought to be manifestations of distinct human races. Such distinctions take on the character of *racism* when they are assumed to reflect different stages of human development and are used to support granting or withholding rights and privileges.

Traditional racism, of course, has not altogether disappeared, but what has largely taken its place is a *neo-racism* grounded not in biology but in anthropology and an ideological commitment to the virtues of difference. In Western Europe, for example, guest workers and new immigrants from the Middle East, the Indian subcontinent, and Africa are targets of this phenomenon.[6] A 1992 United Nations report observed:

> Now, at the end of the twentieth century . . . racist ideology emphasizes the unique nature of the language, religions, mental and social structures, and value systems of immigrants of African, Arab, or Asian origin, for instance, in order to justify the need to keep human communities separate. It even goes so far as to contend that preserving their identity is in the interest of the communities concerned. By asserting a radical cultural pluralism, the new racism based on cultural differences tries, paradoxically, to look like genuine anti-racism and to show respect for all group identities.[7]

Large-group identities are the end result of a historical continuity, geographical reality, a myth of a common beginning, and other shared events: they evolve naturally. They are neither bad nor good, but a normal phenomenon. When ethnic groups define and differentiate themselves, they almost invariably develop some prejudices for their own group and against the others' groups. As members of the Committee of International Relations of the Group for the Advancement of Psychiatry concluded, "Ethnicity has no existence apart from interethnic relations."[8] There is, therefore, a degree of ethnocentrism that appears to be universal, and either end of the spectrum is undesirable. At one end is non-differentiation between ethnic groups, a form of identity confusion (or merging) that would disturb the members' sense of belonging and run counter to mankind's natural need to find similar others. At the other extreme is ethnocentrism, which evolves into malignant proportions until it cannot be distinguished from neo-racism. Ethnic differentiation and ethnocentrism should not be condemned entirely; they are healthy or acceptable within certain limits.

In some cases, there is a distinct link between ethnic groups and nations. The difference between a *nation* and an *ethnic group* is that a nation implies political autonomy and established borders, or at least organizations that create roles, positions, and status.[9] Most nations contain more than one ethnic group, so some scholars refer to ethnic groups as "sub-nations."[10] Other scholars use the term *ethnonationalism* to cover a people's attachment to both concepts simultaneously.

Nationalism, after the birth of the French and American republics in the eighteenth century, became a dominant political movement in the nineteenth century when the emergence of unified nation-states rearranged the map of western and central Europe. Since then, nationalism's "ability to inspire dedicated action in history has been equaled in earlier times only by religion."[11] Yet the politico-legal definition of the term *nation* remains problematic, and since nations were "born" differently, the degree of inclusion and exclusion, of entitlement and grievance, differs from one nation to the next.[12]

In France, nationalism emerged when people banded together to defend the French Revolution from external threats. The age-old role of religion to provide a sense of togetherness was absorbed in the newer concept of nationhood. The French would continue to share religious beliefs with others outside of their nation-state, but the nation now provided a border, a new frame of reference, for their religious togetherness. French nationalism, furthermore, was based on pre-existing bureaucratic structures co-opted in part from the monarchy of Louis XVI and from the church. It took a shared struggle, a very bloody one, to construct the sense of French nationhood. "While the idea of nationalism may be linked to liberty and universalistic ideals," the French psychoanalyst Janine Chasseguet-Smirgel notes, "it also sometimes led to particularism, racism, totalitarianism, and destruction. Indeed, in its National Socialist version, nationalism waged war on the liberal and democratic ideals that developed in the wake of the Enlightenment and the French Revolution."[13]

While the French Revolution descended into a Reign of Terror, other nation-states were formed without bloodshed. Kuwait, for example, was founded in 1759 by the Al-Sabah and two other Arab families who immigrated there from other parts of the Arabian Peninsula in search of a better life. Over the centuries, they were joined by other families, of both Arab and Persian origin, from surrounding areas. Slowly an amalgamation took place, and although there were outside threats that called for unity, Kuwaitis faced few crises that brought the past or future of their nation into question.[14]

Still other nations, asserts Peter Loewenberg, a historian and psychoanalyst, evolved from a synthesis of disparate influences. The United States, Brazil, Indonesia, and Israel are all "invented nations," he says, "each with an assertive, self-worshipping, and aggrandizing nationalism."[15] To mold them out of the rich multiplicity of historical, ethnic, and religious roots, Loewenberg explains, required "acts of mental invention of a mythic common past, usually glorious but sometimes persecuting, and suppression of the 'sub-nations,' units smaller than a nation."[16]

Human beings have always lived in emotionally bonded large groups, such as tribes and clans. Psychoanalyst Erik H. Erikson coined the term *pseudospeciation* to refer to the tendency to portray one's own tribe or ethnic group as human while describing other groups as subhuman. Erikson speculated that primitive humans, as a measure of protection against their unbearable nakedness, adopted the armor of the lower animals by wearing animal skins, feathers, or claws. On the basis of these outer garments, each tribe, clan, or group developed a sense of identity, as well as a conviction that it alone harbored human identity in contrast to its neighbors.[17]

Initially, neighboring tribes were concerned primarily with basic survival, the competition for food and goods. As humankind evolved, in addition to the necessities of nutrition, warmth, and weapons, other meanings were attached to the physical items for which neighboring tribes competed. Some of these items, such as feathers and claws, became symbolic, valued not only for their physical benefits, but also for the psychological benefits they provided, such as enhancing self-esteem. These symbols reflected the group's conscious and unconscious needs and wishes and slowly evolved into the colors, flags, songs, dress modes, and other cultural indicators that keep shared identities alive and reflect the group's realistic and mythical history. Shared language, a sense of attachment to the land where ancestors were buried, and shared religion further shaped the identity of the group and differentiated it from the other, the potential enemy.

Humankind's preoccupation with the other appears in ancient documents and in languages where the concept is elaborated with accrued connotations. The ancient Chinese, for instance, regarded themselves as people and saw other races as *kuei*, or hunting spirits. In the United States, the Apache Indians called themselves *indeh*, the people, and all others *indah*, the enemy.[18] The Mundurucú of the Brazilian rain forest divide their world, with few exceptions, into Mundurucú, who are people, and non-Mundurucú, who are *pariwat*, or enemies.[19] In English, the term *barbarian* refers to foreigners; in other words, those who are uncivilized and ruthless and whose values differ from one's own. Although anthropologists continue to debate the universality of the "we are human and they are less than human" view, clearly it is very common. As W. H. Auden wrote in "The Sea and the Mirror," if we did not have a hated "them" to turn against, there would not be a loving "us" to turn to.[20]

— · —

When one large group interacts with another, "we-ness," whether it is described with reference to religious, ethnic, national, or racial affiliation, acts as an invisible force in the unfolding drama. It may be useful to compare this unseen force to a basic physiological function, such as breathing. Most of us are unaware of our breathing when our lungs function normally. But if we contract pneumonia, we suddenly notice each breath. Similarly, individuals are not usually preoccupied with their large-group identity until it is threatened. When a group is in continuing conflict or even at war with a neighbor group, members become acutely aware of their large-group identity to the point where it may far outweigh any concern for individual needs, even survival. It is the psychology of we-ness that may provide valuable insights into why and how large-group identities can act as an invisible force.

In *Group Psychology and the Analysis of the Ego*, his major work on the subject, Freud distinguished between individual psychology—that is, concerns of the individual that relate to the gratification of and mental defenses against his internal impulses (instinctual drives) and wishes—and group psychology. The group, he found, was different from the sum of its parts.

Freud began by examining the late-nineteenth-century theories of the French sociologist Gustave Le Bon, who postulated that an individual within a group loses much of his distinctiveness and acts instead in accordance with the homogeneous urges that unite the group.[21] Freud believed that the effacement of dissimilarity among individuals that occurs under the domination of collective unity may be traced to the liberation of formerly repressed racial urges common to the group. When individuality is obliterated, these unconscious urges surface in the individual. Since these urges are shared by all members of the group, and they are in fact the fundamental points of contact among them, the group's identity is streamlined and shaped by the dictates of those urges.

Freud associated the increased suggestibility among group members with the libido, that is, the forming and maintenance of loving attachments. Since irrational surrender of the individual's intellect implies equally willing suggestibility to collective emotional impulses, he reasoned that this trade-off would come about only through the power of the libido. If the group mind was structured on or derived from relationships based on familial patterns, then that same libidinal foundation might account for the individual's ready effacement of uniqueness within the group. Suggestibility, in which one permits others to exert inordinate influence over oneself, follows this effacement as a manifestation of the libidinal urge to feel harmonious with the group rather than apart from it.

Freud saw the church and the army as examples of willing effacement of individuality. Both are artificial groups structured around the authority of a single benevolent leader in which members are seen as equal, equality being defined libidinally. To be equal is to be loved equally by Christ or by the commander in chief, respectively. Also, to be equal is to love and to identify with other members of the group.

Individuals perceive the group as seeking to satisfy the same vital needs they themselves want to satisfy. This congruity makes them idealize, identify with, and love the group. They suspend their critical faculties, falsely inflating the group's values. Humility and subjection replace insight, so the many who operate with the same object of love are tied libidinally to it and to one another. Members of the group also want one person to lead them. In a way, man is a horde animal desiring membership in a strong group led by a strong leader.

Freud based his group theories primarily on the Oedipus complex and suggested that any hostility between a member and the leader must be transformed by the member into the kind of loyalty and devotion that comes from a successfully resolved oedipal conflict. Just as the son identified with the oedipal father, so the member identifies with the leader.

But to say that group psychology can simply be explained by analogy to the Oedipus complex ignores the evolving psychological structure of individuals in both their pre-oedipal and later stages, between earlier individual evolution and the beginning of group psychology. Freud's application of his knowledge of individual development to groups is useful, but not complete.

Large groups, like individuals, regress under shared stress;[22] they fall back on primitive ways of behaving. They may see the environment as more dangerous than it is, while expecting others to be more powerful than they are. Freud's explanation of the leader-follower relationship in the army or the church is applicable to the study of the psychology of ethnic or national groups when they are threatened and regressed. But it falls short of explaining the relationship between leaders and followers in normal situations, the role of aggression in human beings, and how and why investment in emotionally bonded large groups sometimes leads to mass violence and horrifying acts.

I like to use the analogy of a large canvas tent to explore large-group psychology in a more comprehensive way. Think in terms of learning to wear, from childhood on, two layers of clothing. The first layer fits snugly. This is one's personal identity. The second layer, the ethnic (emotionally bonded large group) layer, is a loose covering that protects the individual in the way that a parent, close family member, or other caregiver protects one. Because this garment is not formfitting, it also shelters other members of the group and resembles, in a sense, a large canvas tent. While the tent pole (the leader) holds the tent erect, the canvas itself, in its own right, is a protector of the group. In their relationship to the tent, all of the individuals within the group—male or female, rich or poor—are equal. They are connected to one another not only because they love the same leader but because they share this second layer while still wearing the first.

It is the leader's (the pole's) task to prevent the tent from collapsing, but the tent's canvas survives through many a leader. To some extent leaders are selected—openly in a democratic society and through other means in other societies—according to the nature of the canvas. The leaders must be able to shoulder, so to speak, the weight of the canvas, responding to the special needs of the group. The leader's response to his or her own internal demands and personality influences the followers. In turn, the followers' collective wishes and identity create an atmosphere allowing a certain type of leader to come to power.

Freud's theory of group psychology focuses mainly on the masses of individuals when they rally around the pole (the leader) and identify with one another. These activities occur when the group members perceive a shared danger. But the large group takes on an identity of its own, and the canvas of the tent represents the shared large-group identity. It shelters the members of the group in the same way a mother hen provides a safe haven for her chicks by spreading her wings.

Freud's theory must be expanded in order to explain the equally important role of group identity and to examine its psychological components. Large-group identity better explains the cohesiveness of group members in nonthreatening times, when there is no anxiety or regression. When there is shared anxiety and regression, besides rallying around the pole, the members become preoccupied with repairing and mending the tears in the canvas of the large-group tent. In fact, the main reason for rallying around the pole is to protect the large-group identity. Under certain conditions, efforts to stabilize the tent and repair the canvas after it shakes may include violent mass behavior.

— · —

Freud remained cautious in applying psychoanalytic concepts to the workplace of diplomats. In a 1932 exchange that became known by the title "Why War?" Albert Einstein asked Freud if there was "any way of delivering mankind from the menace of war." Freud responded that there was no hope of eliminating humankind's aggressive inclination.[23] Both men favored a central authority like the League of Nations, the precursor to the United Nations, to oversee world affairs and maintain world peace. Freud was disappointed in his exchange with Einstein, and he was disappointed in the League of Nations.

Since Freud, a number of psychoanalysts have made contributions to large-group psychology. But in general, these contributions have dealt with the collective expression of the individual's internal impulses. Neither the assertion that wars are inevitable because of humankind's aggressive drive nor the theory that a state is identified with a parent or sometimes with oneself has had much practical diplomatic use. Then, in 1971, German psychoanalyst Alexander Mitscherlich urged his colleagues to participate in research into the collective behavior of groups by working with scholars in other fields. He warned psychoanalysts not to restrict themselves to an exclusively medical and clinical position. If they did not expand their horizons, Mitscherlich said, psychoanalysts will "have maneuvered [themselves] into an isolation of [their] own making."[24] His plea was largely ignored. Interestingly enough, six years later, it was a politician, Egyptian president Anwar el-Sadat, who indirectly issued an invitation to mental health professionals to work side by side with diplomats. This led to new psychoanalytic insights about emotionally bonded large-group identities and behaviors that could have practical diplomatic implications.

Chapter 2

ANWAR EL-SADAT GOES TO JERUSALEM: THE PSYCHOLOGY OF INTERNATIONAL CONFLICTS OBSERVED AT CLOSE RANGE

In 1977, Egyptian president Anwar el-Sadat stunned the political world by announcing that he would visit Israel. Given the tense state of the Arab-Israeli relationship at that time, such a proposition was bold, almost unthinkable, and many Israelis did not believe Sadat's visit would materialize. As his airplane touched down in Israel on November 19, armed Israeli soldiers, hidden from the public eye, stood ready to spring into action. A suspicion that the Egyptians might send a suicide plane into the heart of Israel persisted until the moment Sadat stepped onto Israeli soil.

The next day Sadat addressed the Israeli Knesset expressing a desire to move beyond political concerns to a more profound reconciliation:

> . . . Yet there remains another wall. This wall constitutes a psychological barrier between us, a barrier of suspicion, a barrier of rejection; a barrier of fear, of deception, a barrier of hallucination without any action, deed, or decision.
>
> A barrier of distorted and eroded interpretation of every event and statement. It is this psychological barrier which I described in official statements as constituting 70 percent of the whole problem.

Today, through my visit to you, I ask why don't we stretch out our hands with faith and sincerity so that together we might destroy this barrier?[1]

Besides making great strides in reconciling age-old differences between the two groups, Sadat's comment resulted in the availability of funds in the United States to study the psychological barrier that was "70 percent" of the Arab-Israeli problem. A subgroup within the American Psychiatric Association—later known as the Committee on Psychiatry and Foreign Affairs—sponsored six major and numerous minor meetings in the United States, the Middle East, and various locations in Europe in an attempt to understand the components of this wall. Palestinians from the West Bank and Gaza began to participate in these gatherings in 1983. The Americans, mostly psychiatrists with a few diplomats, divided themselves among small groups, where they acted as catalysts to keep the dialogue going, to diffuse resistances, and to foster an atmosphere of collaboration.[2] The Israeli, Egyptian, and Palestinian delegates also included psychiatrists, diplomats (such as Ambassador Tahseen Basheer of Egypt), former high-level military officers (such as General Shlomo Gazit, former chief of Israeli intelligence and the mastermind behind the 1976 Entebbe raid), and public servants (such as Mayor Elias Frej, mayor of Bethlehem).

Exploring the Arab-Israeli conflict through a psychological lens during this six-year period, from 1980 to 1986, created an environment for what former assistant secretary of state Harold Saunders called "ideas in the air": creative new ways of formulating peaceful solutions to an international problem. They were in the air in that they did not stem from official government policy, but their presence among a growing circle of influential people had the potential to affect policy. Saunders understood that once government decision makers adopt a policy, they resist those who want to alter it. However, once it becomes clear that current policy is ineffective, one of the first places policy makers look to for new inspiration is public sentiment.

The meetings created lasting relationships among participants, who, because of their influence at home, helped expand a dialogue toward achieving peaceful but realistic coexistence with their enemies. Some veterans of these meetings, such as Shimeon Shamir, who became the Israeli ambassador to Egypt and then to Jordan, later functioned as official diplomats.

When the Israeli and Egyptian representatives first met in the United States in January 1980, they began by reciting past injuries inflicted by the other group, as if competing to see who had suffered more. The competition was literal: representatives interrupted one another, refusing even to listen to the other side. Emotions pertaining to recent injurious or humiliating events activated memories of other such incidents from the past, some from centuries before.[3]

Many of the references to historical events seemed to have no logical connection to the present Arab-Israeli conflict. Historical grievances were recalled that linked the present enemy to the past enemy. The Israelis cited the fact that August Rohling's *Protocols of the Elders of Zion,* the worst kind of anti-Semitic literature, had been translated into Arabic and distributed by the thousands. Even though the Egyptian representatives at the meeting neither were racist nor approved of distributing or reading hate literature, the Israelis indirectly connected them with anti-Semitic Europeans. The kernel of truth that some Arabs had actually translated Rohling's inflammatory work only facilitated the Israelis' association of the two groups of people, former and present adversaries. When the Arabs countered by referring to the hate literature about them in Israel, the Israelis, not surprisingly, were unmoved.

This competition in expressing historical injuries seemed to occur involuntarily. Rarely was there empathy for the suffering of the "enemy" group (whether Israeli or Egyptian); instead, there was an inability to identify with the anguish of the other. There was only an isolated concern with one's own helplessness and losses. In a way, the recitation of past injuries magnified the present perception of threat and danger. It also magnified the participants' sense of group identity, which hinged on apparent need to remain self-centered and focused on prior experiences, even negative ones.

Initially, committee members often prematurely interfered with the flow of grievance listing and tried to stop the emotional assaults. But they succeeded in bringing about a change of topic only temporarily. The intense competition abruptly came to an end on the third day of the meeting, not because of any therapeutic handling of it, but because of a spontaneous interaction between an Egyptian man and an Israeli woman. The turning point occurred in one of the small-group dialogues, but its effect soon spread to the rest of the participants. It consisted in the sudden recognition that all of them shared a negative and threatening emotion: fear. Each group had its own mental image of past grievances. But sharing a similar emotion attached to such experiences need not erase the distinctions between Israelis and Egyptians: they could hold on to their group identities, even while having empathy for the other group. Once both groups came to this realization, mutual recognition of each other's suffering and fear created a positive atmosphere for joint discussions.

The eventful change began modestly enough. Abd El Azim Ramadan, a historian from Monofeia University in Cairo and a journalist, dominated the discussion in his small group as he cited the merits of a Palestinian state, without giving others a chance to speak. Ramadan came across as a religious and serious socialist and an anti-Zionist. (In later meetings, when he no longer perceived Israelis as a major threat to himself or to Egypt, a different side of Ramadan's personality emerged: that of the joker and wit.) Nechama Agmon, a child psychiatrist from Jerusalem, interrupted Ramadan's monologue to ask him how he could convince her not to fear a Palestinian state. Agmon had been born in Atorat, near Jerusalem and the Arab city of Ramallah. In Atorat, Agmon had experienced times of peace, when nearby Arabs and Israelis were friends, and times of conflict, when the surrounding fields were stained with blood. Ramadan's comments had revived her old fears, specifically, of a 1929 Arab attack when a British force that had promised to protect the inhabitants of Atorat failed to do so. Transferring her past emotions to a present issue, the formation of a Palestinian state, Agmon wanted to know how Ramadan could quell her fears. Ramadan answered, "I do not believe that you Israelis are afraid; Israelis are never afraid." Agmon was appalled, and the exchange quickly ended the encounter for the day.

But the next morning, before the same small group, Ramadan asked for permission to speak. He had not slept the night before, thinking about what had happened. Instead he had lain awake grappling with whether he could trust Agmon and whether Israelis were as fearless as he had long believed. He had decided to consult the Qur'an, and there he had found three passages that spoke of Moses' fear. He read these passages to the group in Arabic and in English. He then added, "I never thought that Moses was afraid. But now I know that since Moses was afraid, you can be, too. So I believe you, Nechama."

On the surface, one might expect Ramadan to be pleased to acknowledge that a member of his enemy group had such a negative emotion as fear, but he was unable at first to accept that possibility. His refusal seemed to suggest that he could not tolerate sharing a sense of victimhood with her. If he acknowledged Agmon's fear, he would be granting Israelis the status of an injured party, thereby compromising the unique, injured status of Egyptians.

But the interchange had another, deeper psychological meaning: Ramadan's insistence that Israelis did not have fear was an indication of his belief that Israelis, unlike Egyptians, lacked emotions; they were nonhuman. As a result of coming face-to-face with his "enemy" and discovering some unexpected empathy for Agmon, he consulted his Qur'an for help. Then he experienced the sudden connection between emotional experience and intellectual understanding that rehumanized the Israelis. In acknowledging their human identity, Ramadan also had to acknowledge that they had a grievance and negative emotions pertaining to it.

— · —

Under normal conditions, with the passage of time, individuals mourn losses—of people, land, prestige—associated with past traumatic events and work through feelings of fear, helplessness, and humiliation. Mourning and working through the effects of an injury signify the gradual acceptance that a change has occurred. The "lost" elements—a parent, a country—no longer exist in the present reality; they can no longer satisfy one's wishes.

The traumatic events of the past mentioned at the American Psychiatric Association–sponsored Arab-Israeli meetings sounded as though they had occurred only the day before. The feelings about them were so fresh it was clear that genuine mourning for the losses associated with these events had not taken place. Furthermore, representatives of opposing groups acted as if they themselves had witnessed such events, even though some had taken place before they were born.

This is an example of time collapse, in which the interpretations, fantasies, and feelings about a past shared trauma commingle with those pertaining to a current situation. Under the influence of a time collapse, people may intellectually separate the past event from the present one, but emotionally the two events are merged.

Chapter 3

—·—·—·—·—

CHOSEN TRAUMA:
UNRESOLVED MOURNING

Humans cannot accept change without mourning what has been lost. Mourning is an involuntary response that occurs at the time of the loss of a loved one or loved possession or when a loss appears to be imminent, as with a dying parent. We also mourn the loss of persons and things that we hate, since, like love, hate connects us deeply to one another. Human nature gives us a painful but ultimately effective way to let go of our previous attachments, to adjust internally to the absence of lost people or things and to get on with our lives. When we finish the work of mourning, we feel a new surge of energy and an adaptive liberation that may be expressed in undertaking new projects or developing new friendships.[1]

The prototypical adult mourning reaction to the death of a loved one consists of two stages. The first is crisis grief, which occurs during the initial few months after the death. It includes shock, denial, bargaining, and the sadness and pain of losing access to the deceased. Feeling anger in the first stage is important; it is, in effect, a cry of indignation that says, how dare you leave me! This anger is often displaced and directed toward others—relatives, for example, or a physician who treated the deceased person. Anger marks the realization that what is lost will never come back.

Even before the first stage ends, the second stage—usually known as the "work of mourning"—begins.[2] It aims to help the mourner assimilate and adapt to a changed reality. During the second stage, an internal examination of hundreds of memories, along with their accompanying feelings, begins to take place. There is also pain, this time associated with the emotional acceptance of loss. This process enables the mourner to convert the relationship with the dead person into a memory that no longer eclipses other thoughts.[3]

An adult's mourning process is like the healing of a wound: it takes time and it occurs gradually. Mourning usually comes to a practical end within a year or so, after important anniversaries—of a wedding, birth, or vacation—are experienced without the lost person. But the nature of an individual's response to a loss or change depends on a variety of circumstances, both external and internal. If there are complications during any of the stages of the mourning process, they may prevent adaptive resolution of the loss. A sudden death, for example, usually complicates the mourner's response because he or she is psychologically unprepared for it. Deaths by suicide or homicide also make adjustment very hard, sometimes impossible, as do feelings of guilt, shame, humiliation, and helplessness associated with the death. The more an individual is dependent on a loved one, the more difficult it will be to mourn that person's loss.

If mourning takes its expected course, the mourner identifies with aspects of the dead person, such as his ideals and functions. Thus, the mourner becomes less dependent on the one who is lost and can let the dead person go. (One analogy would be identification with a teacher when a student is trying to master a body of knowledge. Once the knowledge or problem is mastered, the student no longer needs the teacher.) Strong identification with aspects of a departed one is a brutal gift because of the pain involved in the mourning process.

But not all mourning processes are this smooth. Mourning may result in a mourner's turning grief into depression. In this situation, the mourner makes a bad identification with the image of the dead person; he identifies indiscriminately, taking in both the loved and hated aspects of the departed one. The mourner unconsciously wishes simultaneously to keep and to destroy the image of the deceased. An unending internal struggle ensues and is experienced as depression and guilt for wishing to get rid of the deceased's image. The depressed mourner suffers in order to relate to the object of mourning buried within.

Sometimes complications in mourning make people perennial mourners. They remain preoccupied, year after year, with the ambivalently regarded image of the dead one, but they are not depressed in the usual sense because they do not actually identify with this image. Perennial mourners symbolically live in the world of the dead, continuing to have inner conversations with the image of the dead person years after death has occurred. They may also relate to certain possessions of the dead person as though they were magical. A dead father's handkerchief or watch, for example, becomes invested with emotions for his son, who locks the item in a drawer. He cannot use or repair the item, but he needs to know where it is at all times. Such *linking objects* connect the perennial mourner with the dead one. The linking object becomes a meeting ground between the mourner and the person who has died. The perennial mourner unconsciously remains in a state of limbo: he can bring the dead one back to life by relating to him through the linking object or he can "kill" him by throwing away the symbolic object in order to progress with his work of mourning. But he completes neither of these actions and instead remains in a perpetual state of mourning. There are mothers, for instance, who continue to turn down their dead child's bed every night, even though they know intellectually that the child will never return.[4]

—·—

Like individuals or families, large groups also mourn. Members of a group who share the same loss collectively go through a similar psychological mourning process. When the image of the *Challenger* space shuttle explosion flashed across television screens on January 28, 1986, the loss affected Americans personally. At the time of this tragedy, I was treating a patient whose older sister had died suddenly several years before. My patient's response to the *Challenger* explosion centered around astronaut Christa McAuliffe, who, like the patient's sister, had been a teacher. My patient's grief over McAuliffe prompted a renewal of unfinished grieving for her own sister.

The *Challenger* disaster also precipitated a collective response.

McAuliffe had won the privilege to accompany the *Challenger* astronauts through a contest sponsored by the National Aeronautics and Space Administration (NASA); she would teach from space. Children in classrooms all over the United States sat ready to see her on television. Instead, the space shuttle exploded in front of their eyes.

Soon after the incident, Americans began telling the same tasteless jokes from the East Coast to the West. "Question: How can you prove that the *Challenger* astronauts had dandruff? Answer: Their Head and Shoulders were found on the beach." In psychological terms, this and other gruesome jokes signaled the initiation of group mourning. Jokes lightened sadness through laughter and helped Americans accept the reality of the tragedy. By telling or listening to these jokes, Americans also tried to deal with their shock over the failure of U.S. technology. Trust had been lost and people needed to adjust accordingly.

Not long after the *Challenger* disaster, the role of jokes in facilitating grief was demonstrated again when an earthquake struck Mexico City. Many buildings in the middle of the city collapsed. I flew there to investigate the group response to the disaster. Soon after my arrival, my host asked me if I knew the similarity between Mexico City and a doughnut. The answer was that the insides of both were missing. It was a gruesome joke, again reflecting the initiation of mourning.

In the cases of the *Challenger* explosion and the Mexico City earthquake, group mourning was relatively uncomplicated. There were no chronic societal wounds left in their wake. In such cases, after the initial shock and attempts to reverse the feelings of loss, society becomes involved in religious and cultural rituals, usually repeated over time with decreasing intensity, on the anniversaries of such events. The work of collective mourning eventually fades away, and society's adaptation to these shared losses is, on the whole, a silent one.

But some kinds of tragedies result in more complicated group mourning processes, such as those that directly affect a larger cross section of a group or involve longer-lasting damage. In response to the assassinations of leaders such as John F. Kennedy and Martin Luther King Jr., for example, the media have contributed to a piecemeal work of group mourning by ritualistic observances of anniversaries.

When the shared trauma is severe, as it was in the losses of both Kennedy and King, memorial activities may be pronounced for many years. America's reaction to losing sons and daughters in the Vietnam War was also profound, but it was not fully expressed until many years later with the construction of the Vietnam War Memorial in Washington, D.C.[5] Much of the trauma of the Vietnam War was already in the process of being resolved in public venues such as film, literature, and continuing political and news media activity. Nevertheless, building monuments after drastic collective losses has its own special place in societal mourning; such actions are almost a psychological necessity. Structures made of stone or metal function as the group's linking objects. Their indestructibility makes them psychological containers that preserve and limit emotions.

American's losses in the Vietnam War were profound, and the memorial greatly helped the mourning process to resolve the hurts. But in other situations, a shared calamity can leave members of a group dazed, helpless, and too afraid, humiliated, and angry to complete or even initiate a mourning process. In these cases, group members cannot turn their passive submission to the event into responsive, constructive activities.

Severe calamities, besides arousing extensive feelings of helplessness, create another kind of loss that sociologist Kai T. Erikson called the breakdown of "the tissue of community."[6] Two kinds of events can have this effect. The first includes natural (e.g., a typhoon) and man-made (e.g., Chernobyl) disasters, where those who suffer do not feel deliberately singled out by others for victimization or punishment. The helplessness that ensues is unaccompanied by humiliation or loss of human dignity. Such calamities usually affect only a limited geographical area, and not everyone in the large group feels the impact directly.

In the Buffalo Creek disaster of February 1972, a slag dam in the West Virginia mountains collapsed and inundated sixteen towns and many coal camps in a seventeen-mile-long valley, killing 127 people. The dam had been formed of waste from coal mining operations, and its sudden collapse created waves of water as high as thirty feet. The survivors were numb; they couldn't relate to one another. They also felt guilty and blamed themselves for having lived while others perished. In the long run, they found comfort in ascribing a higher meaning to what had happened (declaring that it was God's will,[7] for example). After an event such as the Buffalo Creek disaster, a community actually may regenerate itself through an increase in the birthrate.[8]

The second kind of event that damages the tissue of community is caused by another group of people, the enemy, often a neighboring one. In 1992, Neal Kight and Harold Bare, two pastors from Charlottesville, Virginia, were involved in a project with Navajo Indians. A local newspaper was interested in their work and sent one of its reporters, David A. Maurer, to interview them. The pastors relayed to Maurer their perception that for many Navajo time stopped in 1864 when Kit Carson and his men destroyed their way of life. During that year, approximately eight thousand Navajo Indians in New Mexico were left homeless when U.S. soldiers, under the direction of Carson, burned and destroyed their property. The Indians were then forced on a three-hundred-mile march to Fort Sumner, New Mexico, where they were cruelly imprisoned for four years. During the march and imprisonment, twenty-five hundred of them died. The march became known as the Long Walk. Pastor Bare remarked:

> The Navajo were telling me about the "Long Walk," and at first I thought they were talking about something that had happened the day before. I was really taken aback when I realized they were talking about something that had happened more than 125 years ago. . . . To the Indians, the "Long Walk" is as real as morning sunlight.[9]

Because their ordeal so decimated their population, the Navajo who survived the Long Walk were doomed to pass down the memory of the tragedy and their feelings about it to their descendants, as if later generations could carry out the mourning and adaptation that their ancestors could not.

This type of trauma exacerbates feelings of humiliation and helplessness, which can cause post-traumatic stress disorder (PTSD). In PTSD, the internalized version of a trauma remains in the minds of the victims long after the overwhelming physical danger disappears. The victims relive the trauma in daydreams and dreams, suffer amnesia, or may become hypervigilant or completely dissociated from the idea of danger. Their responses to others are often contaminated with their reactions to their victimizers; they interchange their own identities with those of the aggressors, and they merge aspects of different events. Individuals suffering from PTSD behave as though they have an internal theater where the various actors (victim, victimizer, and rescuer) continuously perform a play. PTSD interferes with the everyday activities of thinking and decision making; it also interferes with the initiation or adaptive accomplishment of the work of mourning. When a whole society has undergone massive trauma, victimized adults may endure another kind of guilt and shame for not having been able to protect their children.[10]

One of the ways to deal with this shared dilemma is for individuals to "envelop" their traumatized (imprisoned) self-representations (images) and externalize and control them outside of themselves. The case of an individual I once treated illustrates the mechanics of enveloping, even though he was not a victim of a shared trauma.

This young man had congenital difficulties with one of his hands. At the ages of five and ten, he had undergone two painful surgical operations. The second operation had also coincided with a third one on his genital area, which had been injured in an accident. The boy's alcoholic father had made fun of his injury and had told the boy that he would never amount to anything. Even if surgery helped him, according to his father, the boy would never grow up to be a man. Naturally, this had been profoundly humiliating to the boy. Surgical interventions had corrected the boy's deformities physically, but, as an adult, he still thought of himself as handicapped. He worked as an orderly in an orthopedic hospital taking care of chronically handicapped individuals.

He dealt with this problem by finding a reservoir for his own traumatized self in chronic orthopedic patients. He enveloped and externalized the unacceptable aspect of himself onto others who fit his perception of his traumatized self. Then he devoted himself with an intense compulsion to caring for the handicapped. In other words, he was trying to "fix" himself through the patients in the orthopedic hospital, who were the reservoirs of his own, now fantasized, handicapped self. The key concept here is the externalization of parts of oneself. As long as this man could retain the hope of effectively rehabilitating these externalized parts (the orthopedic patients), he behaved in daily life as if he were not injured, humiliated, or helpless. But of course, he paid a price for his unresolved humiliation and loss by being stuck in a job that he disliked.

— . —

Transgenerational transmission is when an older person unconsciously externalizes his traumatized self onto a developing child's personality. A child then becomes a reservoir for the unwanted, troublesome parts of an older generation. Because the elders have influence on a child, the child absorbs their wishes and expectations and is driven to act on them. It becomes the child's task to mourn, to reverse the humiliation and feelings of helplessness pertaining to the trauma of his forebears.

I once had the opportunity to study three generations of a family. The details given here are only highlights of a much more elaborate body of information gathered from this family during my study.[11] The man in the first generation had been a prisoner of war in a Japanese camp during World War II. He had been beaten, tortured, and forced to clean up human waste and bury his dead comrades. In short, he had been made to feel extremely helpless, by being humiliated in the extreme. I will call him Gregory. After his release from prison camp, he returned to the United States, where he married a woman who already had a little boy. The woman's first husband had left her when their son was very small, and played no further role in the boy's life.

The little boy, Peter, was being raised by his mother and grandmother, who hated the boy's biological father and, in fact, men in general. They turned their aggression toward Peter by overfeeding him until he was fat. When Gregory joined this family, he felt an uncanny affinity with the little boy, whom he perceived as a prisoner of the two women. Peter, in turn, became a suitable reservoir for the former prisoner's humiliated self-image.

Gregory involved Peter in a rigorous bodybuilding program and began raising him so that he would have exaggerated self-esteem to counterbalance his mother's and grandmother's hateful attitudes. When Peter reached adolescence, Gregory gave him a gun and taught him how to hunt. By "saving" Peter and making him feel above hurt and humiliation, Gregory, like the orderly in the orthopedic hospital, was also trying to repair the damage he himself had suffered. His efforts gave Peter a macho identity, and hunting unconsciously held symbolic importance for both of them. The older man had effectively told the boy through his gestures and actions that "it is better to be a hunter than to be hunted." So Peter became a hunter but not a sports- man. Whenever he felt anxious, he would kill dozens of animals at a time, slaughtering them with a machine gun. "Hunting" became his way of denying his feelings of powerlessness. In the next generation, the meaning of the transmission changed: Peter's own child became a veterinarian who helped injured animals and saved their lives.

The person in the first generation of this family, then, may be said to have had a traumatized (imprisoned) self-representation that he enveloped and externalized onto a member of the second generation in an attempt to repair it. The person in the second generation, who had absorbed the wishes of his elder, in turn externalized his and his stepfather's traumatized aspects onto animals—he would dream of himself as a fat, ugly, hornless deer, for example—and killed them in an effort to erase the bad feelings they represented. His daughter, the veterinarian, once more used predominantly repairing activities, symbolically saving the animals her father had killed (as her grand- father had saved Peter), also in an externalized fashion.

Transgenerational transmissions are not simply the result of hand- ing down stories about a humiliating calamity from one generation to the next. Patterns of behavior and nonverbal messages are intuited and acted upon accordingly. The transmissions of traumatized self- images occur almost as if psychological DNA were planted in the personality of the younger generation through its relationships with the previous one. The transmitted psychological DNA affects both individual identity and later adult behavior. But it is important to remember that what is transmitted may also change as it passes from one generation to the next.

— · —

The influence of a severe and humiliating calamity that directly affects all or most of a large group forges a link between the psychology of the individual and that of the group. In the wake of such an event, a mental representation of it, common to all members, begins to take shape. This mental representation is the consolidated collection of the shared feelings, perceptions, fantasies, and interpretations of the event, as well as the images of relevant characters, such as a fallen leader. Also included are mental defenses against painful or unacceptable feelings and thoughts. When the mental representation becomes so burdensome that members of the group are unable to initiate or resolve the mourning of their losses or reverse their feelings of humiliation, their traumatized self-images are passed down to later generations in the hope that others may be able to mourn and resolve what the prior generation could not. Because the traumatized self-images passed down by members of the group all refer to the same calamity, they become part of the group identity, an ethnic marker on the canvas of the ethnic tent.

Another method of handling the effects of a trauma is to distance oneself from it: sometimes those in a group who were not directly affected by a trauma avoid those who were. After World War II, for instance, many Israelis reacted with shame to certain aspects of the Holocaust and consequently distanced themselves from Holocaust survivors. A large number of the survivors who arrived in Israel in the 1940s without families were put immediately into mental hospitals for depression. Many of these patients' official files did not even mention that they were victims of the Holocaust; among certain mental health professionals, there was a conspiracy of silence.[12]

The reason, according to Israeli psychoanalysts Rafael Moses and Yechezkel Cohen, was "the wish not to have these terrible events be true, not to have them touch us, not to be too closely aware of what took place."[13] In turn, the Holocaust survivors could not relate their experiences openly, which added to the division between those who had been directly affected by the calamity and those who had not. The survivors were given the nickname "soaps," implying that they were weak people who could easily be washed away. It was only years later that a hidden meaning of the nickname became publicly known: Nazis used to make soap out of the bodies of victims.[14] The effort to ignore the Holocaust survivors was short-lived and naturally ineffective.

Today most Jewish people have inherited a legacy to "never forget."[15] The Holocaust is linked to previous incidents of Jewish persecution and anti-Semitic sentiment that have created for Jews the sense of having a special, precarious fate and a shared identity, even for those far removed from the Holocaust. Peter Loewenberg tells a poignant story of how, at a Rosh Hashanah dinner he was attending, a teenager put her parents and other guests on the spot by inquiring in what way she was Jewish, what made her different from her peers and classmates.

> After considerable foundering all over the map of cultural/religious identity, her father asked how Anne Frank knew that she was Jewish. This invocation of a bitter time when identity was defined by a remorseless external world constituting "fate" clinched the argument for the moment. The young lady acknowledged that she was Jewish as Anne Frank was a Jew, irreducibly, because they were potentially subject to the common historical and socio-political forces which would define their destiny.[16]

The psychodynamic explained by Moses and Cohen between those directly affected by a calamity and those who are further removed from it may also appear between a victimized generation and its children. Because of this dynamic, later generations may attempt to erase the memory of the past event. In this case, the memory of the past trauma remains dormant for several generations, kept within the psychological DNA of the members of the group and silently acknowledged within the culture—in literature and art, for example—but it reemerges powerfully only under certain conditions. For instance, a political leader may reignite a dormant group memory that affects collective thinking, perceptions, and actions. When such a shared mental representation of the original injury is reactivated, it may distort a large group's perceptions. New enemies involved in current conflicts may be perceived as extensions of an old enemy from a historical event. Although the original event was no doubt humiliating, the function of the mental representation of it changes, now serving to bond the individuals in the group, paradoxically raising their self-esteem and fueling their attempt to reverse their ancestors' humiliation.

If historical circumstances do not allow a new generation to reverse feelings of past powerlessness, the mental representation of the shared calamity still bonds members of the group together. But instead of raising a group's self-esteem, the mental image of the event links people through a continuing sense of powerlessness, as though members of the group existed under a large tent of victimhood. Indian psychoanalyst Sudhir Kakar found such an example in his study of Hindu-Muslim violence in southern India during the 1990 riots in Hyderabad.

Hyderabad was founded in the late sixteenth century as the capital of the Deccan kingdom of Golconda. It was seen as "a replica of heaven on earth."[17] The city was dominated by Muslims whose mainstream culture had roots in Arab, Turkish, and Persian ways of life. But the Islamic domination did not exclude Hindus from administrative positions and some political power. Hyderabad remained a rich, multicultural city until industrialization caused a demographic shift. As factories and mills were built across the Musi River from Hyderabad proper, many of the Muslim elite left for Pakistan, and the beautiful old city became a ghetto of poverty and deprivation.

When India and Pakistan split in 1947, some argued that Hyderabad should become either part of Pakistan or an autonomous Muslim state since it had a Muslim ruler. However, due to its large Hindu population and its territorial contiguity, Hyderabad became part of India, and subsequently the Hindu population increased to 40 percent.

Violence between Hindus and Muslims broke out in earnest on the eve of the partition in 1947 and has continued into recent years. Concomitantly, the demographic shift between old and new Hyderabad has been reversed; Muslims have fled to the old city "as if to a fortress" where they now make up approximately 70 percent of the population, while Hindus have moved into outlying areas, further separating the two communities.[18]

Muslims dominate the city, but they have lived so long with memories of misery that they continue to perpetuate their legacy. Kakar convincingly describes Indian Muslims in this part of the world, especially those belonging to the upper and middle classes, as suffering from "Andalus syndrome":

> The syndrome, of course, refers to the great Muslim civilization on the Iberian peninsula that ended abruptly [at the end of the fifteenth century], plunging the Islamic world into gloom and leaving a yearning for its lost glory in the Muslim society on the rim of the Mediterranean. . . . In Hyderabad, with its history bearing a striking similarity to the fate of Andalusia, especially in the abrupt ending of Muslim rule, the heartbreak is more widespread than in most other parts of [India].[19]

The shared feelings among indigent Muslims in Hyderabad are closer to depression than to perennial mourning. Their loss of collective self-idealization and the emotional burdens of historical grievances combine to make them act as ready victims of circumstances.

— · —

I use the term *chosen trauma* to describe the collective memory of a calamity that once befell a group's ancestors. It is, of course, more than a simple recollection; it is a shared mental representation of the event, which includes realistic information, fantasizied expectations, intense feelings, and defenses against unacceptable thoughts.

Since a group does not choose to be victimized, some of my colleagues have taken exception to the term *chosen trauma*. But I maintain that the word *chosen* fittingly reflects a large group's unconsciously defining its identity by the transgenerational transmission of injured selves infused with the memory of the ancestors' trauma. For example, Czechs hold on to the memory of the battle of Bilá Hora in 1620 when the Czech nation became part of the Hapsburg monarchy and lost its freedom for nearly three hundred years. Scots keep alive the story of the battle of Culloden, precipitated by Bonnie Prince Charlie's vain attempt to restore a Stuart to the English crown in 1746. The Lakota people retain mental representations of the massacre of the Big Foot band at Wounded Knee in 1890. Jews will "never forget" the Holocaust. Crimean Tartars define themselves by their deportation from Crimea in 1944.

Shi'ites annually perform an extreme form of remembering a chosen trauma by commemorating their religious leader al-Husayn ibn'Ali through ritualized self-flagellation on the anniversary of his martyrdom. Memories and feelings about historic traumas may also be expressed in indirect or even concealed ways. Subtle symbolic protests against the Spanish conquest of Mexico, which took place nearly five hundred years ago, for example, are still enacted throughout present-day Mexico in folk dances. Officially, the dances celebrate the arrival of Roman Catholicism, but surreptitiously they act out a defeat of the conquistadores, a reversal of history.[20]

Chapter 4

ANCIENT FUEL FOR A MODERN INFERNO: TIME COLLAPSE IN BOSNIA-HERZEGOVINA

In December 1994, former president Jimmy Carter went to Bosnia-Herzegovina hoping to play a role in stopping the bloodshed and in obtaining an agreement from the Bosnian Muslims and Bosnian Serbs to return to the negotiating table. If the shooting stopped, even for a short while, it could provide an opening for diplomatic efforts. The former president succeeded in obtaining a four-month cease-fire and an agreement to resume peace talks.

Carter's entourage included Rosalynn Carter; former ambassador Harry Barnes, director of the Conflict Resolution Program at The Carter Center; and Joyce Neu, associate director. They met with Radovan Karadžić, then the Bosnian Serb leader, and Ratko Mladić, then military commander of the Bosnian Serbs. According to Neu, soon after Carter and his group sat down across from Karadžić and Mladić, the Serbs began to explain the victimization that had begun more than six hundred years ago, after the Battle of Kosovo. The former president had already been briefed in Serbian history and was not surprised that in a meeting in 1994 about current, pressing issues the memory of events from 1389 was so prevalent. While Karadžić and Mladić spoke at length of the Battle of Kosovo, Serbian victimization, and their sense of responsibility to protect their group, the Americans remained silent, allowing the Serbs to discharge their emotions concerning a centuries-old memory.[1]

In fact, the Serb grievances have roots that predate the Battle of Kosovo. Between the sixth and eighth centuries A.D., tribes of Slav peoples migrated from the Caucasus region to the Balkan Peninsula and mingled with the local population. They were differentiated into groups such as Serbs, Croats, and Slovenes. By the beginning of the ninth century, the Serbs had been Christianized by Byzantine missionaries and became part of the Orthodox Church based in Constantinople (present-day Istanbul). As the Byzantine Empire declined in the twelfth century, the Serbs developed their own kingdom and established their own autonomous church. For almost two hundred years, under the Nemanjic dynasty, the Serbs enlarged the area of lands they governed. The kingdom reached its climax under the rule of its beloved emperor Stefan Dušan. At the end of his twenty-four-year reign, Serbia controlled a territory from the Croatian border in the north, to the Aegean Sea in the south, and from the Adriatic Sea in the west, to Constantinople in the east. Dušan died in 1355, and the Nemanjic dynasty came to an end after his successor's death. In 1371, Serb feudal lords elected Lazar Hrebeljanović as leader of Serbia. Some sources say that Lazar had been educated at Dušan's court, where he began his career as a low-ranking official. He assumed the title of prince or duke rather than czar, king, or emperor.

On June 28, 1389, Prince Lazar and his army clashed at Kosovo Polje, the Field of Blackbirds, with the army of the Ottoman Turkish sultan, Murat I. Both Lazar and Murat lost their lives. Some seventy years later, Serbia fell under the control of the Ottoman Empire and remained a part of Ottoman territory until it received its autonomy in 1829. Serbia became fully independent in 1878, when it was recognized by the Congress of Berlin. But some areas, such as the province of Kosovo and neighboring Albania, remained under Ottoman control until 1912.

The Ottomans in fact had conquered most areas that later would be included in the former Yugoslavia. Bosnia and Herzegovina were Ottoman territories from the mid-fifteenth century to the late nineteenth century. Croatia and Hungary were conquered in 1526, but the Ottomans remained there only 173 years, at which time Croatia was subjugated to the Hungarian crown. The fact that Roman Catholic Croatia remained under the Ottomans a much shorter time than Greek Orthodox Serbia created both a religious and a historical division between the two peoples. Another rift occurred because some Slavs in Bosnia, beginning with their first century under Ottoman rule, became Muslims. These were the ancestors of today's Bosnian Muslims.

After World War I, the attempt to bring all the southern Slavs into one polity eventually succeeded, and the kingdom of the Serbs, Croats, and Slovenes was founded. Later known as Yugoslavia (meaning "land of the southern Slavs," to distinguish the people there from northern Slavs, such as Poles and Slovakians), it comprised five lands: Serbia, Croatia, Montenegro, Slovenia, and Bosnia. As one might expect, the kingdom was fragmented by frequent quarrels among its different groups. Orthodox Serbs sought to extend their domination, and the Catholic Croats were determined to resist it.

During World War II, Yugoslavia was occupied by the armies of Nazi Germany, and a puppet Croat government consisting of members of the fascist Ushtashi movement was set up by the occupying forces. The Ushtashi declared the independence of Croatia and unilaterally enlarged its territory to include some Serb lands. However, a three-sided war was fought in Yugoslavia by the Nazi-backed Croatian Ushtashi, the Serb monarchist Chetniks, and the communist Partisans. Various sources state that the Ushtashi massacred between 350,000 and 750,000 Serbs during the war. The Chetniks massacred Croats and Bosnian Muslims, many of whom were supporters of the Ushtashi. The Partisans also killed some 100,000 people. All sides committed extreme acts of violence. But in terms of numbers, the Ushtashi killed the most and also established Nazi-style death camps. During this conflict, one-third of Bosnia's population perished.

In 1945, a second Yugoslavia was organized as a communist state, with the former Partisan leader Marshal Tito at its head. Tito was ethnically half Croat and half Slovene. Communist Yugoslavia, like the post–World War I kingdom before it, included the five lands just mentioned, now called republics, plus Macedonia, once part of Serbia but granted status as an independent republic under Tito. Bosnia-Herzegovina was the only republic not clearly dominated by one ethnic group.[2] Kosovo, in southern Serbia, was an autonomous province, populated mostly by Albanian Muslims. The province of Vojvodina in northern Serbia, with its large population of ethnic Hungarians, also had independent status.

Under the communist regime, Serbs, Croats, Slovenes, Montenegrins, Bosnian Muslims, and others lived together without overt conflict. But this harmony was only superficial—internecine discord still existed but was not allowed to be verbalized under communism. Subtle quarrels took the place of outright disputes. In 1967, for example, some Croat intellectuals worked to elevate the status of the Croat Latin script to equal that of the Serb Cyrillic script. In the late 1960s and early 1970s, Croat nationalists demanded the formation of an independent Croatia.

To combat these problems, the communists promoted the concept of the Yugoslav Man, similar to the Soviet ideal of the Soviet Man in which all peoples were connected through the higher objectives of communist ideology and so were equal. In some respects, the project of creating the Yugoslav Man succeeded. In Bosnia-Herzegovina, before the breakup of communist Yugoslavia, more than one-fourth of marriages were mixed and less than 3 percent of Muslims attended prayers in mosques,[3] demonstrating some degree of detachment from the Muslim identity and an apparent attachment to an overarching communist identity.

During the 1984 Olympics at Sarajevo in Bosnia-Herzegovina, visitors could buy one ticket that would allow them admission to selected mosques, Croatian Catholic churches, Serb Orthodox churches, and synagogues. Watching the Olympics on television, Americans might have got the impression that in Sarajevo a multiethnic and multireligious population of Yugoslavs lived in harmony. Yet also during this period Serbs in Belgrade were watching films depicting World War II, reliving the atrocities of the Ushtashis and the "glories" of the Serbs and inflaming their enmity toward their Croat neighbors. The same media that was portraying a harmonious image to the outside world—television—was the key instrument in exacerbating divisiveness within the former Yugoslavia.[4]

The official breakup of the former Yugoslavia began in June 1991 with Slovenia's bid for independence. This occurred rather peacefully, in large part because there were few Serbs to be protected in Slovenia; the war between the Slovenes and the Yugoslav People's Army (JNA) lasted only five days. The JNA, which had come into being in 1945, was dominated by Serbs: 60 percent of its officers were Serbian, even though Serbs represented less than 40 percent of the total population in the former Yugoslavia.[5]

When Croatia declared independence in the same month, a very different situation arose. First, there were many Serbs living in Croatia, and conflict between Orthodox Serbs and Catholic Croats escalated. Both sides began to recall more acutely their centuries-old historical grievances, their suffering during World War II, their religious differences, the pain inflicted by the other. Politics and emotions merged. A war broke out between the Croats and the JNA, which began to disintegrate and was completely dominated by the Serbs. Croats were ethnically cleansed from Croatian areas that Serbs considered traditional Serb homelands. The European Community, especially the Germans, (re)interpreted the notion of self-determination (which had its birth in the fragmentation of colonial rule) and recognized the independence of Slovenia and Croatia in January 1992, perhaps prematurely.

In December 1991, the government of Bosnia-Herzegovina announced that it, too, would seek independence. Bosnia-Herzegovina, however, had three major ethnic groups living within its borders: Muslims, Serbs, and Croats. In a referendum conducted on March 1, 1992, Muslims and Croats chose independence; however, the 1.2 million Serbs in Bosnian territory, who made up 31 percent of the population, boycotted the referendum, and their leader, Radovan Karadžić, warned of civil war between ethnic groups if the independence of Bosnia-Herzegovina was recognized. Bosnian Serbs did not wish to become a second-class minority in a newly independent Bosnia-Herzegovina. Talks concerning the possibility of partitioning Bosnia-Herzegovina failed in March 1992. The following month, one day after twelve European Community foreign ministers and the U.S. government announced their recognition of Bosnia-Herzegovina as an independent nation, the carnage in Bosnia began. The JNA directly or indirectly supported the Serbs in Bosnia and their ethnic cleansing agenda.

What replaced the former Yugoslavia, then, was the creation of new states: Slovenia, Croatia, Bosnia-Herzegovina, and the third Yugoslavia, called the Federal Republic of Yugoslavia, which consisted of Serbia and Montenegro, along with the formerly autonomous republics of Vojvodina and Kosovo. Macedonia, which had been included in the first Yugoslavia until becoming a separate republic of the second Yugoslavia under Tito, became independent without resorting to armed conflict and was named the Republic of Macedonia.

In November 1995, the United States hosted negotiations in Dayton, Ohio, between Slobodan Milošević, president of the Federal Republic of Yugoslavia; Croatian president Franjo Tudjman; and Bosnian president Alija Izetbegović (a Muslim). On November 21, 1995, they agreed to make peace. According to the Dayton Agreement, Bosnia-Herzegovina's boundaries would remain the same, but about 49 percent of the land would be controlled by a Bosnian Serb state, and the rest would be controlled by a Muslim-Croat federation that would include Sarajevo. Furthermore, they agreed to ban indicted war criminals from holding office. Soon after, the United States, Belgium, Great Britain, France, Turkey, and other NATO countries, as well as Russia, sent soldiers to Bosnia-Herzegovina as peacekeepers. Now that American men and women were stationed in this foreign land, Americans could no longer consider Bosnia simply a remote hell zone; it had become a place of emotional and intimate concern for many Americans and other peoples worldwide.

— · —

Such a brief overview of recent events in the former Yugoslavia cannot do justice to the many factors contributing to the conflicts there. The situation is like an onion: you peel off one layer of skin only to discover many more beneath it. Focusing on the mental representation of the Battle of Kosovo suggests not that this chosen trauma actually caused the armed conflicts of 1992–1995 in Bosnia-Herzegovina, but rather that it provided fuel for the fire once Bosnia began to burn. The details of the story of this battle are known by many involved in the Bosnia-Herzegovina crisis, but the story's underlying significance remains largely unexplored.

People often interpret the thinking and behavior of those who live within different political systems or who have different traditions and shared histories according to the parameters of their own political system, tradition, and history.[6] Similarly, in studying an event from another culture or era, one needs to keep in mind that it happened in

THE FORMER YUGOSLAVIA
Dayton Peace Accord

AUSTRIA

HUNGARY

• Zagreb

CROATIA

EASTERN
SLAVONIA

YUGOSLAVIA
Serbia

•Bihac   •Banja Luka   Belgrade•

Tuzla •

BOSNIA

Srebrenica •

Sarajevo •

CROATIA

Mostar •

YUGOSLAVIA
Montenegro

Adriatic Sea

ALBANIA

AGREED ZONES OF CONTROL

Muslims   ⎫
             ⎬ Muslim-Croat
Croats   ⎭ Federation

Serb Republic

0 Miles   50   100
0 Kilometers   100   150

© 1997 Jeffrey L. Ward

a "foreign" context and that one cannot truly understand the event without understanding the thinking and behavior of that place and time.

During the medieval times of the Kosovo battle, nationalism as we know it today did not exist. In the Balkan Christian world, there were czars and czarinas, princes and princesses, lords and ladies, and common people serving their masters. Religious belief and the church dominated thinking. But religious boundaries were fluid enough that Christian royalty or nobles would marry their daughters to neighboring Muslim royalty. In Serbia, the Serbs lived in clans composed of large, extended families of up to a hundred people under the same roof. This tradition caused two seemingly contradictory phenomena: family ties were close, and yet there were constant feuds. Seesawing relationships led to the formation and re-formation of alliances and hostilities. Blood and kinship relations, court intrigues, and the personal whims of leaders played important roles in political and military events.[7]

In the Middle Ages, perceptions of life and death were different as well. In 1348, just forty-one years before the Battle of Kosovo, the Black Plague swept through the Balkan Peninsula, ravaging entire populations. Death was everywhere, and with it came heightened beliefs in heaven and hell, identification with religious figures, and belief in angelic visions. Since science as we know it did not exist, the causality of events was explained by folk traditions and divine intervention.

The Serbs' antagonists, the Ottoman Turks, were rather new to history when the Battle of Kosovo took place. Their ancestors were central Asian pastoral nomads who relied on sheep and camels for wealth and on their ability to shoot from horseback with bow and arrow for their military superiority. In the ninth and tenth centuries A.D., some Turkish tribes began migrating westward. Along these journeys, the Turks were Islamized. After defeating a Byzantine army at Manzikert (today's Malazgirt) in eastern Anatolia in 1071, the Seljuk Turks established a Turkish empire in Anatolia and mixed with the local population. After this empire collapsed, a group of Turks who had taken up residence on the frontier facing what was left of the Byzantine Empire emerged as the new Turkish power under their founder, Osman. This group would become known to history as the Osmanlis or the Ottomans. Osman's son Orhan (who ruled from 1326 to 1359) married the daughter of the Byzantine emperor John VI Cantacuzenus, forming a Byzantine-Ottoman alliance. By 1352, the Ottomans established a bridgehead in Gallipoli, on the European side of the Dardanelles, and served as mercenaries in Byzantine political struggles. Soon they began to act on their own interests in Europe and converted conquered Bulgarian and some Serb Christian overlords into vassals. The reasons behind the battle at Kosovo Polje are not clearly recorded; however, the best guess is that the Serbian leader, Lazar, refused to be a vassal of the Turkish sultan, Murat I, or that he had been a vassal and now wanted independence.[8]

Early Ottoman society was characterized by a social egalitarianism—which would disappear by the fourteenth century and be replaced by a new social structure. The sultan had a hereditary right to rule, and contemporary religious belief compelled him and his followers to conquer the infidel lands for Islam. Under the Ottoman system, the conquered people were categorized by their religion, not their ethnicity. One was Orthodox or Muslim, not Serb, Greek, or Bulgarian. Once under Ottoman control, all were equal—Christians, Jews, and Muslims alike—although Muslims were more equal.[9] In the Balkans much of the land was held by monasteries, and feudalism existed. Raphaela Lewis, who has studied everyday life in the Ottoman Empire, remarked that "by wiping out the big land-owners the Turks put an end to the old feudalism in the Balkans and opened new horizons to small farmers, who settled gratefully under Turkish rule and rewarded their benefactors with their loyalty."[10]

Most of the Serbs, with their own history of recent greatness and expansion, were hardly ready to submit to the Turks and declare their loyalty to the conquerors. They chose instead to resist. While Lazar was the most powerful of these Serb lords, his authority did not extend over all free Serb leaders. In order to make strategic alliances, he gave his daughter Mara to Vuk Branković and his daughter Vukosava to Miloš Kobilić (or Obravitch). Both bridegrooms were Serb lords who later participated in the Battle of Kosovo.[11]

Since no eyewitness reports are available, the historical truth about the battle at Kosovo Polje remains unknown. The story of the battle has been told by many chroniclers, Serb, Turkish, Greek, and others.[12]

What is clear is that there was a full-fledged battle at Kosovo Polje. Some sources state that the Turkish forces outnumbered the Serb forces, and some say the opposite.[13] The Turks were accompanied by Greeks and other Christian soldiers from the European areas they had already conquered and by Slavic soldiers who were already under the Ottomans. Lazar's forces included Bosnians, Hungarians, and Germans, in addition to Serbs.

It seems that the main battle was fought on two consecutive days during which time both sides suffered serious losses, including the two sons of Sultan Murat. On the second or perhaps the third day of the encounter, Miloš Kobilić fatally wounded the Turkish leader.[14] In the most prevalent version of the assassination story, Miloš pretends to defect to the Turkish side and is brought to the sultan. When the sultan offers him his right foot to kiss, as was the custom, Miloš bows as though to kiss it, but suddenly draws a knife from his sleeve and stabs the sultan instead.[15] As might be expected, Miloš was apprehended and later executed by the Turks. Meanwhile, as the sultan lies dying, Lazar is captured and brought to the sultan's deathbed. Either Murat himself, or his son and successor, Bayezit, orders Lazar's execution.[16] The prince is beheaded. At least one Serb source adds that Murat admired Lazar's courage so much that he wanted him killed so that the two of them could be together in heaven.

Because of the chaos following the deaths of both leaders, the immediate outcome of the Battle of Kosovo was not clear. The new Turkish sultan, Bayezit, took his army back to Edirne (Adrianople), not far from Constantinople, temporarily withdrawing the threat against the "free" parts of Serbia.

— · —

After the battle, Murat's body—with the exception of his internal organs—was returned to Bursa (in Anatolia), which was then the Ottoman capital, and buried next to his ancestors' graves. At Kosovo, a tomb with a dome was erected over the burial site of Murat's internal organs. Inside, a stone casket was draped with a beautiful green cloth and with a white turban mounted at the head.

An Ottoman soldier named Hacı Şefik, who had married a local woman and was originally from Buhara in central Asia, was assigned to care for the grave. His descendants took the surname Türbedar (grave keeper), and for six hundred years this family has watched over the buried organs of Murat.

The remains of this tomb have fallen into ruin; today one can barely discern the yellow paint of the walls or the blue paint of the dome. In front of the tomb stands an ancient tree, four centuries old, whose trunk is divided in two at ground level, as if symbolizing the many separations of the Battle of Kosovo: the severing of Lazar's head, the separation of Murat's organs from his body, the splits between the Ottoman and Serbian armies and between Islam and Christianity.

While the Ottomans still possessed this part of the world, the monument held magical significance for Muslims. A crystal chandelier hung above the casketlike structure. Legend claimed that the chandelier would turn one way or the other according to whether a visitor's wish would be granted or not. Today, a remnant of the chandelier lies in one corner of the tomb.

Every night throughout the centuries, ancestors of the Türbedar family placed a cup filled with water in front of the turban, and each morning visitors discovered that Murat—or his spirit—had drunk the water. Fahri Türbedar, a man with a black mustache who wears a fez like the Turks of the late Ottoman period, presently oversees the tomb. He lives with his wife and daughter in a house in the garden of Murat's monument. He complains that the present Turkish government has been negligent in providing funds to repair the place. His grandmother had a vivid dream toward the end of World War II in which a strong man, representing Murat, appeared at her bedroom window and told her, "I am leaving. *Gavurs* (nonbelievers) now occupy this land. I am returning to Bursa." From that day forward, the cup of water placed by the grave keepers next to the turban stayed full, signifying that Murat was, indeed, gone.[17]

The story of Fahri's grandmother's dream and the end of the family's tradition of "magically" filling and emptying the water cup parallels Turkish investment in this part of the world. It reflects the sense that this part of Europe no longer belongs to Turks. For them, the mental representation of the Kosovo battle has become a memory as pale as the sun-bleached yellow paint on the walls of Murat's memorial tomb.

What happened to Lazar's body—and head—is another story with significant psychological implications. Lazar's body and severed head were returned to the central Serbian monastery of Ravanica, and there, in a religious ceremony attended by the hierarchy of the Serbian Church and the surviving nobles, he was canonized. Meanwhile, Lazar's wife, Princess Milica, and her young son, as well as her surviving son-in-law, Vuk Branković, continued to rule their respective territories but suffered from family infighting and Hungarian invasions from the west. In the east, the Turks continued to put pressure on the Serbs. In response to this pressure, Milica wed her youngest daughter, Olivera, to Bayezit. Once more, marriage was used to attempt a political solution. This time, the son-in-law was a former enemy, a Muslim Turk, and quite possibly the man who had ordered his new wife's father's execution.

Meanwhile, Milica's other son-in-law, Vuk Branković, gave in to Bayezit's power. True to the customs of medieval times, political matters intertwined with family matters, and Lazar's son Stefan Lazarević and his men also later joined his father's enemy, Bayezit, in fighting against the conqueror Tamerlane, in Anatolia, near present-day Ankara. The Ottomans were defeated, and Bayezit was taken prisoner by Tamerlane's men. He died in captivity. But Stefan Lazarević survived the battle, returned to Serbia, and combined his father's territory with that which had belonged to his sister's husband, Vuk Branković. Apparently feuds between the Lazarević and Branković families continued, but under Stefan Lazarević, Serbia enjoyed economic and cultural prosperity until 1459, when the Ottoman Turks brought Serbia to an end. Six years earlier, they had captured Constantinople (today's Istanbul) and put an end to the Byzantine Empire.

Despite the gap of seventy years between the Battle of Kosovo and the fall of Serbia, a popular belief gradually developed that equated the two events. It is not the historical truth (or even one of the many versions of it) that matters in the collective Serb psyche. What is important is the shared mental representation of the Battle of Kosovo and of the characters who played key roles in it. As decades and centuries passed, mythologized tales of the battle were transmitted from generation to generation through a strong oral and religious tradition in Serbia, reinforcing the Serbs' sense of a traumatized, shared identity.

This chosen trauma is an observable part of the contemporary Serb identity. When Albanians settled on the "holy earth" of Kosovo, it "took on the character of a festering wound in the national self-esteem."[18] Political scientist Marko Marković states that for Serbs the memory of Kosovo is a "sacred grief" and that "mere mention of that name suffices to shake a Serb to the depths of his soul." He suggests an analogy: "That which the destruction of the Jerusalem Temple is for Israel, and Golgotha is for the Christians, so Kosovo is for the Serbs."[19]

— · —

After his execution and canonization, Prince Lazar was seen as a martyr, and a local cult of Lazar was established by the monks at Ravanica. Then his son Stefan Lazarević died and was succeeded by a Branković family member, and the influence of Lazar's cult diminished greatly. Most likely the tensions between the Lazarević and Branković dynasties contributed to the general disinterest in the memory of Prince Lazar, but the monks of Ravanica remained faithful to the cult and continued to transmit the memory of Lazar, Miloš, and the Battle of Kosovo to new generations. Memories of Lazar and Kosovo have also been kept alive through *guslars,* folk singers who play a one-stringed fiddle called the *gusle,* through a strong oral tradition, and later through schools that taught the story as a part of the Serbian cultural heritage.

As Turkish rule settled in Serbia, many Serbs began migrating north. In 1690, the few remaining monks at the monastery of Ravanica took the corpse of Lazar and joined the northern migrations. Lazar became an "exile." The monks enshrined his mummified body and separated head at a location in the Fruska Gora region, northwest of Belgrade. With his remains, it seems, traveled the myth about him to wherever Serbs resided. Saint Lazar and the mental representation of Kosovo now belong to all Serbs.

In the Serb chosen trauma, Lazar had to be forgiven for sealing the fate of Serbia. According to legend, Saint Ilya, in the shape of a gray falcon, appeared before the prince on the eve of the battle with a message from the Virgin Mary. Lazar was given two choices: he could win the battle and find a kingdom on earth; or he could lose the battle, die a martyr's death, and find a kingdom in heaven. A common Serb folk song memorializes Lazar's dilemma:

Dear God, what shall I do and
Which kingdom should I choose?
Should I choose the Kingdom of heaven
Or the Kingdom of earth?
If I choose the kingdom,
The kingdom of the earth,
The earthly kingdom is of short duration
And the Heavenly is from now to eternity.
The Tsar chose the Kingdom of Heaven.[20]

Through the proliferation of this legend, Serbs collectively tried to deny feelings of shame and humiliation. But helplessness and victimization could not be denied since they, under Ottoman control, had no power to bring back their glorious past. Serbs held on to the martyrdom of the legend and identified with it. In fact, a sense of martyrdom corresponded to their pre-Ottoman self-perception. Even during the Nemanjic period, Serbs felt that they had sacrificed themselves for other Christians in Europe since they had served as a buffer against the advancing Muslim Turks. However, the Serbs, who belonged to the Greek Orthodox Church, won no recognition of their sacrifice from their Roman Catholic neighbors in Europe.

The events and characters of the Battle of Kosovo mingled with elements of the events and characters of Christian mythology. As the decades passed, the story even included a symbolic Last Supper.[21]

Before the battle, Prince Lazar's daughters, Mara and Vukosava, quarrel over whose husband is greater. Vukosava insists that Miloš is the better man. Offended, Vuk's wife, Mara, slaps her sister on the face, and Vukosava runs to her husband, Miloš, to inform him of the insult. Miloš, being an honorable medieval lord, quickly seeks out Vuk, insults him, and challenges him to a joust. Lazar tries to make peace between the two men but to no avail. The two lords face each other on horseback. At one point, Miloš knocks Vuk from his horse and prepares to finish off his opponent, as custom then dictated. But a family tragedy is prevented when Lazar and other nobles force the two brothers-in-law to make peace. The opponents make a show of reconciliation, but not a genuine one. Vuk continues to hold a grudge against Miloš and slanders him at every opportunity.

Meanwhile Murat enters the scene. Vuk tells Lazar that Miloš cannot be trusted, that he is secretly plotting with Murat and the Ottomans. "Miloš is a traitor," Vuk announces. Lazar begins to suspect that Vuk is telling the truth, and he decides to test Miloš's loyalty. The night before the Battle of Kosovo (or, according to one source, during the Battle of Kosovo), the prince gives a big dinner party attended by a number of lords, including the embittered brothers-in-law. The stage is set for a Last Supper, with Lazar as Christ and Miloš as Judas. As the supper gets under way, Lazar stands up and, holding a goblet of wine, tells Miloš that he is accused of treason. He then offers the goblet to Miloš. Without hesitation Miloš drinks the wine, demonstrating no fear that the wine is poisoned. He passes the test.[22] A nineteenth-century lithograph depicts a halo of sunlight over a saintly Lazar, with Miloš bathed in the same light.[23]

Some chroniclers suggest that Miloš killed Sultan Murat in order further to prove his innocence. When he himself was killed in retaliation by the Turks, he became a martyr, an ironic reversal of his former status.

— · —

Under Ottoman rule, Serbs became perennial mourners. The "defeat" of June 28, 1389, became the shared loss that could not be mourned but that had to be recalled continually. Kosovo Polje evolved in the minds of Serbs as a kind of shared, abstract monument. A folk story sprang up speaking of the flowers on the mountainous plain of the Kosovo battlefield that were "crying" for Serbia—referring to the fact that their stems were bent and the flowers appeared to be bowing their heads in grief. The Serbs held on to their victimized identity and glorified victimization in song:

> Drink, Serbs, of God's glory
> And fulfill the Christian law;
> And even though we have lost our kingdom,
> Let us not lose our souls.[24]

During the first centuries after his death, Lazar's image was closely associated with the image of the crucified Jesus. Overtly, Serbs, like Lazar, chose to hold on to the idea of a kingdom in heaven. The idea that they could change their minds and choose a kingdom on earth was not articulated until the awakening of nationalism in Europe in the nineteenth century and the decline of the Ottoman Empire. While the painted icons of Lazar and Miloš from the Renaissance typically depict them as saintly or Christlike, with sorrowful visages and carrying scrolls and crosses, images from the late nineteenth and early twentieth centuries more frequently feature strong warrior figures, with angry eyes and swords raised. Lazar began to be perceived as a resurrected savior; he and Miloš were being transformed from tragic martyrs to heroic avengers.

After much political scheming and several wars, the European powers helped Serbia achieve autonomy in 1829;[25] the Ottomans lost Bosnia to the Austrians in 1878 when Serbia became fully independent. The province of Kosovo remained under Ottoman control. The influence of Austria-Hungary increased in this region (in 1909 the Ottoman Empire and Serbia recognized Austria-Hungary's annexation of Bosnia-Herzegovina). The Austrians attempted to suppress Bosnian Serbs' Kosovo spirit so that they would cease to contemplate rebellion, using Lazar's avenger image as a kind of mascot.

Serbia soon found itself in the Balkan Wars of 1912–1913. It was during these wars that Kosovo, after more than five hundred years, was liberated. A young soldier recalled this liberation:

> The single sound of that word—Kosovo—caused an indescribable excitement. This one word pointed back to the black past—five centuries. In it exists the whole of our sad past—the tragedy of Prince Lazar and the entire Serbian people. . . .
>
> Each of us created for himself a picture of Kosovo while we were still in the cradle. Our mothers lulled us to sleep with the songs of Kosovo, and in our schools our teachers never ceased in their stories of Lazar and Miloš. . . .
>
> My God, what awaited us! To see a liberated Kosovo. . . . When we arrived in Kosovo . . . the spirits of Lazar, Miloš, and all the Kosovo martyrs gazed on us.[26]

For this soldier, and for others like him, "to kill many Turks mean[t] not only to avenge his ancestors but also to ease the pains which he himself fe[lt]."[27] Conquering the territory associated with the heroic images of Lazar and Miloš seemed to reverse the shared sense of victimization and powerlessness, at least temporarily.

Less than two years after Kosovo's liberation, on June 28, 1914, the anniversary of the fourteenth-century Battle of Kosovo, a Bosnian Serb named Gavrilo Princip assassinated Archduke Francis Ferdinand of Austria-Hungary and his pregnant wife in Sarajevo, thereby beginning World War I. What is known about Princip is that as a teenager he, like most other Serb youths, was filled with the transformed images of Lazar and Miloš as avengers. The fact that the archduke had dared to enter Sarajevo on the anniversary of the Battle of Kosovo was perceived by many Serbs as an intentional insult.[28] By shooting the archduke, Princip felt he was attacking Austria-Hungary, which had replaced the Ottoman Empire as the "oppressor" and which had tried to suppress the Kosovo spirit. The archduke's visit on the anniversary of the Battle of Kosovo combined two "oppressors" in a time collapse. After World War I, the kingdom of the Serbs, Croats, and Slovenes was founded.

— · —

One of the carriers of the mental representation of Serbian history was Slobodan Milošević, a stodgy, middle-aged lawyer, banker, and politician. In April 1987, as a communist bureaucrat, he attended a meeting of three hundred party delegates in Kosovo. At the time, only 10 percent of the population of Kosovo was Serbian. The majority was, as it is today, Albanian Muslim. During the meeting, a crowd of Serbs (and Montenegrins) tried to force its way into the meeting hall to express grievances about the hardships for Serbs in Kosovo. The local police blocked the crowd's entry. At that moment, Milošević stepped forward and told the people that no one had the right to suppress them. The crowd responded with a frenzy and spontaneously began singing "Hej Sloveni," the national anthem, and shouting, "We want freedom. We will not give up Kosovo." In turn, Milošević stayed in the building until dawn—for thirteen hours—listening to their tales of victimization. He would later declare in a speech that Serbs in Kosovo were not a minority since "Kosovo is Serbia and will always be Serbia."

Milošević came out of this experience transformed, wearing the mantle of Serb nationalism. I do not know enough about him personally to know whether this transformation occurred suddenly. Most likely, he had been considering the idea of inflaming nationalism for political purposes for some time.

Those who know Milošević describe him as alternately aloof and angry, a shrewd and self-centered politician. A saying in Belgrade goes something like this: Have pity on the person whom Milošević has called a friend.

Milošević was the second son born to an Eastern Orthodox theologian during the Nazi occupation of 1941. He married his teenage sweetheart, Mirjana Marković, but is not known to have many other lasting and trusting relationships. Like her husband, Mirjana had a traumatic childhood. Her mother, having been accused of divulging information about Partisans while arrested by the Nazis, was executed by the communists after World War II. Mirjana remained a communist and became a kind of spokesperson for communist ideology.

There is evidence to suggest that Milošević comes from a dysfunctional family: when he was seven, his favorite uncle, an army officer, killed himself with a bullet to the head; when he was twenty-one, his father, separated from his wife after World War II, did the same. When Milošević was in his early thirties, his mother, who was a schoolteacher and a communist from a prominent upper-middle-class family, killed herself.[29] Whatever his personal motivations, Milošević has transformed himself from anonymous apparatchik to visible nationalist, rousing the patriotic feelings of the Serbian people. He played a role in re-igniting the flames of the Battle of Kosovo and further strengthening this collective memory as a tool for entitlement to revenge.

As the six hundredth anniversary of the Battle of Kosovo approached in 1989, Milošević and his associates were determined to bring Lazar's body out of "exile." Lazar's remains were placed in a coffin and taken on tour to every Serb village and town, where they were received by huge crowds of mourners dressed in black.[30] Whether Milošević's initial intentions were to provoke desire for genuine revenge is unclear. It appears that he wished to increase the cohesion of Serbian group identity and pride and to secure his political position, and he succeeded. Serbs began to feel as if the defeat at Kosovo Polje had occurred only recently, a development made possible by the fact that the chosen trauma had been kept effectively alive—although sometimes dormant—for centuries.

The communist era was one such dormant period, but even then there were signs that the psychological DNA of Kosovo continued to be passed down from one generation to the next. The Battle of Kosovo was presented to elementary school children as the most important event in Serbian history. In the 1970s, a movie about the battle aroused Serb interest but was soon discredited because the director was a Croat. In a bronze figure of Prince Lazar made in 1971, the exaggerated frown and the arm beginning to lift a sword are unambiguously bellicose.[31] Serbian red wines were even sold under the labels of Czar Lazar and Czarina Milica, with pictures of Prince Lazar and his wife on the bottles. Symbolically speaking, their "blood" was consumed by the population.

Milošević's focus on Kosovo reactivated this DNA. With his encouragement, Serbs felt within their bosoms the traumatized self-images of their ancestors. As they greeted Lazar's body during its tour of Serbia, they cried and wailed and gave speeches; never again would they allow such a defeat to occur.

Milošević ordered a huge monument to be built on a hill overlooking the Kosovo battlefield. Made of red stone symbolizing blood, it stands one hundred feet over the "grieving" flowers. Lazar's words before the battle are inscribed on it, calling every Serb to come to the Field of Blackbirds to do battle against the Turks. Any Serb who fails to respond to this call, Lazar's words warn, will have neither a child nor fertile land where fruits and crops will grow. The monument consists of a platform surrounded by "bullet-shaped cement towers inscribed with a sword and the numbers '1389–1989.' "[32] By linking 1389 with 1989, Milošević was resending Lazar's ancient message and merging the interpretations and feelings associated with the Battle of Kosovo with those of 1989.

On June 28, 1989, the six hundredth anniversary of the Battle of Kosovo, a helicopter brought Milošević to the Field of Blackbirds. After descending from the helicopter, he "took the podium from dancing maidens in traditional folk costume and transported the crowd to heights of frenzied adoration with a simple message: 'never again would Islam subjugate the Serbs.' "[33] In a photograph of this rally, one can see that Lazar's message telling Serbs to come to the battle-field to fight against the Turks was imprinted on the T-shirts of many of those present.

———

In 1990, the six Yugoslav republics held elections. The communists were defeated everywhere except in Serbia and Montenegro. In Serbia, the communists were now called the Serbian Socialist Party, and Mil-ošević was elected to lead them. The province of Kosovo became a police state. Meanwhile, Turks once more became the clear and pres-ent enemy. The Turkish embassy in Belgrade was led by Hasan Ay-gün, who, in the absence of an official ambassador, fulfilled that role. In this atmosphere of heightened Serbian nationalism, he found him-self considered public enemy number one in the Serb capital city. Everywhere he went, Serbs asked him, "Why are you [Turks] planning to invade us?"

It seemed to Aygün as though almost every Serb believed in the imminence of a Turkish invasion, and he was afraid for his own safety. This was a kind of "shared paranoid disorder";[34] a large percentage of the population perceived Turks as enemies and Bosnian Muslims as Turks, consciously and unconsciously.

Aygün also noticed that many Serb youths had developed a new game: playing Russian roulette with loaded pistols. Many of these teenagers ended up in the hospital—dead or with head wounds. Like Lazar, the youths were experiencing two choices: death and martyr-dom or life and revenge on Turks.

Horst Grabert was the German ambassador to Belgrade who would sometimes dine with Milošević. The German wanted to warn the Serb about the danger of spreading nationalism, so one day he told Milo-šević a cautionary tale—Johann Wolfgang von Goethe's "Der Zaub-erlehrling" ("The Sorcerer's Apprentice"). When his master is away, the story goes, the apprentice experiments with the sorcerer's magic and orders a broom to do his chores and carry water to a basin. But once the basin is filled with water, the apprentice does not have the magical skill to stop the broom, so he chops it in half. No sooner does he split the enchanted broom than both pieces spring back to life and begin the chore anew, in duplicate.

Ambassador Grabert reminded Milošević that without the old master, Marshal Tito, Milošević might not be able to stop the doubling and spreading of nationalism. Obviously, Milošević did not appreciate this advice; instead, he continued to fan the flames, even accusing Tito of having pursued an anti-Serb policy.

In June 1992, Milošević accused his "friend" and mentor Ivan Stambolić, then the president of the third Yugoslavia, of not protecting the Serbs in the province of Kosovo. Milošević engineered the downfall of Stambolić and was himself elected the next president. Earlier, Milošević had summoned Radovan Karadžić and others to meet with him.

— · —

Karadžić himself is an interesting case study. He was born in 1945 in Petnjica, an isolated mountain village in the western part of Montenegro. The people of Petnjica are proud of their history: four hundred years ago, their ancestors refused to pay taxes and rebelled against the Ottomans. Karadžić's father was a Chetnik who fought during World War II against communist Partisans led by Tito. Later, during Tito's reign, Karadžić's father was imprisoned for five years. Some villagers say he was jailed for being a traitor to Tito's communist government; others, however, report that he had been convicted of incest with a cousin.[35]

Because her husband was in prison, or perhaps due to other circumstances, Karadžić's mother, Jovanka, was left alone with few resources to raise five children: four boys and one girl. When Karadžić was eleven years old, the family moved to Nikšić, where the children could get an education.

Karadžić went to Sarajevo at the age of fifteen and found it difficult to find acceptance in urban social circles. Sociologist Beverley Allen referred to the young Karadžić as "an uncouth bumpkin with offensive manners" who had "come down from the mountains."[36] But he later studied medicine and psychiatry and married a fellow psychiatrist. For a while he worked as a physician to the Sarajevo Football Club, under a Bosnian Muslim with whom he was friendly. There are stories of his gambling and drinking.[37] The best man at his wedding was also a Muslim.[38]

Karadžić was a poet. In 1974–1975, he attended a graduate creative writing program at Columbia University in New York. Little is known about his life in New York, however, except that he once had a Columbia University library card.

He began to publish poetry in his early twenties, and he also wrote some children's books. His first three volumes of poetry were written before his transformation into a nationalistic, political leader. But the early poems carry themes of victimhood, ancestral longing, and mythical heroism. He has, on occasion, sung his poems to his own accompaniment on the gusle—like the traditional guslars.[39]

The story of Karadžić's transformation begins in 1985 when he was convicted of fraud (misuse of public funds for home loans) and, like his father before him, was put in jail, where he remained for eleven months before being freed by a Serbian judge. While in prison, he developed ideas of an imminent Islamic jihad (holy war) in Bosnia. He thought that the Muslims would murder him and other Serbs.[40] He either really believed in this danger or found it useful to increase his influence as a nationalistic leader. Karadžić's personal transformation crystallized when he condensed in his mind his imprisoned identity with the imprisoned identity of his ancestors—he was not immune from the effects of a time collapse and from being a carrier of the Serbs' chosen trauma. After release from prison, he was ready for revenge.

In 1990, after his prison experience, Karadžić published his last book of poetry, *Crna bajka* (The black fable). Psychiatrists Kenneth Deklava and Jerrold Post, who studied the poems in *Crna bajka*, observed in them a marked change in language. While Karadžić's previous writings had reflected "a collective sense of myth and sacrifice," *Crna bajka* expressed "his grandiose fantasy and sense of destiny."[41] Most likely Karadžić was wounded psychologically when he was in prison. It was there that he wrote "A Man Risen from the Ashes," a poem in which he claims he can tolerate humiliation if he can enjoy a kind of rebirth. In another poem, "Kalemegdan," the situation is inverted. This time his ancestors are imprisoned. Eventually they would have their freedom. By aligning his plight with the fate of his ancestors, Karadžić bolstered his own sense of nationalism. He describes Serbs trapped in the eponymous Belgrade fortress, surrounded by advancing Turks. The Serbs are helpless, able to do nothing but "await the Czar's [Lazar's] return, which will crown our destiny, as if marked at birth."[42]

In *Crna bajka* the image of the motherland to which he returns is full of sorrow. Karadžić also wrote of the assassin Gavrilo Princip, likening Princip's shooting of Archduke Ferdinand to shooting "into the wound of an era" that would lift "our [the Serbs'] spirits."[43]

When Joyce Neu met Karadžić during Jimmy Carter's cease-fire talks, she asked him about his psychiatric specialty. Karadžić replied, "I specialize in group therapy and the treatment of depression."

— · —

After the collapse of the former Yugoslavia, Serbian leaders in the Yugoslav Federation and in Bosnia collaborated on preparations to "purify" Bosnian Serbs from Bosnian Muslims (as well as Croats). Scholars such as Dobrica Cosić at the Serbian Academy of Arts and Sciences joined the politicians and feverishly incited Serb nationalism. Separating Serbs from Bosnian Muslims and stabilizing a rigid psychological border between the two became a necessity.

The Bosnian Muslims who were victims of ethnic cleansing were descended from southern Slavs who had converted to Islam within a century of the Ottoman conquest. While the Serbs remained Christian, many Slavs in Bosnia changed their religion, an apparent anomaly that some historians explain with the so-called Bogomil hypothesis. Bogomilism began in Bulgaria in the late tenth century and prospered in Bosnia in the thirteenth and fourteenth centuries. Converts to this religious reform movement named after a Bulgarian priest, the Bogomils believed that God and Satan had equal power; they rejected the Crucifixion and did not believe in the holiness of the Virgin Mary. Because of this, they were viewed as heretics, enemies of both Catholics and Orthodox Christians. When the Muslim Ottomans arrived, the Bogomils chose Islam over Catholicism or Orthodoxy. Some historians, however, do not subscribe to this theory.[44] They contend that southern Slavs became Muslims merely to avoid paying certain taxes the Ottomans demanded of non-Muslims.

Under the Ottomans, Bosnian Muslims developed epic songs reflecting their past glories. Sarajevo housed many Muslim treasures, including the Gazi Hüsrev Bey mosque, an architectural marvel built in 1530. This mosque, and a library of the same name that held more than four thousand manuscripts in Arabic, Turkish, and Persian, was destroyed during the Bosnian conflict of the 1990s.

Bosnian Muslims, seen as an extension of the Ottomans, served as a reservoir for the massive projections of Serbs' unwanted qualities, including aggression. One should not minimize, however, the role of the Bosnian Muslim leadership in establishing Bosnia as an attractive target for these projections, a factor that received scant attention in the media.

Though Tito, for political reasons, showed tolerance of the Muslim faith by allowing three hundred mosques to be built between 1945 and 1968 (with money supplied by Arabs), Bosnian Muslims did not invest much in their religion during the communist era. The large increase in the number of mosques did not translate into a drastic increase in mosque attendance. Radical, fundamentalist Islam was supported from outside Yugoslavia, and there were both secular and radical segments in Bosnian Muslim society. As the former Yugoslavia began to collapse, radical Islamists gained political power. Bosnian Muslim leader Alija Izetbegović, a religious man, expressed in writings going back to the 1970s his dream of an Islamic power, or an Islamic empire, extending from Morocco to Indonesia. That dream provides an opportune reservoir for the Serbs' projections.[45]

Serb propagandists began accusing Muslims of preparing to launch a jihad against them. In reality, however, Muslims had no military power and insufficient weapons to consider such a move. The more such projections occurred, the more Bosnian Muslims were perceived, consciously and unconsciously, as Ottoman Turks, the enemy in the Serbs' chosen trauma. The more the Bosnian Muslims' "dangerousness" evolved, the more the Serbs feared them. They also feared a boomerang effect: namely, that their projected aggression would come back to them. Thus, the collective idea that Muslims had to be exterminated began to emerge,[46] and the emotional atmosphere was such that Serbs as a group responded easily to their political and military leaders' manipulations. In fact, these leaders were acting according to the group's existing psychology. The stage was set for the ethnic cleansing of Bosnian Muslims.

In November 1995, while Slobodan Milošević, Franjo Tudjman, and Alija Izetbegović were meeting with then U.S. assistant secretary of state Richard Holbrooke and his staff in Dayton, Ohio, two Turkish newspaper reporters, a woman named Münire Acım and a man named Ali Koçak, were captured by Bosnian Serb forces and imprisoned for nineteen days before being released. Although not physically tortured, they were made to fear for their lives. During repeated interrogations, the Serbs demanded of the Turkish reporters: "Didn't you rule our lives for five hundred years? Do you still want to rule us?" The captors believed that many of the NATO pilots who bombed Serb positions in Bosnia (in order to force Serbs to come to the negotiating table and accept a political settlement) were Turkish. They continued threatening the two reporters: "We will do to you what your ancestors did to us—break your fingers one by one and hang you by a silk rope,"[47] which refers to the Ottoman method of execution.

The phrase "We will do to you what your ancestors did to us" offers a clue about the psychological impetus behind the systematic rape of Bosnian Muslim women *and* men during the Bosnian conflict. Rapes often occur in riots and wars, where heightened expressions of aggression unconsciously intensify expressions of sexuality, and aggression and sexuality become confused. Rape then becomes the enactment of a primitive and humiliating form of aggression, while on a conscious level it is intended as a strategy to intimidate the enemy.

In Bosnia the rapes were vengeful and planned, as if the entire Bosnian Muslim culture had to be desecrated and destroyed. Sociology professor Ruth Seifert explains: "In 'dirty wars' it is not necessarily the conquest of the foreign army, but rather the destruction of a culture that can be seen as a central objective of war actions, for only by destroying it—and that means by destroying people—can a decision be forced."[48]

On an unconscious level, systematic rapes were connected with the Ottoman institution called the *devşirme*. Its mental representation was added to that of the Battle of Kosovo and submission to the Turks. Beginning with the reign of Murat I in 1359 and continuing for the next four centuries, the devşirme involved conscripting state servants from the empire's Christian Orthodox population. Christian youths were collected as an extraordinary tax levied by the sultan. They were taken from their families, converted to Islam, and educated to serve the sultan. The number of youths—male, unmarried, and between the ages of eight and eighteen—averaged one out of forty Christian households in selected communities. Ottoman officers sought out only the physically strong and left behind orphans, boys with trades vital to the local economy, only sons, and those with behavioral or physical problems.

Professor Norman Itzkowitz, a leading authority on the history of the Ottoman Empire, describes the rigid rules that were followed: The authorities went to Christian areas in the Balkans and

> . . . sent criers to the villages to notify local officials. . . . Fathers were told to bring their sons in for inspection, and they were accompanied by the priests, who brought along the baptismal records. The janissary [military—in Turkish *yeni çeri* means "new troops"] officers then examined the youths. The name, age, parentage, residence, and description of each boy selected was recorded in a register, of which a duplicate copy was made. The chosen boys were then collected in groups of 100 to 150, dressed in special garments, and dispatched to Istanbul in the care of a janissary escort, who was entrusted with one copy of the register, the other copy remaining with the collecting officer. At headquarters in Istanbul, after all the youths were collected, the two registers were compared to ensure that no substitutions had been made en route, because it was common knowledge that some parents sought to buy their children out of levy. Later, when the personal advantages offered by the *devshirme* had become evident, others would try to buy their sons in.[49]

The fate of the boys depended on the career track selected for them. Some received the finest education available in the Islamic world and were prepared for administrative positions in the empire; they would learn religious sciences, Turkish, Persian, Arabic, music, calligraphy, mathematics, miniature painting, horsemanship, archery, and wrestling. One of the greatest grand viziers of the Ottoman Empire, Sokollu Mehmet Pasha (born Bajca Sokolović), was originally a Serb who had risen within the devşirme system. He served three consecutive Ottoman sultans, including Süleyman the Magnificent, during the greatest Ottoman expansion. Most youths were hired out to Turkish farms, where they would learn Turkish and be enrolled in the ranks of the military as members of the empire's feared janissary force. According to Prince Lazarovich and Eleanor Calhoun, "By the middle of the sixteenth century, the heart of the Turkish army was composed of janissaries of Serb blood, their swords turned against their own mothers and fathers."[50]

Even though the boys may have received personal advantages under the devşirme, we can imagine that the families from whom the boys were taken not only grieved for their loss but also experienced great ambivalence toward their sons, who now belonged to the dominant group and the very administration and army that kept their ethnic group subordinated. The parents' pride in their sons' accomplishments would have conflicted with their shame for their new role and religion. In the Serbs' historical grievance, the devşirme was eventually equated with social rape.

The systematic rapes of the 1990s reflect the urge to reverse the shame and humiliation connected with this social rape by doing to Bosnian Muslims—and by extension to the Turks—what the latter had done to them. The shared unconscious sense of entitlement to revenge created a collective and regressive morality that supported the consciously planned atrocities.

When in 1991 journalist Roy Gutman of *New York Newsday* visited Banja Luka, the future capital of the Bosnian Serb state, he investigated Serb propaganda that helped pave the way for the atrocities to come. One piece of propaganda read:

> By order of the Islamic fundamentalists from Sarajevo, healthy Serbian women from 17 to 40 years of age are being separated out and subjected to special treatment. According to their sick plans going back many years, these women have to be impregnated by orthodox Islamic seeds in order to raise a generation of janissaries on the territories they surely consider to

be theirs, the Islamic republic. In other words, a fourfold crime is to be committed against the Serbian woman: to remove her from her own family, to impregnate her by undesirable seeds, to make her bear a stranger and then to take even him away from her.[51]

The missive aimed to create fear among Serbs that Bosnian Muslims intended to resurrect the devşirme and create a new janissary army. There is a kernel of truth in this idea; Bosnian Muslim leader Izetbegović had intimated in his speeches and writings the possibility of an Islamic enterprise in Bosnia.[52] However, the possibility of resurrecting a janissary army is pure Serbian fantasy.

When Gutman spoke with Major Milovan Milutinović, a key figure in the Serb propaganda machine, Gutman was shocked by references to janissaries:

What raised my eyebrows was the reference to janissaries. . . . "Which century are you talking about?" I asked. He replied: "It is a new and recent phenomenon. This is a crime against women. It has ugly aims that can hardly be imagined in the civilized world. They are trying to do what they did centuries ago."[53]

Gutman considered Milutinović's explanation "the most bizarre I ever heard from a military man."[54] The concept of time collapse, however, provides a way to understand Milutinović's seemingly irrational explanation and the effects of a sense of a shared entitlement to revenge.

Further evidence for the connection between the atrocities in Bosnia-Herzegovina and the events of centuries ago was shown in a British Broadcasting Corporation documentary on the massacre of Muslim men at Srebrenica, which occurred in July 1995.[55] One surviving witness of the massacre reported seeing Muslim men being taken to a building, where they were shot. Upon hearing the moans of one man who had not been killed, a Serb went back into the building and said, "Are you still alive? Fuck your Turk mother!" and shot him dead.

Serbs expected Bosnian Muslims to destroy them, and this fiction led them to attempt to increase their own population through raping Bosnian Muslim women. Serbs decided that a child born to a non-Serbian woman raped by a Serb would be a Serb and not carry any vestige of the mother's identity, genetics notwithstanding.[56]

When Serb boys were conscripted under the Ottoman devşirme system and turned into Muslim Ottomans, the biological genes from their parents were rendered irrelevant. Now Serbs were trying to devalue the biological genes of non-Serbian women, by using them as vessels to produce more Serbs to fight against Muslims (and Croats). Meanwhile, they were also killing existing Muslim sons of Bosnian women; their new sons would be "Serbs," and the number of Serb men would increase.[57]

A particular method of killing young Muslim men also was clearly associated with the devşirme system. In Ottoman times, when Christian youths were collected to become Muslims they underwent circumcisions, which their new religion required. During the war in Bosnia-Herzegovina, some of the captured Muslim men, in addition to being raped, were forced to castrate fellow Muslims. One example is reported by Alexandra Stiglmayer: "On June 17, 1992, Serbian guards forced the 21-year-old Emin J. to drink a litre of motor oil and then bite off and swallow the testicles of three fellow prisoners who had already been beaten half to death."[58] In religious circumcision, the foreskin of the penis is removed as a symbol of a shift in male identity, a rite of passage, and also connects the individual to his ethnic or religious group. What Serbs did in Bosnia was infused with aggression; this act of revenge no longer constituted merely doing to the other what was done to them but now included murderous rage. The act of circumcision was elevated to castration and death.

— · —

The story of the Battle of Kosovo illustrates the various ways a chosen trauma can affect a group. Adopting a chosen trauma can enhance ethnic pride, reinforce a sense of victimization, and even spur a group to avenge its ancestors' hurts. The memory of the chosen trauma is used to justify ethnic aggression. As the images of the Battle of Kosovo and its Serb heroes were kept alive throughout six centuries, the story became a frequent and significant subject for countless artistic expressions. It emerged and continues to appear in icons, folk songs, poems, paintings, sculptures, plays, movies, monuments, and scholarly discussions, like a religious symbol that supports the Serbs' sense of being a "chosen people."[59]

By holding on to the memory of the Battle of Kosovo, when manipulated by their leaders following the collapse of the former Yugoslavia, Serbs also fueled a shared feeling of entitlement to revenge, which sanctioned official propaganda and atrocities. But the world did not agree with Karadžić's and Mladić's sense of entitlement, and they were declared war criminals by the International War Crimes Tribunal because of their roles in the atrocities. In 1996, both were removed from their official positions, though still at large in the Serbian-held territory of Bosnia-Herzegovina.

But after the Dayton Agreement, world opinion, especially that of the United States and Europe, was inclined to legitimize Milošević's political power instead of holding him responsible for the tragedies in the former Yugoslavia. Former UN secretary-general Boutros Boutros-Ghali believed that Milošević could become a partner in efforts for peace in the former Yugoslavia. The West moved toward helping Milošević transform himself once more—this time into a democratic leader—using excuses such as national interest and world order to justify such decisions. Milošević was accepted as an actor in maintaining world peace.

But then, in the November 1996 elections, a coalition of political parties opposing Milošević called Zajedno (Together) won the municipal vote in Belgrade and in fourteen of the nineteen largest cities throughout Yugoslavia. Protests were sparked when Milošević moved to overturn the results, and university students began parading noisily, braving frigid weather in the streets of Belgrade. Eventually, the protesters were confronted by police. In December, a delegation from the fifty-five-nation Organization for Security and Cooperation in Europe (OSCE) arrived in Belgrade at Milošević's invitation. The OSCE group confirmed that massive electoral fraud had occurred, but they had no mandate to mediate in Yugoslavia's internal affairs. Zajedno leaders Zoran Djindjić, Vuk Drasković, and Vesna Pesić urged continuation of the protests. The U.S. and European governments began to take a second look at Milošević. In February 1997, he accepted the results of the fall elections.

In view of the tendency of ethnic groups under stress to rally around their leaders, the fall 1996 developments in Yugoslavia are curious. They suggest that the link between the leader and a portion of his followers had been broken.[60] Even if Milošević were to lose power in Yugoslavia, it is difficult to predict the fate of malignant nationalism there. The most important opposition leader, Vuk Drasković, was once the leader of a rightist paramilitary band. Zoran Djindjić used to be friendly with some Serbian fanatic nationalists, and his political alliances have undergone many transformations. *Washington Post* reporter John Pomfret writes that Djindjić's "remarkable string of transformations from anarchist in the 1970s to liberal in the 1980s to nationalist in the early 1990s to democrat today puts him in line to become the first Teflon Serb. . . . When Milošević switched his policy to embrace peace, Djindjić coddled the Bosnian Serb warriors. When Milošević signed the Dayton peace treaty ending the conflict in Bosnia, Djindjić gave it only half-hearted support."[61]

Four years after it began, an international war crimes investigation has convicted only one Serb soldier of crimes against humanity, the low-ranking Dusko Tadič. In May 1997, a London news service reported that British government officials (under then prime minister John Major) had refused to turn over British intelligence intercepts that allegedly showed links between Milošević and the 1992 "ethnic cleansers" in Bosnia. Apparently they assumed that the world would be better served if sleeping dogs were left to lie. This may be good realpolitik, since Serbia and surrounding areas could fall into greater chaos if Milošević were officially discredited. Nevertheless, the "protection" of war criminals could have grave psychological consequences because the collective morality remains tainted. If leaders directly associated with atrocities are not punished, Serbs will internalize shame and guilt, whether they acknowledge it or not, and such feelings will be passed down to later generations. For victims, such as the Bosnian Muslims, not bringing the victimizers to justice could fuel the urge for revenge. When external peacekeeping forces leave Bosnia, efforts at retaliation could take place, especially since the Bosnian Muslims are better armed now than before. At best, this new wound in the heart of Europe will leave an ugly scar. At worst, it will fester.

Chapter 5

—·—·—·—

WE-NESS: IDENTIFICATIONS AND SHARED RESERVOIRS

The mental representation of a historical event that induces feelings of success and triumph, what I call a "chosen glory," can bring members of a large group together. Usually such triumphs are deserved victories over another group. The adjective "deserved" is necessary here because some events that may at first seem triumphs are later seen as humiliating. Nazi Germany's "triumphs," for instance, were perceived as criminal by most of the succeeding generations of Germans.

Chosen glories are reactivated as a way to bolster a group's self-esteem. Like chosen traumas, they become heavily mythologized over time. The Jews remember the legendary story of the Maccabees, who restored the defiled Temple of Jerusalem and lifted the spirit of an oppressed group, and the British remember the Battle of Britain, in which the Royal Air Force successfully held Hitler's forces at bay. After the Soviet empire collapsed and triumphs of the communist era (such as the October Revolution) were devalued, Russians clung all the harder to their mental representation of the great patriotic war against the Nazis as a key marker of their group identity.

During the Gulf War, Saddam Hussein depended heavily on chosen glories and even associated himself with past heroes in order to persuade his people to follow him. He once likened himself to Sultan

Saladin, who rose to power in Egypt in 1169 and united Islamic opposition to defeat the crusaders. Interestingly, Saladin was not an
Arab, but a Kurd. During the Iran-Iraq War of the 1980s, Hussein
had not blinked an eye in killing Iraqi Kurds with poisonous gas.
Now, for the sake of glory and omnipotence, he found it expedient to
"reincarnate" himself as a Kurd.

Both chosen glories and chosen traumas are easily absorbed by
the children of a group. Chosen glories influence identity less per-
vasively than chosen traumas, however, because their effect is less
complex. Chosen traumas bring with them powerful experiences of
loss and feelings of humiliation, vengeance, and hatred that trigger a
variety of unconscious defense mechanisms that attempt to reverse
these experiences and feelings. Chosen glories, however, simply involve enhanced libidinal attachment, with no need for reversal.

This is not to say that chosen glories cannot be integral to large-
group identity. An event that succeeds in making a positive change
in a country's political system or a cultural revolution can become an
important aspect of a group's identity. The shared mental representation of a war for independence, for example, is a powerful ethnic or
large-group marker. Symbolic representations of chosen glories are
proudly displayed.

The late Boris Lomov, who in the late 1980s was director of the
Institute of Psychology at the USSR Academy of Sciences and previously a key behavioral scientist in the Soviet space program, wore
a Lenin pin on the lapel of his jacket whenever he visited the United
States. In 1989 and 1990, he participated in unofficial meetings to
discuss Soviet-American relations and to consider establishing an ongoing dialogue between social scientists from each country. Whenever
he felt that his group identity was being threatened, he would ritual-
istically play with his Lenin pin. I concluded that this pin, an inanimate object, was Lomov's way of symbolically linking himself to his
Soviet tent whenever he was on American soil.

In 1984, I had observed a similar phenomenon during our Arab-
Israeli dialogues. In one small-group session, I happened to sit between General Shlomo Gazit, formerly the top-ranking Israeli officer
in charge of the Gaza Strip, and Eyad Sarraj, a Palestinian who later
headed the Palestinian Independent Commission for Citizens' Rights

in Gaza. Attending the meetings for the first time, Dr. Sarraj had been frustrated by difficulties in obtaining Israeli permission to travel to Austria for the dialogue. Although we had tried to provide a safe environment for discussion, where enemies could feel equal, I sensed this proud man's uneasiness. As the small-group session began, he turned to the Israeli general and said:

> You were the last Israeli military officer in charge of Gaza who was fair in dealing with Arabs. I don't like living under Israeli occupation one bit, but I respected you as a man. After your tenure was over, however, none of the new military commanders were as fair to us as you had been. Now, to be assigned to Gaza as the Israeli military chief is the end of a person's career. The Israelis send their unwanted officers to us. These officers know this, and they have been frustrated and unjust toward us.

As he spoke, Dr. Sarraj's emotions overtook him. He put one hand into his pocket and stated loudly, "As long as I have this, you can't take my identity away from me." While it was clear that he was speaking about an object in his pocket, he did not reveal what "this" was. It turned out to be a small stone with the Palestinian colors painted on it. Later, without showing it to me directly, he described the stone and told me that most Palestinians in Gaza carried one like it. They had developed an invisible network to which they belonged, signified by carrying these objects in their pockets. When they felt threatened—upon approaching an Israeli checkpoint or group of soldiers, for example—they could put their hands in their pockets and touch the stones.

—·—

An ethnic marker is used by members of a group to protect and maintain the canvas of the ethnic tent and to keep individual members loyal. The marker may be related to present or past leadership (the tent's pole), but its primary purpose concerns the canvas itself. Ethnic markers may be abstract concepts, such as chosen glories, or concrete objects, such as Dr. Sarraj's stone. In all cases, they serve to enhance members' sense of belonging to a group.

While the role of fetishistic objects in reflecting sexual conflicts and protecting sexual identity was recognized in the 1920s by Freud,[1] it was not until 1953 that psychoanalysts identified the progenitor of all psychologically magical inanimate objects—the transitional object.[2] A perfect example of a transitional object is the blanket Linus carries in Charles M. Schulz's *Peanuts*. Many children become attached to a blanket, a teddy bear, a special pillow, or even part of their own body (hair, for example). These children often cannot go to sleep without their "magical" teddy bear or without twisting their hair in a ritualistic fashion.

The attachment to a transitional object not only helps children have a sense of controlling their surroundings, but also gives them confidence as they explore their world. The transitional periods during which children start to find their place in the world require stimuli from the outside, but too much can overwhelm them and arrest emotional growth. When children are feeling vulnerable and unable to process the new information and experiences that will eventually form their identity, they can move into a magical, controlled world for a while, with the help of a transitional object. Magical objects allow children to control the pace of their developmental progress.

Think of a lantern with transparent and opaque sides. When children are awake, fed, and alert, they use the transparent side of the lantern to illuminate their surroundings and allow access to the people around them. When children are sleepy, angry, or hungry, they turn the opaque side toward others, including their mother, and wipe them out. Now the children's world outside of themselves is limited to a relationship with the lantern. When the children are alert again, they shed light on others once more. Slowly children get to know others and climb the developmental ladder, eventually finding their own identity so that they no longer need the magic of the transitional object. These transitional objects are normal; they disappear as children grow up, but memories of them may not be forgotten.

If children have difficulties in their early years and their developmental attempts are interfered with, they may exhibit a different form of transitional object, usually referred to as a "childhood fetish" or "psychotic fetish." In these instances, children carry around not soft objects like teddy bears, but tough, cold objects, like stones.[3]

Problems with caretakers and difficulties in this early stage of identity development are at the root of the meaning of these objects: they serve to "patch up" deficiencies in a child's nascent sense of identity. A piece of rock or other fetish that a child feels compelled to carry around is a temporary support system, a kind of identity scaffolding, that is used until it is no longer needed or until it is replaced by another method of shoring up the sense of self.

While dependence on such bizarre objects of attachment is considered pathological in individuals, the use of similar inanimate objects by members of a group is a relatively common reaction to a perceived threat. Like the Gaza Palestinians' colored stones, these objects connect individuals with their group and strengthen and define the border between their group and others. They are not pathological, because the use of shared inanimate objects by members of a large group under threat is only a partial regression to the use of childhood fetishes. The primary regression involves reactivating a device used in childhood around the age of three. This device is called a "suitable reservoir of externalization,"[4] which is but one of a series of magical inanimate objects that people use. Suitable reservoirs, like all magical inanimate objects, have at the lowest level a transitional function in boundary and initial identity formation. Always shared by children in the same group, they are crucial tools in connecting individual psychology with group psychology in the pre-oedipal period.

— · —

Professor Robert Emde, a child psychoanalyst and researcher at the University of Colorado, has postulated the concept of "the executive we": an "idea" that exists in the infant's mind that he or she is acting in concert with caregivers.[5] There is no firm sense of "self" or "I." The infant's mind is in a creative state of confusion, and his sense of "I" (which will clearly differentiate him from other people in his surroundings) evolves only slowly, crystallizing by the age of three. Innate potentials (including the "executive we," sophisticated thought, relationships, discrimination between feelings, and identity construction) are developed through experiences with important people, especially parents. After the first weeks of life, for example, a newborn smiles automatically in response to a wide range of external stimuli, such as his mother singing a lullaby or touching his face. With further maturation, smiling becomes a selective response to specific stimuli and a more meaningful expression in the baby's developing human interactions.[6] The child begins to absorb experiences with important others. This absorption is called *identification*.

Identification is an old concept in psychoanalysis. Although Freud spoke of identification in his letters to his friend Wilhelm Fliess in 1896 and 1897, it was not until *Three Essays on the Theory of Sexuality*, published in 1905, that he made a theoretical formulation about it, suggesting that sucking provides essential gratification that is associated with the mouth (or oral zone, as he called it).[7] The taking in of the breast became a prototype of identification. Later, Freud spoke of this concept as "the earliest expression of an emotional tie with another person."[8]

Initially, Freudian theory focused on the internal world of the individual, emphasizing the subject's impulses (instinctual drives) and defenses against these impulses. The influences of others (i.e., mother or father) in the development of the child's internal world were seen as peripheral stimuli. The child was the active agent, identifying with a "passive" adult, whose role in the child's mind was "interpreted" by the child. The child's impulses, fantasies, and expectations made the relationship with adults either nurturing or inhibiting. Not until after Freud's death was the crucial role of the conscious and unconscious interaction between the primary caregiver and the child fully appreciated by psychoanalysts, such as Erik H. Erikson, Edith Jacobson, and Margaret Mahler. Identification involves not only the active role of the child, but also the influences of the person with whom the child is identifying.

By identifying with another person, the child does not become an exact replica of that person. Rather he absorbs experiences with that person. Through identification, children take on functions that previously were performed for them by others, thereby enriching their own mental lives. Identification opens the way for relative independence from others and leads to further psychological growth as well as more effective methods of dealing with the demands of one's environment. This type of enriching identification is usually referred to as "ego identification," indicating a child's growing ability to do things the way his mother did.[9] Ego identification helps explain how a child who receives good parenting has greater potential to be a good parent himself.

Before ego identification can take place, a child has to accomplish a task called *differentiation*. This refers to the baby's separating his existence from that of the mother or other caregiver. During the first months of life, before differentiation gradually takes place, the child's mind generally does not know where the child ends and the mother begins. Ego identification can be enriching only when the child identifies with someone from whom he has been differentiated. Identification after differentiation therefore means that something new from the outside comes into the child.

Integration is another task that the child negotiates early in life while he is involved in establishing ego identifications. Newborn babies can tell the difference between pleasant and unpleasant physical experiences. They enjoy the taste of sugar but spit out lemon, for example. Similarly, they can sense the difference between pleasant and unpleasant emotional experiences. Yet small children do not fully realize that they are the same person when they are having a satisfying experience as they are when having a frustrating experience. They feel good when they are loved, fed, kept warm, complimented, and made to feel secure, and they associate these feelings with a certain "I." But they do not have the same strong connection to this "good" self when they feel rejected, hungry, scared, humiliated, or threatened. Instead, under such bad conditions, they behave as if they had a different sense of "I." Only slowly does a child become capable of knowing that he is the same individual when he feels pleasure as when he feels frustrated or devalued. This process is called integration, and it is completed for practical purposes by the age of thirty-six months.

With integration completed, a child can, at least unconsciously, say to himself, "I am the same person when I am adored as when I am scolded." We can envision integration as a process of making gray by blending one's black and white parts. Through gray-making, the child becomes more realistic about himself. He is neither entirely kind nor entirely cruel, not just Dr. Jekyll or just Mr. Hyde, but a combination of both aspects of his personality. The child now has an *identity*.[10]

While the concepts of identification and identity are related, they are not the same. Unlike the concept of identification, identity is a rather new concept in psychoanalysis. Freud did not mention it often, and when he did it was in a colloquial or literal sense.[11] Erik Erikson once remarked that "identity formation . . . begins where the usefulness of identification ends."[12] Revising Erikson's statement, it is more accurate to say that formation of identity begins when the integration of early identifications is solidified: it is a subjective experience that starts with a sense of "persistent sameness within oneself."[13] The child shares with other people some essential characteristics, but his own wishes, memories, thoughts, and appearance make him unique.

As a child continues to mature, he discovers anatomical differences between the sexes and adds to his personal identity new elements pertaining to gender. During the oedipal period, more complicated identifications, called superego identifications, enrich his identity. The child absorbs his parents' prohibitions as well as their values and cultural and group heritage. He learns to move from acting to avoid punishment to acting to fulfill his parents'—and by extension his group's—values. When the child goes through adolescence, he experiences what is called an identity crisis. During this period, he unconsciously reexamines, modifies, and even discards some identifications from childhood, then remixes them, lets them settle, and reassimilates them with modifications and additions.[14] What results is his now crystallized personal identity: the formed personality that will remain his core until he dies.

Throughout his life other sub-identities are added to this core. An adult, for example, can present himself as a husband, a father, a Virginian. He may also be a businessman, an amateur photographer, a Republican, and a member of the Rotary Club. Individuals have multiple sub-identities that they can either embrace or reject without causing much harm to their internal world or physical environment. The person who is a father, a Virginian, a Rotarian, an amateur photographer, and a Republican, for instance, may give up photography and instead develop a sub-identity as an amateur carpenter. He can also change political party or social club affiliations without much inner turmoil (unless for personal reasons he thinks that a particular affiliation will make or break him).

It is the core identity, however, developed around age three, enriched with gender-specific elements during the oedipal period, and crystallized in adolescence, that we hold on to. If this core identity is ever lost or destroyed, as it is with adult schizophrenics, the experience is terrifying. As one schizophrenic patient explained it:

> The whole world begins to shatter and you see yourself lit up like a thousand-watt light bulb traveling a million miles an hour. . . . It's no longer a problem of whether to wear a shirt or wash your jeans. . . . You fly into your world and all else diminishes in importance.[15]

This patient is describing a psychological death more horrifying than a physical one. Because of the schizophrenic's response to this threat, it seems to observers as though he has pushed a button and created a new identity, albeit a false one. Now, he says, "I am Richard Nixon," and makes the victory sign with his arms as the former president used to do. While everyone else knows this identity is false, the person clings to it (unless he gets well again) in order to avoid the terror of not having an identity of his own.

— · —

When the core identity initially forms, some unintegrated fragments of the self, both positive and negative, always remain unintegrated.[16] Because these unintegrated black and white fragments threaten to throw a child's established grayness off center, keeping them inside his identity is a bothersome reminder, a thorn. Failing to rid himself constructively of these unintegrated parts will destabilize a child's identity. There are a variety of ways that a child unconsciously deals with these unintegrated aspects of self. One way is mentally to sweep them under a rug. Called *repression*, this is a form of hiding away unintegrated fragments of the self as well as troublesome impulses, thoughts, and feelings. However, another method, the process of *externalization* (an early form of the broader concept *projection*), particularly applies to ethnicity.[17] In externalization, remnant black and white fragments are deposited in people or things outside oneself.

As a child integrates his internal world and develops his identity, it is easy to understand why he wants to rid himself of unintegrated "bad" aspects of this world. It is not as easy to understand why he would want to get rid of unintegrated "good" aspects. If he kept them, however, he would tend to idealize himself unrealistically and would expect the world to idealize him, too, and recognize his greatness. Life, with its cruelties, would make him miserable because it would seem to ignore his special status. Furthermore, failure to rid himself as much as possible of unintegrated parts makes the identity precarious. This is why a person behaves as if he is afraid that these loose fragments will clash or threaten the grayness (reality) and why he externalizes them for safekeeping. Yet because they are a part of him, he does this without completely eliminating them. Having become more realistic, for example, a child knows that he is no longer "the greatest," but he may begin to idealize his grandmother or uncle now because he has externalized these feelings of greatness onto them. By seeing himself as an extension of this grandmother or uncle, the child can then feel great through association. As he grows older, he begins to recognize that this grandmother or uncle is not quite so wonderful, and, in a sense, he takes back and absorbs some of these unintegrated good aspects, allowing his own grayness, his realistic identity, to grow. He does this also with his unintegrated bad aspects. Nevertheless, a need for some externalization always remains.

This process in itself does not create an ethnic identity; it is all simply part of the personal developmental experience. The reservoirs into which the unintegrated good aspects of children are externalized must have two characteristics in order to be containers of ethnicity: they must be shared, as by all children in a group, and they must be constant, like a national flag or national colors. A Cuban lullaby, a Finnish sauna, a German nursery rhyme, and matzo ball soup are all examples of ethnically shared reservoirs. By investing unintegrated good aspects of themselves in these reservoirs, children develop an invisible network, a we-ness, by which they are connected to the same reservoir. Without knowing it, they become part of an emotionally bonded large group. Just as a child experiences pleasure when he sees himself as an extension of an idealized grandmother, the children in a large group feel secure by connecting themselves to a positive reservoir.

This investment of parts of individuals in shared reservoirs—the song, the sauna, the rhyme, the soup—is another example (like mental representations of chosen traumas and glories) of psychological DNA in the canvas of the ethnic tent. Through the shared reservoirs, ethnicity or large-group identity is intertwined with personal identity at the pre-oedipal level. The more abstract concepts of Cubanness, Finnishness, Germanness, or Jewishness slowly become associated with these reservoir objects, which are, indeed, at the foundation of large-group identity.

A child's intense involvement with his parents, other family members, and teachers functions as a bridge to his ethnic reservoirs because the adults in his environment are also attached to these items that enhance group identity. As the child's mental capacities enlarge, these adults help him to form more sophisticated ideas about belonging to a group. Depending on the focus of a large group's identity, a child's investment might be in ethnicity (I am Arab), religion (I am Shi'ite), nationality (I am French), or some combination of these. A child born in Hyderabad, India, for example, would focus on religious and cultural issues as he develops a large-group identity, since adults there define their dominant large-group identities according to being Muslim or Hindu. A child born in Cyprus would absorb a large-group identity defined by ethnic and national sentiments, because what is currently crucial in that part of the world is whether one is a Greek or a Turk, with less emphasis on whether one is Greek Orthodox Christian or Sunni Muslim. Questions of investment in ethnicity versus religion, or nationality versus race, are not as crucial to understanding large-group identity as is the psychodynamic process of linking individual selves to the canvas of a large-group tent.

Eventually, a shared way of feeling about one's large group becomes more important than the concrete symbols themselves. Going to the sauna (a suitable reservoir of we-ness) remains a national habit for a Finn, but he is proud of being a Finn even when he is not in the sauna. Though one element of Finnish ethnicity may begin with an inanimate object, such as a sauna, beyond the concrete object lies an abstract ideation of Finnishness, with a history of chosen traumas and glories and a set of abstract values. For the Finn, the link between himself and shared Finnishness will always remain with him; his sense of self will rise and fall with the rise and fall of Finland's fortunes in areas such as sports, academic achievements, political events, and artistic endeavors, whether or not he continues to use the sauna. Should Finland or his Finnishness be threatened, however, he will adhere more stubbornly to his sense of ethnicity, because to give it up would feel like giving up part of his own being, part of his own identity. He will also exaggerate his tradition and perhaps go to a sauna more often to affirm his concrete link with his shared we-ness.

Most shared reservoirs remain constant for a long time, but certain events may shift the group's investment in them. In Scotland, Highland dress dates from the thirteenth century. An event in the eighteenth century transformed the tartan kilt into a shared reservoir of Scottishness. When England defeated Bonnie Prince Charlie at Culloden in 1746, the English banned the wearing of the kilt in Scotland under the Act of Proscription. The act was repealed thirty-six years later, and the kilt was adopted as Scottish military dress. When George IV made a state visit to Scotland in 1882, the wearing of the kilt reached a peak that lasted thirty years. One could say that his visit crystallized the Scottish investment in the kilt, which served to enhance Scottish unity in the face of a visit from the figurehead of the powerful other—England. Many Scottish families have their own tartan design, which they sometimes use in their personal clothing; in this case, the cloth of the ethnic tent is literally worn by members of an ethnic group. Efforts to suppress the wearing of the kilt have been unsuccessful; the dress continues to serve as an ethnic reservoir signifying Scottishness.

— · —

The positive unintegrated aspects of group members include both "good" self-fragments and "good" parts of caregivers. A child before age three is not fully capable of integrating discrete experiences; he cannot recognize that sometimes the source of pleasurable and unpleasurable experiences can be one and the same person. The mother who satisfies her child by feeding him and the mother who frustrates her child by not feeding him are not experienced as the same source in the infant's or young child's mind. As the child integrates his own black and white parts, he also becomes capable of making the caregiver's representation gray. Integrating the caregiver's representation is never a total process. Unintegrated "good" caregiver images are included among the positive aspects that group members externalize onto suitable reservoirs.

In examining groups whose ethnic tents are threatened, one can see how members of such groups attempt to re-create this method of childhood bonding. When Dr. Sarraj reported how other Palestinians in Gaza were carrying stones similar to his, he was describing the way in which the stones had become an adult form of a shared reservoir. The Palestinians' externalized "we-ness," in the form of these stones, was tucked securely out of sight, put away for safekeeping while the Palestinians in Gaza were under Israeli rule.

In childhood, reservoirs are chosen because they have been culturally invested in by parents and other adults, and these adults direct the children to choose them. Adults who regress, however, choose reservoirs that symbolically relate to their existing and threatening (adult) environment. In two very different situations, Kuwaitis chose Chevrolet Caprices and Cypriot Turks chose parakeets as shared reservoirs for their groups.

In the early fall of 1993, three years after Operation Desert Storm and the liberation of Kuwait from the Iraqi invasion, Kuwait City showed little evidence of war damage. What had been ruined in 1990 was fully repaired by 1993. As far as I could observe, only a few houses in the city bore marks of destruction, such as bullet holes in the walls and burned windows. I was told that a couple of them would be left as they were, as tributes to the tragic events.

What touched me emotionally about Kuwait City was that in this modern place, built on a desert, many trees had been destroyed, perhaps by fire but more likely because they had not been watered during the seven months of invasion and occupation. Trees lined both sides of some main streets in the city, and dead ones had been replaced by new trees much smaller than the original ones planted years ago. The breaks in uniformity created an image that stuck in my mind. It reminded me of the stuttering of a terrorized person whose normal flow of speech is broken. Here, the flow of trees was broken. Otherwise, nothing I saw in Kuwait City, except the houses mentioned above, attested to the horrors that had taken place there.

When a group from the Center for the Study of Mind and Human

Interaction conducted more than 150 in-depth interviews with Kuwaitis in order to understand post-traumatic societal responses in that
country, denial of the horrors of the war and difficulties in mourning
losses quickly surfaced.[18] One of the study team members, psychiatrist
Gregory Saathoff, became fascinated with how the Kuwaitis, after the
invasion of Saddam Hussein, used cars as a shared inanimate object
that both united them as members of a shaking ethnic tent and represented a source of supernatural power in the face of an overwhelming enemy. Some Kuwaitis had escaped from the invading
Iraqis to Saudi Arabia by car. One man showed Dr. Saathoff a rusting
1989 Chevrolet Caprice that he had enshrined as though it were a
museum piece. It was the car he had driven in his escape to Saudi
Arabia, and now he would let no one touch it. As Dr. Saathoff looked
at the car and listened to the man speak, he realized that, while all
he saw was a rather common, badly rusted automobile, to the Kuwaiti,
this was a magic carpet.

This sentiment toward cars had generalized into a kind of obsession with them, especially reconditioned 1989 Chevrolet Caprices,
which, as rumor had it, could tolerate desert conditions better than
any other model. That the cars could withstand the heat and aridity
of Kuwait made them an object that the Kuwaitis could rely on, a kind
of security blanket that could be invoked on command. The Caprice
became a symbol of safety, a "good" object. The efficacy of the Caprice
in desert conditions is not the issue. The *meaning* of the Caprice is.
The Kuwaitis began to keep such cars as "good" objects, as magic
carpets that could take them away from their anxiety. Reportedly, a
dealership in the United States has benefited from the myth, providing
Kuwaitis with a steady supply of reconditioned Chevrolet Caprices.[19]

A more complicated example of reservoir sharing took place during the 1960s among Turks living on the Mediterranean island of
Cyprus.[20] This island, where I was born to Turkish parents and spent
my childhood and teen years, is a splendid "laboratory" for interethnic
studies. Under Turkish rule for more than three hundred years, Cyprus
was first "leased" to the British and then legally given to them after
World War I. It has been home to two major ethnic groups, Greeks
and Turks, who originally lived side by side along with a few other,
much smaller ethnic groups. After a period of terrorist activity aimed

at the British by Cypriot Greeks, a Cypriot republic in which both Greeks and Turks were partners was established in 1960. The islanders continued to consider themselves either Greek or Turkish, however, and within three years, a bloody conflict broke out between the two groups.

Between 1963 and 1968, Cypriot Turks were forced by Cypriot Greeks to live in enclaves under subhuman conditions and eventually occupied only 3 percent of the island, instead of the 35 percent they had previously owned. They became caged prisoners, surrounded by enemies. Because Cypriot Turks were forced to live in enclosed areas, they returned to living with extended families, as had been their previous practice. One way for them to tolerate this situation psychologically was to create reservoirs of externalization. For Cypriot Turks, these shared reservoirs turned out to be, oddly enough, parakeets.

During the summer of 1968, when I visited Cyprus after having lived in the United States for twelve years, I found four families crowded into my family's house. There were also sixteen birds in three homemade cages, living as an extended family like their caretakers. The original pair of parakeets—the mother and father—was pointed out to me, along with a "bride" who had just been moved into her new home. One enormously fertile, but crippled, hen was a special pet; her fecundity more than made up for her imperfections. My family fed the birds, gave them names, and kept track of their genealogy. They particularly noted which birds were fertile so that more birds could be born, sing, be happy, and live in extended families.

When I went out the day after my arrival, I found that the hobby of parakeet raising was not unique to my family but was enjoyed by the entire enclave. I felt as if I were walking onto a movie set full of strange props. There were hundreds and hundreds of caged birds everywhere, and parakeets are not even native to Cyprus. Although some people had kept pet birds previously, I learned that beginning in 1963 almost every Turkish household, coffee shop, and grocery store in the Nicosia enclave adopted parakeets, with which the owners were invariably preoccupied.

The caged parakeets may be seen to symbolize the unpleasant aspects of the imprisoned Turks. By externalizing these unpleasant parts, Cypriot Turks were able to tolerate living in such difficult conditions. Also, a shared reservoir unconsciously provided a network for them, a path for bonding. Cypriot Turks went one step further, however. By taking good care of the parakeets and giving the birds positive attributes, the people reversed, at least symbolically, their bad feelings. The birds came to symbolize their hopeful, good parts. As long as the birds were fertile and sang happily, Cypriot Turks unconsciously felt assured that they themselves would not become extinct. In the long run, the birds of Cyprus became reservoirs of "we-ness" for the new Cypriot Turkish ethnicity existing under unbearable conditions.

In 1968, the political situation on the island changed, and Cypriot Turks were allowed to move out of their enclaves. The door of the cage had been opened, and the preoccupation with the parakeet hobby soon began to disappear. In 1974, the mainland Turkish army landed on the island to protect the Cypriot Turkish population, which was facing new threats of annihilation. This action resulted in the de facto partitioning of the island into a Turkish section in the north and a Greek section in the south, and living in the enclaves ended for good.

— · —

The utilization of shared reservoirs from childhood on for the bad and unintegrated parts, as well as projections of unacceptable thoughts and feelings, also helps create an ethnic marker for the recipient group. Here the marker of we-ness is provided by the opposing group, the other. To illustrate this, I will refer to a delusion that used to be commonly found among African Americans suffering from various kinds of psychosis. But first, I will explain the process on an individual level.

Imagine an anxious mother who for her own reasons decides that her child is handicapped in one way or another and then treats him as such. The child may indeed have some problems, but the mother experiences her child's problems in an exaggerated way. In turn, the child identifies with his mother's view of him and performs below his potential. In a clinical setting, when the other's (in this case, the mother's) conscious and unconscious fantasies play a role in her offspring's identity, the effect can be seen clearly, especially in individuals with exaggerated identity problems.

A married woman gave birth to a child while having an affair. She did not know who the father of the child was, her husband or her lover, and fantasized that the child was the product of both men. She could not share her fantasies with anyone, but when the child (a boy) was born, his name sounded like a combination of both men's names, and she related to her son as if he were two people. Nine years after his birth, when I clinically examined the boy and his mother, I saw that the son had a severe identity problem—his mother's unconsciously sent messages resulted in a split in his personality organization. He had, literally, a double personality, one that fit his mother's perception of her husband and another that fit her perception of her lover.

Like a child who identifies with the way his mother perceives him, a large group may develop an ethnic marker that is placed there by a dominant opposing group. Picture two large-group tents side by side. Individuals in the first tent throw mud, excrement, and refuse—the externalization of their unintegrated bad elements and projections of unacceptable thoughts—onto the canvas of the second tent, and inhabitants of the second tent do the same. If the people in the first tent are dominant and the externalizations and projections are powerful, to some extent what they throw onto the second tent is absorbed into that canvas and intertwined with the existing threads. The resulting stain then evolves as an ethnic marker, which individuals collectively and often unconsciously hold on to. Often the group experiences anxiety for having this marker since it is made of bad or undesirable elements.

An ethnic marker among the African American community illustrates this phenomenon. Psychiatric literature in the United States before the early 1960s includes many references to a type of delusion common among African American patients with various psychoses: a delusion of being white. Most writers were following the lead of an American psychiatrist named John E. Lind, who in 1914 had published papers on the "color complex" of African Americans.[21] Lind apparently was a product of his time, for he also conceived of African Americans as "little children" whose dreams, according to then-prevailing Freudian analysis, were simple wish-fulfillments. After studying the dreams of some African Americans, Lind concluded that they suggested the subjects' simple desire to be white, an interpretation he found supported by the delusions of the African Americans he studied.

Several decades later, with changing attitudes toward African Americans, psychiatrists saw Lind's work as lacking a sound cultural and sociological basis. But they continued to observe the prevalence of delusions of whiteness among their African American patients. Sometimes patients openly described their belief; at other times, their belief had to be rationalized in bizarre manners. One schizophrenic African American said that indeed he was white and that his skin had been burned by a flamethrower. Another patient became obsessed with taking showers in order to wash away his "sunburn."[22]

These later psychiatrists and other mental health professionals tried to explain away the reason for such delusions and referred to a variety of external factors but not white racism. Most explanations put the responsibility of causation on black parents, minimizing the role of the other. Social worker S. W. Manning stated that, since these parents were carriers of knowledge that preferential treatment was given to slaves of mixed ancestry, they wanted to have light skin and passed such sentiments on to their children during early mother-child interactions.[23] The parents were bombarded with advertisements for products to bleach their skin, straighten their hair, and "correct" distinction.

An individual's delusion has specific meanings for him. The shared delusion of being white stems from the mental representation of common experiences in race relations. In the early 1960s, I worked at Cherry Hospital in Goldsboro, North Carolina, when this hospital was still segregated. Many black patients I saw there with a wish to be white simultaneously experienced anxiety about the idea of containing or being contaminated with white blood. Their whiteness was due to something put in their body from outside and was desirable on one level and dreaded on another.

But the shared delusion of being white was really related to the externalization and projection by dominant whites onto the African American ethnic tent. By wanting to be like the mud throwers, African Americans were trying to identify with the oppressor and deny the pain of being reservoirs of bad elements. This defensive attempt at identification could only be openly expressed by those who had psychoses, breaks with reality, and yet it was often evident that this identification also induced anxiety.

In the late 1960s and early 1970s, a handful of African American psychoanalysts and psychiatrists began expressing in print what it was like for an African American to be a reservoir of white people's externalizations and projections.[24] These scholars also exposed myths by showing, for example, that all impoverished children were prone to fail in school, not just black children. W. H. Grier and P. M. Cobbs wrote:

> There is nothing in the literature or in the experience of any clinician known to the authors that suggests that black people *function* differently psychologically from anyone else. Black men's mental functioning is governed by the same *rules* as that of any other group of men. Psychological principles understood first in the study of white men are true no matter what the man's color.[25]

Meanwhile, legal and social changes were taking place that attempted to reverse the role of African Americans as targets of externalization and projections. Ideas such as "black is beautiful" rendered the African American tent less suitable for whites' externalizations and projections. Indeed, since my work at Cherry Hospital, I have not encountered African American mental patients with delusions of being white.

In spite of many positive changes since the 1960s, the long history of the use of African Americans as targets of externalization and projection can still be seen, in modified forms, in their ethnic tent. Psychoanalyst Maurice Apprey has tried to tease out shared unconscious psychological processes pertaining to the mental representation of slavery. His studies trace the evolution of an ethnic marker "designed" by whites and follow it through many generations. He theorizes that this process is involved in black-on-black crime, incest, and pregnancy among young blacks. Many aspects of the victimization and humiliation of blacks by whites become internalized, he argues, as self-destructive behavior through which African American teenagers unconsciously recount the calamity of slavery that befell their ancestors.[26]

But not all groups who have been victims of slavery or of political or economic oppression resort to internecine violence. When Cypriot

Turks were forced to live in enclaves from 1963 to 1968 without being able to move from one place to another, they also internalized aggressive impulses and developed psychosomatic symptoms. But the pressure from their enemies was not long in duration. Cypriot Turks, moreover, could hold out the hope of liberation.

Chapter 6

ENEMY IMAGES: MINOR DIFFERENCES AND DEHUMANIZATION

When representatives of large groups in conflict meet to attempt reconciliation, the movement one observes in their deliberations is not a steady progression toward "togetherness" but rather an oscillation between closeness and separation. During the first meeting of the Arab-Israeli dialogue series sponsored by the American Psychiatric Association, the participants at first remained aloof toward one another, except when competing in listing their historical grievances. Their opposition was made physically manifest by their sitting on opposite sides of the conference room, as though facing off. Then the dialogue between Abd El Azim Ramadan and Nechama Agmon, described in chapter 2, broke down one level of resistance between them, and soon the participants began to intermingle and sit next to one another. However, after a period of marked physical closeness ("We are all brothers and sisters, descendants from a common grandfather—Abraham") they would once again separate, usually as a result of some boundary being breached or too closely approached, for instance, when an Israeli said, "What is Egypt? Without the Nile, it is nothing!" It would take a while for a degree of trust to be reestablished, and then the cycle of contradictory attitudes would continue.

I call this nearly rhythmic oscillation between togetherness and distancing the "accordion phenomenon,"[1] which was especially pronounced when the Palestinians joined the group and aligned themselves physically and emotionally with the Egyptians. The ritual first represented an unconscious effort on the part of the participants to deal with their aggressive feelings. Confined in a room with "enemies" with whom they were charged to work closely, both Israelis and Arabs sat apart, unconsciously avoiding any harm they might do if they sat near one another. While they verbally suppressed their aggression, the participants' behavior indicated that they still harbored antagonistic feelings.

The conscious aim of the dialogue, of course, was to forge a path toward peace. After denying their aggression, both Arabs and Israelis could achieve an illusory sense of brotherhood through a mechanism called *reaction formation* (unconsciously doing something contrary to one's true but hidden wish). When this union became too much to tolerate, distancing again took place. The extension and contraction of the accordion gradually became less pronounced as Arabs and Israelis felt less of a need for reaction formations and greater freedom to express constructively both their aggression and their goodwill, without fear that their dialogue would come to an end.

The accordion ritual also reflected a need to maintain a border between the antagonists. Their togetherness was tolerable up to a point, but too much togetherness created palpable anxiety. This was reflected in even minor differences. For example, during lunch, when all the participants ate together by design, an Israeli might recount having eaten a certain dish in an Arab restaurant in Jerusalem and would explain that Israelis ate that dish, too, but that the recipe was slightly different. While people of different cultures like to talk about what makes their recipes unique, the importance of small distinctions in food preparation habits testified here to the importance of maintaining separate group identities. To understand better the need to maintain a border and to preserve identity from contamination with enemy images, a closer look at the development of enemy images is helpful.

— · —

The human body contains biological pairs of opposites—both physiological and anatomical. Digestive functions are in opposition to excretory functions. Some nerves (called sympathetic and parasympathetic), belonging to the autonomous nervous system, perform opposite but paired functions. Psychoanalyst Charles Pinderhughes maintains that human "us and them" behavior has a biological foundation and is modeled after the dichotomies in the body.[2]

Regardless of whether or not the existence of such a biological foundation for allies and enemies can be proved, as far as individual psychology is concerned, the infant's first enemy is the mother or caregiver who does not or cannot respond to the infant's needs, leaving the infant in a state of accumulated frustration and rage. A severe earache that persists despite a mother's efforts to console may lead to an infant's creating an enemy image of the mother. The child only slowly integrates mother's good and bad aspects into one image, a process that for practical purposes is completed when the child is about three years old.[3]

When a child is about eight months old, he experiences what is known as "stranger anxiety."[4] He clings to a parent in the presence of a stranger, even though the person has done nothing to warrant such a response. By this time in his development, the child has come to know the first big love of his life, his mother (or her substitute), and to distinguish her from others. What bothers the child is not who the stranger is, but who the stranger is *not*: the stranger is not the good mother. Stranger anxiety shows that the child is capable of putting out there—onto the stranger, for example—something scary that comes from within himself. The child is capable of creating individual "enemies," thus an externalization mechanism is at work at this early age. As he matures, the child will have a more realistic sense of the degree to which his individual enemies are real and the degree to which he has fantasized them as undesirable.

Child psychoanalyst Henri Parens saw evidence at about nine months of age of a striking "biological upsurge" in a child's aggressive drive that accounts for obstinacy and willfulness. This upsurge includes a need to master and channel angry impulses because they threaten to cause the loss of the mother's love should they be directed at her. Parens found that because children cannot tolerate losing their mother's love they quickly learn how to displace their anger onto someone else. According to Parens, the biological upsurge of aggressive impulses and a child's way of handling them through displacement create the foundation of prejudice.[5]

As far as ethnic enemies are concerned, children belonging to one large group externalize their unintegrated "bad" self-fragments (as well as their "bad" images of caregivers) onto the canvas of another group's tent. While influential adults, such as family members and teachers, direct children to songs, dances, foods, and colors to be used as positive shared reservoirs, they also, through verbal or nonverbal behavior, tell the children how to find stable reservoirs in the enemy tent for their bad unintegrated parts. The beginning of the formation of social and political enemies is an extension of this phenomenon. For example, Muslim and Christian "enemies" have different religious beliefs, but they also have stable, shared reservoirs.

Muslims, like Jews, are forbidden by their religion to eat pork. Children born in Kuwait or Saudi Arabia, where the population is almost entirely Muslim, may grow up never having seen a live pig because farmers there do not raise them. Imagine, however, a place like the island of Cyprus before its de facto division between Muslim Turks and Christian Greeks in 1974. Here opposing ethnic groups lived side by side, and a Muslim child invariably became aware of the existence of pigs. According to their religion and tradition, his parents taught him that the pig is dirty and foreign. Like the adults in his group, the Muslim child was forbidden to eat pork. Eating or even petting a pig would have been unpleasant because the child would risk being reprimanded by his parents—not being loved—by his family, and, by extension, other members of his ethnic group.

Therefore, a Muslim child used a pig as a reservoir for his bad parts and externalized his unpleasant aspects onto the animal. Family members, teachers, religion, tradition, and culture all supported this process, ensuring the permanence of the shared reservoir. Putting the pig into a category of the uneatable improved its utility as a reservoir for negative externalization. (In the unconscious, the act of eating—taking something in—is associated with identification. This is reminiscent of the Armenians refusing Azerbaijani blood.) The Muslim child therefore avoided identifying with the pig; the animal clearly belonged to the other, i.e., Christian group. In Cyprus, perceptions and feelings about pigs—associated with the bad Christian other— linked all Cypriot Turkish (Muslim) children in an invisible way, just as their good reservoirs did.

— · —

Observing two ethnic tents side by side reveals rituals that occur between their members. Erecting a psychological border between the two tents that prevents each group's externalizations and projections from boomeranging back to the sender is one ritual. Without a psychological border, each tent would become a replica of the other. In that situation, the externalizations and projections needed to provide cohesion for group identity would be unstable. Sometimes these invisible borders are made manifest in attention to physical borders. When neighbor groups are not in conflict, physical borders are flexible and large groups reduce their investment in them accordingly. For example, crossing the border between Canada and the United States is little more than a formality since no threat is involved in moving from one large group's territory to the other's. Under stressful conditions, however, physical borders serve a double duty: they provide practical, physical protection, and they are "psychologized" to represent a symbolic thick skin that protects large groups from being contaminated.

In late 1986, before the Jordanians and Israelis made peace and when tensions between the two countries were still high, I spent half a day near the Allenby Bridge, which spans the Jordan River and separates Israel from Jordan. One could see a definite "us" and "them" attitude on the part of border patrol and customs officials in the elaborate precautions they took. Trucks that went over the bridge looked as though the factory had forgotten to finish them: doors and hoods were missing, the upholstery had been removed to allow fewer places to hide contraband items. Even though the trucks seemed incapable of hiding a mouse, the Israeli customs officers spent hours taking them apart and putting them back together to assure that nothing was smuggled in from Jordan.

Another precaution involved Israelis routinely sweeping a dirt road that ran parallel to the border in order to detect the footprints of people trying to cross it. While this may at first sound quite rational, it should be noted that the border was amply supplied with sophisticated electronic surveillance devices, minefields, and the natural barrier of the river Jordan. In view of these protections, actions such as sweeping the dirt road seemed to reflect an unconscious need to protect a psychological border, not just a legal one. Some Arabs, in turn, encouraged this obsessive vigil by constantly attempting to find weak spots in the border. When passing through Israeli customs, for example, they concealed in children's dolls small metal items that could conceivably be used to build a bomb, as though tricking the Israelis was a great game. There was some justification for this military preoccupation and constant alertness, but more than likely the need for psychological borders between neighbors lay at the root of these elaborate rituals, or at least was intertwined with real security concerns.

The U.S.-Mexico border—unlike the U.S.-Canada border—has also been psychologized. Issues of legal and illegal immigration concern government officials as well as U.S. citizens in states bordering Mexico.

Harvard University's Marcelo M. Suárez-Orozco sees "pro-immigration scripts [as] myth-making. . . . They are about (re)creating a sacred language to inscribe the eternal ideals and values that constitute our cultural soul . . . Immigrants are our alter super-ego. Celebrating immigration is a kind of pseudo-xenophilia: we love them for reminding us of what we once were." But in anti-immigration scripts, "humble foreigners become 'illegal aliens' abusing social services and successful immigrants become sneaky competitors 'stealing our jobs.' "[6]

During the 1996 U.S. presidential campaign, the anti-immigration script was fueled with references to economic concerns. Some politicians helped turn the southern border of the United States into a psychological boundary as well. Seeing the U.S.-Mexico border in the way that some Israelis viewed their border with Jordan, they expected a dangerous influx of criminals and potential abusers of the welfare system into the United States. Consequently, many politicians competed to present ideas for fortifying the "fallen" southern wall by increasing patrols and other militarizing measures.[7]

Some mental borders take the form of a shared mythical belief in a fantasized physical structure that protects the group, like an invisible wall that keeps dangerous elements out. The late William Niederland, a psychoanalyst who did work on the psychology of Jewish Holocaust victims and who coined the term "survivor syndrome," once told me how concentration camp survivors had, while imprisoned, believed in the myth of a secret weapon that would save them from extermination. This fantasy might have had another function—that of providing a protective barrier that united the prisoners and protected their identity under horrible conditions.

Cypriot Turks living in the Nicosia enclave surrounded by Cypriot Greeks between 1963 and 1968 also believed in a great weapon that they "knew" was located in Saint Hilarion Castle, atop the only mountain in the enclave. In children's drawings, it was pictured as a great cannon.[8] The secret weapon, like Ronald Reagan's Strategic Defense Initiative, would provide an umbrella of protection, a safe area with definite borders.

Because of the need to preserve differences and delineate one group's members from another, it is more effective to make borders flexible, accessible, and negotiable than to remove them. The late president Anwar el-Sadat saw the psychological barrier between Egyptians and Israelis as undesirable—a problem that needed to be removed. Although the barrier certainly was an obstacle on the path to peace, removing it entirely would have caused further complications because a sense of shared identity without a border induces aggression as each group tries to recover its individual identity.

— . —

The anthropologist Howard Stein maintains that "enemies are neither 'merely' projections, nor are they 'merely' real."[9] They are both. After all, a neighbor group that attacks us, bombs our land, kills our people, is real. But because we externalize and project our unwanted elements onto enemies, they are also products of our fantasies.

If the enemy absorbs the externalizations and projections, the situation becomes more complicated. At this point, though a group insists that it is not the same as the enemy, on an unconscious level, it is, at least in those areas where externalizations and projections have been absorbed. Although the antagonists "hate" each other, psychologically they need each other. When neighbors become enemies, they

do not wish to acknowledge any degree of similarity, for that conces-
sion would diminish the distinctions between them. Enemy neighbors
who do share similarities will stress and elevate the importance of
major differences, such as language, skin color, religion, history, food,
music, dance, or folklore and exaggerate the importance of minor differences.

In 1726 Jonathan Swift satirized the obsession with minutiae in
his fictional account of a war between the Lilliputians and the Ble-
fuscudians over the proper way to break an egg. Swift knew that humans would kill over trivial differences; and in *Gulliver's Travels*,
eleven thousand people choose to die rather than submit themselves
to breaking their eggs at the small end. Literature, of course, predates
psychology, and it would be nearly two centuries before psychoanalysis explored the psychology of minor differences. In 1917 Sigmund Freud wrote in "Taboo of Virginity":

> Each individual is separated from others by a "taboo of per-
> sonal isolation," and . . . it is precisely the minor differences
> in people who are otherwise alike that form the basis of feelings
> of strangeness and hostility between them. It would be tempting
> to pursue this idea and to derive from this "narcissism of minor
> differences" the hostility which in every human relation we see
> fighting successfully against feelings of fellowship and over-
> powering the commandment that all men should love one an-
> other.[10]

Freud's 1917 remarks were in relation to individual relationships.
But in 1921, in *Group Psychology and the Analysis of the Ego*, he
briefly commented on the role of minor differences in the international
arena. He noted that communities with adjoining territories, such as
Spaniards and Portuguese, English and Scots, and North Germans and
South Germans, were engaged in constant feuds and in ridiculing each
other.[11] According to Freud, the narcissism of minor differences was
a convenient and relatively harmless way of satisfying the inclination
to aggression, by means of which cohesion among members of the
community is made easier.[12] But his emphasis was on the identification of group members with one another. He did not mention the

potential collective anxiety over the loss of a group's identity. Furthermore, he seemed unaware that under certain stressful conditions investment in minor differences by emotionally bonded large groups in conflict is not always a harmless satisfaction of the inclination to aggression. As Swift pointed out two hundred years earlier, and as the blood shed during countless ethnic conflicts reminds the world, people will kill to reinforce their ethnic or national group's distinction from the enemy group, however minuscule that distinction may be.

An example in the extreme occurred during the 1958 riots in Sri Lanka, where Sinhalese mobs methodically sought out men wearing shirts over their *vertis,* a style adopted by the Tamils. In the absence of distinguishing characteristics such as skin color, the Tamil manner of dress stood out and enabled the Sinhalese to identify and victimize their enemies.[13] By the same token, in troubled Bosnia-Herzegovina, even after the 1995 Dayton Agreement, Muslims, Croats, and Serbs continued to have distinguishing emblems and even different alphabets (Latin or Cyrillic) on their car license plates. To be caught outside the safety of one's own area with the wrong license plate might mean trouble in the form of bodily harm.

Similarly, during British rule in Cyprus, and even into the early years of the republic, it was customary for Greeks and Turks to take evening strolls in Nicosia and elsewhere. The sidewalks that lined the main streets in front of cafés and pastry shops were favorite gathering spots, and although the two groups usually congregated separately according to ethnicity, both could be found here. To a stranger, even after the ethnic tensions began, the crowd of Cypriot Greeks and Turks appeared to be a homogeneous group of Mediterranean people dressed alike and taking pleasure in the cool evening air. But to the islander, minor differences among members of the crowd were obvious and important.

Cypriot Greeks and Turks could distinguish each other at a glance by such seemingly insignificant details as the brand of cigarettes they carried. Greeks usually preferred those packaged in blue and white, the Greek national colors, a suitable good reservoir of externalization for their group. Turks smoked brands packaged in red and white, the Turkish colors. In the villages, where the usual masculine farmers' dress consisted of baggy black trousers and shirts, the Greeks wore black or blue sashes and the Turks red (although nowadays it is rare to see either Cypriot Greek or Turkish farmers in such dress). In "normal times," a breach of this color code might be tolerated, but when ethnic relations were strained and group cohesion (and therefore individual identity) was threatened, a Cypriot Turk would rather die than wear a black or blue sash, and a Cypriot Greek would be just as adamant in his refusal to wear a red one.

Color that has psychological implications can be seen in other countries, too. In Northern Ireland, Catholic villages distinguish themselves from Protestant ones by a subtle color code to which every member of the village adheres: Catholics paint their front doors and gates green; Protestants paint theirs blue. There is no direct correspondence between the two colors and the two religions; the colors are simply unalterable minor differences that separate the two groups and that each group preserves under the influence of tradition. In India, the traditional Hindu saffron and Muslim green cannot be used interchangeably.

Sadhavi Rithambra is a well-known spokeswoman of the Hindu revivalist movement and in her speeches highlights minor differences between Hindus and Muslims to separate further the identities of the two communities:

> The Hindu writes from left to right, the Muslim from right to left. The Hindu prays to the rising sun, the Muslim faces the setting sun when praying. If the Hindu eats with the right hand, the Muslim eats with the left. If the Hindu calls India "mother," she becomes a witch for the Muslim. The Hindu worships the cow, the Muslim attains paradise by eating beef. The Hindu wears a mustache, the Muslim always shaves the upper lip.[14]

But there are minor differences, as well, among Hindus themselves. The neighboring Indian states of Gujarat and Maharashtra, for example, composed a single large state until civil unrest forced their separation in 1960. Although both states are predominantly Hindu, each has its own distinct language and customs. Women in both states wear saris, but Garati women wear the shoulder section of their saris on the right, whereas Marathi women wear it on the left.

In the former Yugoslavia, Croats and Serbs are both southern Slavs, but there are major cultural differences between them: Croats are Catholic and use the Latin alphabet, and Serbs are Orthodox and use the Cyrillic alphabet. When conditions led them to hold on to their respective identities more stubbornly, they too focused on minor differences. For example, during the economic decline of 1967–1968, the Croats—as well as the Slovenes—felt that too much of the foreign currency earned in their coastal resorts and businesses was directed to projects in Serbia and Macedonia. They could not complain about this publicly because of the threat of jail sentences. So instead, Croat intellectuals began to insist that their language was different from the Serb language. Thomas Butler, a specialist in the Serbian language and the history of Yugoslavia, observed:

> No matter where I traveled, in inner Croatia or on the Dalmatian Coast, I never had trouble being understood by Croats, even though I had learned my language in Serbia. The basic difference between the two dialects involved the pronunciation of one syllable, the Croats pronounce it as *je* or *ije* and the Serbs in Serbia as *e*. For example, Croats say *mlijeko* for milk and Serbs say *mleko*, although the Serbian minority in Croatia may also pronounce it *mlijeko*.[15]

Butler recalled talking to a Croatian woman in the winter of 1967–1968 who insisted that the Croatian dialect was superior to the Serb dialect. She cited the *ijekavian/ekavian* distinction as evidence "proving" that the Croatian pronunciation was more musical. Butler stated: "Boring as such a discussion may be to the outsider, it alerted me once again to the fact that for Croats the language question carried a very heavy political-cultural load."[16]

—·—

The more stressful the situation, the more neighbor groups become preoccupied with each other. Groups in conflict may then enact malignant rituals associated with regressed collective morality. To understand regressed collective morality, we should look first at how morality evolves in an individual.

Personal morality depends not simply on what parents and teachers insist on, nor merely on religious admonition; it is connected with internal aspects of human development. At the oedipal age, when a child competes with the parent of the same sex and expects punishment for it, his or her morality develops as a matter of feeling, thinking, and behaving in ways to avoid being punished.[17] The child becomes "moral" as he unconsciously attempts to minimize anxiety and depressive feelings.

As children grow, they develop more sophisticated moral codes unrelated to the fear of punishment. Now the moral code of their group is taken into account and interacts with the developing personal morality. At times an individual's moral code may not conform to his group's code. The population may approve a war against an enemy while an individual's conscience prohibits him from participating. Even when the group and individual values do not mesh, the group's shared moral code always has an effect on the individual.

Given this evolution of morality, it is not surprising that in situations when individuals regress, their morality also regresses to an earlier stage. Once more, to be moral means to avoid internal punishment by the superego and the resultant sense of anxiety. A group's shared conscience is also prone to regression. When members of a group experience mass regression, their fears are transformed into fear of punishment by the enemy. Shared morality is then modified to focus on minimizing group anxiety. Eventually, the ability to kill the enemy without remorse is created.

At this point, the regression of collective morality is often masked by intellectual rationalizations for actions taken to destroy the enemy. Since both irrational and rational elements are part of human nature, to understand the irrational does not mean to reject entirely the validity of reasonable motivations, such as ensuring the protection of one's group. Conversely, there are times when regressed morality is truly the dominant force leading to complete dehumanization of the enemy.[18] Members of a group, when they regress in the face of stressful conditions, come close to experiencing their enemy as the original reservoir of unintegrated bad parts (punishers) of their childhood selves. Such reservoirs typically contain nonhuman objects, such as a pig for a Muslim child or the turban for a Christian child. Similarly, adults, when regressed, reactivate a sense of experiencing the enemy as nonhuman.

To effect this dehumanization, group members attach sophisticated symbols to enemy images. These symbols originally evolved in childhood when individuals struggled with anxiety-provoking developmental tasks. When, for example, a child learns to appreciate cleanliness, he disowns, psychologically speaking, his waste and begins to see it as dirty. Likewise, a group will often perceive the enemy or other, consciously or unconsciously, as dirty. When one group insists that the enemy has a darker color, smells bad, or does dirty deeds, they are rejecting their enemies as if they were feces.[19] They make this assessment even when their own aggressive activities are as bad as or worse than those of the opposing group. The association of the other with objects that inspire revulsion fuels feelings of prejudice, which originated at the age of nine months, when the child displaced the upsurge of his aggressive impulses away from loved ones.

Prejudice serves to differentiate one group from another; it helps people retain their group identity, which, in turn, supports their individual identity. Therefore, rituals that foster prejudice—telling ethnic jokes, for example—psychologically help to secure group identity. Prejudice is normal when it is used to differentiate one's self and one's group from another without causing humiliation or destruction of the other. Prejudice is a human reaction, however, that ranges in intensity from normal to malignant. Feelings of malignant prejudice accompany malignant rituals in the relationships of emotionally bonded large groups.

The process of dehumanizing an enemy group may be done in stages. First the enemy is demonized but still retains some human qualities. Later it may be rendered as vermin and completely dehumanized. In Rwanda, Hutu first referred to Tutsi as evil, and later began calling them *cafards*, meaning cockroaches.[20] Hurting or killing cockroaches does not induce the guilt feelings that hurting other human beings would. Furthermore, getting rid of the enemy would result in absolute differentiation from the enemy and cause the first group's collective bad aspects to disappear with the dead enemy, thereby prohibiting a boomerang effect.

A more twisted variation, one so illogical that it rarely reaches consciousness, is the belief that by killing the enemy the aggressor is doing the enemy a favor. The aggressor begins to think that the enemy recognizes that he is entrapped in badness and so would welcome the release from it by death. In 1985 when Iran and the Christian West, especially the United States, were facing off, the late Ayatollah Ruhollah Khomeini came up with the bizarre rationale that "if an infidel is allowed to pursue his nefarious role as corrupter on earth until the end of his life, his moral sufferings will go on growing. If we kill him, and we thus prevent the infidel from perpetuating his misdeeds, this death will be to his benefit."[21]

Beliefs and activities that dehumanize the enemy naturally create a hostile atmosphere. War may break out if this hostility is accompanied by realistic sovereignty and border disputes—as well as underlying psychological identity issues—that are perceived as unsolvable by diplomatic means. Sometimes when the ethnic tent shakes, public opinion about the dehumanized enemy becomes so strong that the leadership may have no other choice than to go along with popular sentiment. In other instances, the leadership may be the impetus behind the inflammation (or taming) of these sentiments. The group will evaluate whether it can afford to go to war, but a warlike atmosphere is conducive to irrational perceptions and poor decision making.

When such an atmosphere prevails, any break in the physical border may translate into a break in the whole group's psychological "border" or identity. The possibility of disturbing that identity (an internal danger) brings about shared anxiety in the group. The fear of physical death (an external danger) is seen as the lesser evil when compared to this unbearable mass anxiety. Although mass anxiety is sometimes expressed openly, it may also be reflected less directly in phenomena such as psychosomatic physical complaints (e.g., back pain or headaches) among many members of the regressed group.

Irrational actions by a group are often another expression of mass anxiety. Peter Loewenberg cites the internment of Japanese Americans in 1942 as an example of mass anxiety in the United States. The government's decision was irrational and illegal. "It was not founded in reality because there was not a single demonstrated case of espionage by a Japanese American. It was irrational because the relatively large Japanese Nisei and Sansei populations of the exposed Hawaiian Islands were not interned."[22]

When anxiety about identity occurs, members of a large group may consider killing a threatening neighbor rather than endure the anxiety caused by losing their psychological borders and having holes in the canvas of their ethnic tent. In such a climate, chosen traumas and chosen glories, mourning difficulties, and feelings of entitlement to revenge are reactivated.

Wars can then be considered curative in the sense that the aggressor party—and sometimes both sides are aggressors—tries to cleanse itself of externalized and projected bad elements that threaten to return and contaminate the group identity and in turn the individual identity.[23] But the cure itself is pathological and is associated with destructive activities. The situation here is like the dilemma of the potential schizophrenic who is threatened with losing his identity. He feels terror, regresses, loses his identity, and in his attempts to cure himself develops a new one. But the new identity is unrealistic.

As a warlike atmosphere develops, or as an actual war begins, a group's psychological processes are not usually in the forefront of diplomatic concerns, because most psychological processes are unconscious. When preparing for or engaging in war, the large group's regressed psychology is masked by considerations that require high-level (non-regressed) thinking. The business of preparing and making war, with activities such as assessing economic and military power, buying new weapons, organizing troops and materials, planning defense strategy, finding allies, and so on, requires logical thinking and rationalizations. Involvement in these preparations deflects attention from psychological processes, and that, of course, carries a new set of dangers.

Chapter 7

TWO ROCKS IN THE AEGEAN SEA: TURKS AND GREEKS IN CONFLICT

In January 1996, Turkey and Greece came perilously close to starting a war over two rocks—unpopulated islets occupying no more than ten acres in the Aegean Sea. Three miles from the Turkish coastline, they are called Imia by the Greeks, and Kardak or İkizce by the Turks. The incident started when a Turkish vessel nearby ran aground, and the captain called the Turkish authorities for help. The Greeks complained that he should have called the Greek authorities since the islets belonged to Greece. The Turks did not agree.[1]

A short time after the incident was publicized, Greek and Turkish newspapers carried a photograph of a group of civilian Greeks accompanied by a priest who had landed on the Kardak/Imia rocks and planted a Greek flag in a gesture reminiscent of the American astronauts planting an American flag on the moon. Two boys, also carrying flags, accompanied the group on its mission to demonstrate Greek possession of the islets.

The Turks, meanwhile, were busy protecting their claim. A popular Turkish newspaper, *Hürriyet*, sent reporters and photographers in a helicopter to Kardak, where they managed to raise the Turkish flag. Soon, Turkish and Greek navy ships and air force planes faced off across the islets. The situation was ominous: a war between two NATO partners could have erupted over a mere ten acres of real estate. President Bill Clinton and then assistant secretary of state Richard C. Holbrooke called the Turkish and Greek authorities in an attempt to de-escalate another Greek-Turkish imbroglio.[2] The crisis ended, but the conflict over the islets was not resolved.

The Kardak/Imia incident is just one more in a long series of sovereignty conflicts between Greece and Turkey. Considering how often altercations over sovereignty have resulted in war throughout world history, the preservation of peace between Turkey and Greece is a significant accomplishment. Compared to many other states in this region, Turkey and Greece have some crucial advantages that allow them to maintain peace. To a great degree, their membership in NATO has helped enforce stability, but even more important is their long-standing relationship, which is one of both familiarity and caution.

Modern Greece was born after the Greek war of independence (1821–1829), when the new Greek state separated from the Ottoman Empire. Modern Turkey was born in the early 1920s after the Ottoman Empire collapsed and the Turks pushed the invading Greeks out of Anatolia (Asia Minor). Since 1930, Turks and Greeks have negotiated and concluded treaties, agreements, conventions, joint communiqués, and other understandings. During this time they have managed to avoid war, with the exception of the brief 1974 war in Cyprus, which may actually be considered a displaced war since it was not fought between Turkey and Greece proper. On the other hand, despite avoiding all-out war, the long-standing Turkish-Greek relationship has not fostered a durable settlement between Turkey and Greece. This relationship cannot be understood by focusing only on real-world factors, such as economic, military, legal, and political circumstances. For the real-world issues are highly "psychologized"—contaminated with shared perceptions, thoughts, fantasies, and emotions (both conscious and unconscious) pertaining to past historical glories and traumas: losses, humiliations, mourning difficulties, feelings of entitlement to revenge, and resistance to accepting changed realities. The process by which the modern Greek and Turkish nations were born has also influenced present-day nationalism in both countries.

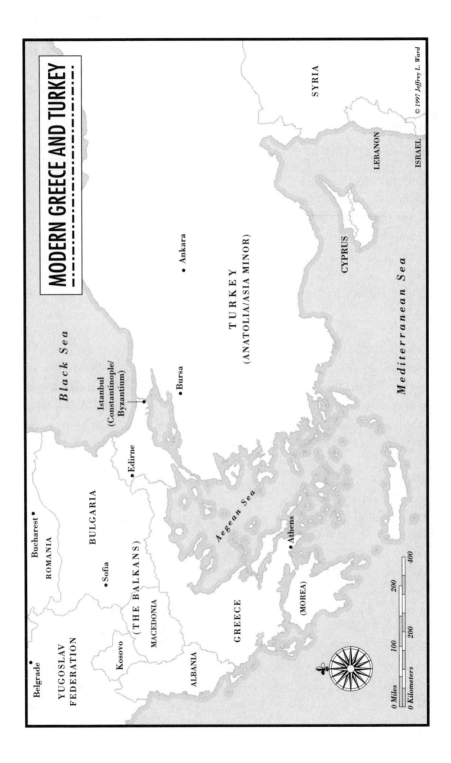

— ·—

After the 1071 battle at Malazgirt in eastern Anatolia during which Seljuk Turks, originally from central Asia, defeated the Byzantine army, Turks began to settle in Anatolia in earnest. They mingled and intermarried with the existing inhabitants, including Greeks who belonged to the Orthodox Church. Since Greeks had been for a long time under the rule of the Byzantine (Eastern Roman) Empire, the newcomer Turks called them *Rum* (Roman), as did the Greeks themselves. In any case, the identifying affiliation of Anatolia's inhabitants was primarily religious, not what today we would call nationalistic. Within a century or so, Anatolia was Turkified. Since the Turkish tribes had become Muslims during their migration, the Muslim religion was established in Anatolia alongside the already existing religions.

The Byzantine Empire, though shrinking, lasted some three hundred years after the battle of Malazgirt, until Constantinople (present-day Istanbul) fell to the Ottoman Turks on May 29, 1453.[3] Even before the fall of Constantinople, however, some areas that are now Greece, and had been part of ancient Greece as well, had come under Ottoman domination. But with the collapse of the Byzantine Empire, the entire Greek world was now part of the Ottoman Empire. For practical purposes, from 1453 until the emergence of an independent (modern) Greece in the 1830s, Greeks and Turks lived under a mantle of "togetherness."

The Ottoman Empire was a multireligious, multilingual, and multicultural conglomeration with the sultan as its supreme ruler. Identity in the Ottoman Empire was corporate rather than individual; one's primary identity derived from one's religion. It was not until the sixteenth century, when the Ottomans conquered the Arab world, that the Ottoman Empire became a society in which Muslims held the majority.

Christians and Jews, as well as their religions, were protected in the empire since they were considered people of the holy book. They were included in a system called the millet system.[4] The word *millet* came to mean nation in the nineteenth century, but earlier it referred to an organized religious community whose head was responsible to the Ottoman government for the good behavior of its members, payment of the *cizye* (special capitation) tax, and other obligations. There were the Orthodox Millet, the Jewish Millet, and the Armenian Millet. Muslims constituted the Ummah, the community of God or of Muhammad.

Greeks belonged to the Orthodox Millet, or Millet-i Rum (the Roman Millet). Also under this category were Serbs, Vlachs, and others, but Greeks were dominant in the church's hierarchy. Over time, Turkish words entered the Greek language. The resulting dialect could only be understood by those who had a knowledge of both languages. Many Greeks also became Turcophone, speaking Turkish but writing it in Greek letters.

During most of the Ottoman period, Turks and Greeks cooperated more than they fought.[5] Many Ottomans of Greek origin (and many more of Greek Orthodox origin, such as Serbs and Bosnians) had been levied and educated through the devşirme process to hold office in the Ottoman establishment. Other Greeks retained their Christian religion while serving the Ottoman state. Greek family names such as Mavrocardatos, Ipsilanti, and Capodistrias are familiar in the annals of Ottoman affairs.

From the 1850s on, the Ottoman Empire was seen by European powers as the sick man of Europe. In 1821, Greeks in Morea rebelled, signaling the beginning of the Greek war of independence, which led to the formation of an independent Greek nation-state carved out of the Ottoman Empire. After the establishment of a Greek state, many Greeks still remained within Ottoman territory; a few of them would serve as Ottoman ambassadors to Athens, London, and Saint Petersburg, and another would govern what is now southern Bulgaria. Alexander Carathéodry, an Ottoman Greek, represented the sultan at the Congress of Berlin in 1878.

Coexistence does not mean that relations between Greeks and Turks of the Ottoman Empire were congenial. Conquerors and conquered may have mingled blood for four centuries, but differences in ethnicity and nationality depend more on historical processes, belief systems, shared traumas, glories, and myths than on blood ties and cooperation in administrative matters.

Naturally, the circumstances surrounding the birth of modern Greece in the 1830s affected its identity as a nation. The Greeks had not been a separate nation since the Middle Ages. To achieve independence as a nation-state, they had to accomplish three tasks: to fight for independence against the declining Ottoman Empire; to reclaim members of their ethnic group in remaining and former territories of the empire (irredentism); and to create a culturally homogeneous people. These three necessities were also applicable to other Christian nation-states born out of the Ottoman Empire.

Greece's movement to build a national identity, however, contained a unique element not shared by others: external support, and even pressure, for a specific kind of new identity. The British, French, and Russians demanded that the modern Greek identity be Hellenic and respond to the Europeans' nostalgia for the restoration of a pre-Christian Hellenic civilization that had been in eclipse for some two thousand years. Europeans confidently expected to see the characteristics of Homer in postliberation Greeks, in spite of the ebb and flow of history over such a great span of time.[6] The neoclassicism that rose in seventeenth- and eighteenth-century Europe as an aesthetic and philosophical idea was to be physically embodied in modern-day Greece. The idealistic and hopeful attitude of neoclassicism that would later be imposed on the Greeks was succinctly expressed in 1822 when American president James Monroe declared: "The mention of Greece fills the mind with the utmost exalted sentiments and arouses in our bosoms the best feelings of which our nature is susceptible."

In reality, however, just before the Greek war of independence, most Greeks still referred to themselves as Romans. Vlachavas, the priest rebel leader who rose against the Ottomans, declared, "A Romneos I was born, a Romneos I will die."[7] A ballad composed a few years later for Diakos, another rebel leader, had him declare, "I was born a Greek, and a Greek I will die."[8]

The villages in what later became known as Greece had Greek ethnic compositions, and the villagers retained their Orthodox Christian religion, customs, and language. Greek women, married at twelve or thirteen years of age, did farmwork, spun and wove, and helped with the harvest. Greek men raised sheep, and those near the sea were sponge divers.[9] Some Europeans, and the few Americans who came to help Greece start a new nation-state, were disappointed, even indignant, to discover that among Greece's peasants there were no warrior-heroes like Achilles or Ajax, no statesmen like Pericles, no philosophers like Socrates or Plato, and no poets of the caliber of Aeschylus or Sophocles. There was, in fact, little likeness between nineteenth-century Greeks and the idealized Greeks from ancient history that had such a hold on the imaginations of European liberators.

Nevertheless, the idea of a Greek renaissance persisted, perpetuated and embellished by the romantic figure of Lord Byron and his coterie of poets and adventurers. Furthermore, a small group of elite Greeks who had been educated in Europe also longed for the revival of a long-forgotten Hellenic identity and rejected a Romaic one. Theirs was no easy task.

The folklore scholar Michael Herzfeld has identified three major obstacles to the project of re-Hellenizing Greece.[10] First, the people in the new nation-state found it difficult to accept that they should resemble the long-lost inhabitants of their land; most of the common people had no idea what they were supposed to be. Second, they could not be "Hellenic" in the old, pagan sense of the word, since they strongly adhered to the Christian faith in their Orthodox church. Finally, it was hard to be Hellenic while using a Romaic language, mixed with many words of Turkish, Arabic, and Persian origin.

To deal with these difficulties, Greek intellectuals sought a continuum of Greek life from ancient Greece through the Byzantine period to the nineteenth century. They studied folk tales, dances, poetry, and lifestyles to substantiate this continuum. Hellenism was embraced, but under the three obstacles listed above, in a special way. It was made "intimately personal,"[11] identified as a mystical sensibility that could not be understood by even Western supporters. George Evlambios in 1843 declared that foreigners should not attempt the impossible by trying to fathom the mysteries of Greekness.[12] It was ironic that the Hellenism thesis, although initially externally directed, would in practice ultimately lead Greeks to differentiate themselves from the very others who had helped to define them. Absorbing Hellenism made modern Greeks proud of their uniqueness.

Differentiation from the Turks would be more rigidified. A shared and mostly unconscious psychological mechanism was needed for the maintenance of Hellenism: the wholesale externalization and projection of the unwanted aspects of "togetherness," which was perceived as oriental (therefore inferior) by the West. In the Western view, "oriental" meant being lazy, dirty, and lacking a civilized background. Turks provided a handy reservoir for the Greeks' massive externalizations and projections; during their togetherness, they had shared some similar characteristics and cross identifications. Upon separating from the Turks, the Greeks wanted to retain only the good and civilized aspects of their former togetherness that could fit into Hellenism and get rid of the bad or oriental aspects by externalizing and projecting them onto the closest reservoir.

After embracing the Hellenic identity for most of the first forty years following the war of independence, Greeks began to weave in elements of the cultural and religious heritage of Byzantium. The urge to retain this aspect of Greek heritage was articulated in the mid- and late 1800s by intellectuals, especially Spyridon Zamblios and Nikolaos G. Politis, who reclaimed glorified aspects of Byzantium.[13] Now Greek identity became a composite of Hellenic (ancient Greek) and Byzantine (Christian Greek) elements. With this development came a second wave of massive externalizations and projections of the unwanted aspects (laziness, orientalness) of the Eastern Romaic identity onto the Turks. Once made, these externalizations and projections became part of the foundation of the modern Greek identity. It was impossible for Greeks to feel together with Turks again, because maintaining the externalizations and projections kept the new identity in place. Meanwhile, through the efforts of Adamantios Koraïs and others, a neoclassical form of the modern Greek language, Katharevusa, was developed that rejected Ottoman Turkish words.

Greeks had to rid themselves of the Turk *within* that had been formed during the time of togetherness. No one explains this better than the Greek writer Nikos Kazantzakis in his *Report to Greco*:

> To gain freedom first of all from the Turks, that was the initial step; after that, later, this new struggle began: to gain freedom from the inner Turk—from ignorance, malice and envy, from fear and laziness, from dazzling false ideas, and finally from idols, all of them, even the most revered and beloved.[14]

—·—

Around 1868, the idea of incorporating adjacent regions populated by Greeks or felt to belong to the Greek world became a national passion. What made Greek irredentism special was its connection with the political ideology later called the Megali Idea (the Great Idea), namely, "the doctrine . . . whereby all the lands of Classical and Byzantine Hellenism should be reclaimed for the reborn nation."[15] The Megali Idea did not become an ideology until the mid-nineteenth century, but Greeks reached back to the fall of Constantinople as its origin and reactivated the chosen trauma of the collapse of the Byzantine Empire. As Kenneth Young observed, the seeds of the Megali Idea were sown soon after the Turkish conquest of Constantinople.[16]

When the Turks attacked Constantinople in 1453, the Byzantine Empire had already shrunk to little more than the city itself. Its ultimate collapse was inevitable, but what matters here is the mental representation of the event and not the historical reality that Byzantium's fall was well under way. The psychological implications of the capture of Constantinople by the Turks created shock waves among European Christians.

The seizure of Constantinople by the Turks was seen as a reflection of God's judgment on the sins of Christians everywhere.[17] Since Constantinople had been taken on a Tuesday, every Tuesday thereafter was regarded as an unpropitious day for Christians. In spite of the fact that Rome had refused to provide support to Constantinople against the Turks, word of Byzantium's fall was received with disbelief. The Turkish victory was seen as a knife plunged into the heart of Christianity. Enea Silvio Piccolomini (later Pope Pius II) wrote to Pope Nicholas V on July 12, 1453, that the Turks had killed Homer and Plato for the second time.[18]

The desire to undo the sense of loss associated with the fall of Constantinople expressed itself in rumbling about organizing another Crusade. Nothing came of such talk, but the idea persisted. Christians of the Ottoman territories sang of their lands, "Again, with years, with time, again they will be ours."

Denial appeared in other ways. Some sought a continuous link between the Turks and the Byzantines, which would lessen the need for Byzantines and other Christians to feel pain. Even Westerners contributed to the project of finding good ancient origins for the Turks. Francesco Filelfo, an Italian humanist, declared that Mehmet II, the sultan who had seized Constantinople, was a Trojan. Felix Fabri, a German scholar, explored the idea that Turks descended from Teucer, son of the Greek Telamon and the Trojan princess Hesione. Fabri did not accept Teucer as the forefather of the Turks but believed, instead, that they descended from the mythological figure, Turcus, a son of Troyas, whose grandfather was Laomedan.[19]

While these pseudohistorical efforts to forge a link between the two sides continued as a way to make loss and change tolerable, there was a counter-attempt to separate them so that Byzantines could maintain *their* identity. This, in turn, led to stereotypes of Turks as the aggressive other. Some Christians referred to Sultan Mehmet II as the beast of Apocalypse, or Satan, whose people were sharply differentiated from good Christians.

In the case of the fall of Constantinople, Turks *were* the aggressors; but to Western Christians, Turkish aggression was different: it was more "uncivilized" and imbued with sexual symbolism. The epitome of this symbolism was the image of the virile, young Turkish sultan Mehmet II, who was only twenty-one when he seized Constantinople and is known as Mehmet the Conqueror, or the Grand Turk. He was the fourth son of Murat II and grandson of Murat I, who was assassinated at Kosovo Polje. Mehmet's mother is thought to have been a Serbian or Macedonian slave who was brought to Murat's harem and became a Muslim and wife to Murat.

In 1444, Sultan Murat II abdicated to allow his twelve-year-old son Mehmet to reign with the assistance of two mentors and his grand vizier, Halil Çandarlı Pasha. Murat had arranged a peace treaty with the Serbs and Hungarians and hoped to devote the rest of his life to cultural pursuits in the company of poets, theologians, and other men of letters. But military conflicts with the Serbs in the Balkans soon heated up and presented new challenges to the Ottoman leadership. Within two years, Murat retook the throne from young Mehmet, a move that was engineered in large part by the grand vizier Halil Çandarlı Pasha.

Halil's actions humiliated Mehmet, who must have felt as if the grand vizier were saying: "You are not good enough for a grown-up's job. Your father is better than you, and you cannot compete with his power and prestige." Mehmet's internal response to this affront may later have pushed him to excel and surpass his father—a kind of "second individuation"[20]—by conquering Constantinople, something his ancestors had not been able to do. Because Sultan Murat remained friendly toward his son and took him on various campaigns, it seems likely that to a great extent the boy displaced the bad oedipal father image (associated with being dethroned and demoted) onto Halil and onto the Byzantine emperor. When Mehmet was nineteen, his father died, and he again became sultan. His mother had passed away between his first and second enthronements.

Mehmet's preoccupation with Constantinople and his seizure of the city, of course, should not be attributed solely to his unresolved oedipal strivings. His internal motivations no doubt found expression in his political and military activities. What is important here, however, is not the accuracy of this assumption, but rather the fact that shared fantasies about Mehmet's oedipal motivations are reflected in the images of this Turkish victory that have been passed down through the generations.

Young Mehmet addressed the task of defeating the Byzantine Empire with youthful zeal, and the Turks constructed the largest cannons ever made in order to blast a hole in the impenetrable wall protecting Constantinople. The Byzantine emperor Constantine was killed as the final Ottoman assault surged through the opening in the city wall. His head was cut off and shown to Mehmet.

After Constantine's death, Mehmet declared himself the new chief protector of the Christian Church (the mother), his own mother originally having been a Christian. Here a son was replacing his father. It was widely believed—as shown in pseudohistorical accounts of the event, in oral histories, and even in modern fictional renditions of the fall of Constantinople—that Mehmet the Conqueror slept with Constantine's daughters.[21] Whatever the truth of the matter, such a conjecture echoes an oedipal theme wherein the father (Constantine in this case) having been killed, the son (young Mehmet) sleeps with his women. It is interesting to note, also, that soon after the emperor's death the triumphant young sultan ordered the arrest of Halil Çandarlı Pasha, the other displaced bad father, and had him put to death.

The seizure of Constantinople by the youthful and virile sultan who opened a hole in the city wall was perceived as a rape. This helped foster the image, among Christians, of Turks as lustful people. And what was particularly difficult to assimilate was the fact that the rape was performed not by the father but by the son. A noted nineteenth-century historian, Joseph Freiherr von Hammer-Purgstall, went so far as to claim that the young sultan lusted after the younger son of Grand Duke Lucas Notaras, who had led the Byzantine fleet in defense of Constantinople.[22] Similar characterizations in serious history books were later repeated by other Christian writers; boundless lust was ascribed to Mehmet the Conqueror. Historical fact, by contrast, describes him as a highly educated man who had been taught by special tutors in his youth. He spoke six languages, including Greek,[23] was familiar with Greek mythology and well read in history. Like his father, he loved to have discussions on religious and metaphysical topics.

Mehmet was known as a generous person and after capturing Constantinople worked to restore economic, social, and religious (both Islamic and Orthodox Christian) stability in the city. He brought Turks and Greeks from other parts of the empire, including many artisans and merchants, to revitalize the new Ottoman capital. He named a new patriarch to the Greek Church, a monk named George Scholarios, who became known as Gennadius II Scholarios. The Turkish sultan established a close personal relationship with the Greek patriarch. Nevertheless, the image of Mehmet as wanton prevailed. Over time Constantinople (Istanbul) was symbolized as a fallen or grieving woman and was celebrated as such in folk-songs and poems for centuries.[24]

Two waves of massive externalizations and projections by "new" Greeks onto Turks have led to the perception of Turks as lazy and dirty. These characteristics were adjoined to projections of lustfulness and aggressiveness that accompanied the chosen trauma of the fall of Constantinople when it was reactivated by the Greeks in the nineteenth century. Even today, when political problems between Turkey and Greece arise, the Greek press, as well as politicians and military men, often refer to Turks as rapists.[25]

— · —

During the Greek war of independence, Greeks had many captains, but no nationally recognized leader. This was due, in part, to the way the war evolved. By 1821, the Ottoman Empire was no longer functioning as a unified state. It faced outside threats from Austrians, Russians, and Persians whose territories surrounded it. The sultan's authority was in decline and local notables had begun to act independently of Istanbul. Gangs of bandits roamed the countryside.

Greek bandits were known as klephts. The Ottoman authorities enlisted the help of loyal Greeks, called *armatoles,* to fight them, and there were many skirmishes. Although initially the klephts did not perceive their struggle as one of national liberation, they were soon viewed as heroic freedom fighters, and in 1821 the Greek war of independence had begun.

Several sources contributed to the transformation of the klephts into freedom fighters. Among those were Phanariot Greeks who claimed to be descendants of noble Byzantine families; most historians believe the families died out in the sixteenth century. Some of them held high positions in the sultan's court, serving as translators or other advisers. Others were appointed governors of Walachia and Moldavia, regions in present-day Romania.

In 1821, while the klephts were busy fighting the Ottoman authorities, ideas of Greek nationalism and independence were hotly debated among Greek intellectuals and religious leaders, mostly outside the Ottoman Empire. In Crimea, Alexander Ypsilantis, a Phanariot Greek and a general in the Russian czar's army, had been influenced by a clandestine organization called Philike Hetairia (Society of Friends) that promoted the notion of Greek independence. Inspired by such thoughts, Ypsilantis led a Greek force across the Prut River into Moldavia, which was previously ruled in the name of the sultan by a Phanariot Greek governor. Ypsilantis's efforts failed because the local people, tired of Phanariot misrule, refused to support another Phanariot. Czar Alexander I, meanwhile, was infuriated and dismissed Ypsilantis when he learned of his venture.

Ypsilantis escaped to Hungary, but his actions gave new life to the idea of a Greek war of independence in Europe. Groups of elite Greeks living in Europe and liberals, such as Lord Byron, traveled to Greece to join the cause, which resulted in the establishment of the modern Greek state.

Although there were Greek heroes during this war—and foreign ones like Lord Byron—no enduring leadership emerged. President

Ioánnis Kapodístrias, who was elected in 1827 for a seven-year term, attempted to turn Greece into a new, centralized state, but he earned the hostility of most of the population for his efforts, and in the end he was reviled. He was assassinated in 1831 by the Mavro Michili family, important landowners in the Morea, where the war of independence had begun.

The absence of a supreme parent figure to consolidate Greece's new identity had a profound effect on its development. When a strong and lasting leader is present during a large group's passage from one political or social belief system to another, he confers legitimacy and establishes boundaries for the transition. The function of the leader is analogous to that of a good oedipal father for the developing child. The child drastically transforms the self at the oedipal age, a time when the role of the father (in the traditional family) or parents is essential in setting limits for this change. Without these boundaries, there is the risk of anxiety about overstepping one's place and facing unknown "territories" and dangers.

The newly formed Greek state experienced just that. Without a supreme leader, Greeks continued to adhere to irredentism as a psychological and political force. The physical borders of classical Greece and the Byzantine Empire were fluid, so how could modern Greeks decide which lands to reappropriate and when to stop? The Greeks tended to press for continual expansion, but nervously. They incorporated into modern Greece more and more Ottoman territories up until the empire collapsed and modern Turkey was born. One characteristic of this expansion was that, except for their Asia Minor campaign (1919–1922), Greeks generally employed irregulars rather than organized, disciplined troops in almost all undertakings against the Ottoman Empire, keeping alive the tradition of the Greek war of independence.

— · —

The Turkish war of independence occurred about one hundred years after the beginning of the Greek war of independence and followed the Ottoman defeat in World War I. This largely resembled nineteenth-century Western European revolutions in that it aimed at removing a monarchy and restricting the scope of religion.

The Ottoman millet system worked, for practical purposes, until the nineteenth century, when it was challenged due to an increase in nationalistic sentiment in Europe. The Ottomans' response was too little and too late. The last century oí the Ottoman Empire was marked by attempts at reforms (such as Tanzimat, a process similar to the Russian one of perestroika), conflicts and uprisings within the borders, wars with external enemies, political and social suppression, and human suffering.

During the last and troubled century of the empire, Turks made serious efforts to reconsider their identity. There were three alternatives. The first was to extend the Ottoman identity to all its citizens, regardless of their ethnic and religious adherence. There would be no division between the rulers and the ruled. This was unsuccessful since citizens with various ethnic backgrounds did not wish to melt into one entity. The second alternative, advocated by Ottoman grand vizier Said Halim Pasha, was to put all Muslims in the empire under the umbrella of Pan-Islamism. Ideas about the last alternative came from Yusuf Akçura, a Tartar from Russia, and Ahmed Ağaoglu, a member of a prominent Turkish family. They hoped to focus on the expansion of the Turkish identity alone so that Turks, and those who felt like Turks, would be combined. This process was known as Pan-Turanism, *Turan* meaning the land of Turks.

Since there were Turks or Turkic peoples throughout Asia and Europe, the third option, an expanded Turkish identity, might appear to have had the potential to create a mighty political and cultural force. But this idea remained a fantasy because of major and minor differences among the Turkic peoples, the weakness of the Ottoman Empire at the time, and the restrictions that an existing government could put on expansionist ideologies.

All three alternatives had one aim in common—to keep the sultan in place and in power. A radical change, which would establish a new Turkish identity apart from the sultan and the Ottoman traditions, had to await the end of World War I and the Turkish war of independence.

The Turkish struggle for independence contrasted greatly with that of the Greeks. During World War I and the Turkish war of independence, Turks fought major European Christian powers as well as Muslim Arabs in the Middle East. Unlike the Greeks, the Turks had an indisputably charismatic leader in Mustafa Kemal (Atatürk, or Father

Turk), who united the military during the struggle and provided political cohesion after the war was won. The Turkish war of independence was fought with a disciplined regular army, so it was not burdened with the individualistic adventurers and lawlessness that afflicted the new Greek state because of its dependence on irregular forces.

In 1919 Atatürk and his associates created a national pact (Misak-i Milli) that drew concrete borders (and, in a sense, psychological ones) indicating the geographical scope of new Turkey (with the exception of the Hatay [Alexandretta], which was incorporated by means of a plebiscite in 1938). Turkey would harbor no irredentist aspirations toward former territories of the Ottoman Empire nor toward territories outside the empire inhabited by Turks. The new Turkey did not have the problems that Hellenism and the heritage of the Byzantine Empire had raised for Greece. On the contrary, the national pact contributed greatly to the establishment of a new Turkish identity.

Internal homogeneity was of utmost importance to the new Turkish identity. A large part of the population of the Turkish state consisted of those who had been forced out of their centuries-old Balkan lands through numerous ethnic purification operations similar to those seen in Yugoslavia after its collapse. There was also a mandatory exchange of population between Turkey and Greece engendered by an agreement reached at the conference between Turkey and the Allied powers in Lausanne, Switzerland, in 1923. The Lausanne Treaty fixed modern Turkey's borders and legalized the concept of Misak-i Milli.

Although more than 95 percent of the citizens of the new Turkish republic were Muslims, modern Turkey was established as a secular state. All citizens were to be equal, regardless of their ethnic backgrounds, and all—including the Kurds, who played an important role in Atatürk's victories—were put under the Turkish umbrella.

— · —

The new Turkish nationalism was not to be a continuation of Ottomanism; secularism sharply differentiated the Turkish republic from the Ottoman Empire. Instead, Turkey was to adopt a westernized identity, in spite of the fact that during World War I and the Turkish war of independence the Turks had fought mainly against Europeans. Because of Atatürk's interest in modernizing Turkey, the country became engaged in a vigorous process of westernization under his tutelage. Within five years of the founding of the Turkish republic in 1923, Turkey adopted European criminal and civil laws, changed its dress code, and substituted the Latin alphabet for Arabic script.

The new Turkish Ministry of Culture sponsored translations of Western scholarship, novels, and poems, producing massive volumes of books to be read by Turks and their children. Included were ancient Greek myths and the works of Homer. Jewish refugees who fled to Turkey to escape the Nazis also contributed to Turkey's westernization; they helped found a Turkish opera and ballet, and some became university teachers.

The westernized Turkish revolutionary elite thought of themselves as "enlightened ones" and kept their distance from the traditional and conservative segments of the population. The societal and political implications of the division were not at first apparent.

The revolution from above was supposed to seep down to the masses. But externalization and projection of unwanted elements were necessary for the cohesion of the new identity formulated by the enlightened ones. This was a difficult task. For the leaders of modern Turkey, the West was both a former enemy and an object of idealization. As the latter, it could not easily serve as a suitable reservoir for the Turks' unwanted elements.

Although the parent figures (Atatürk and his successor, İsmet İnönü) limited externalizations and projections onto former enemies, some projections did occur and in an unusual way, especially when directed toward Greeks. Greeks were divided into two segments: the idealized ancient Greeks who founded Western civilization, and the modern Greeks, who were seen as "clamorers"—people who, though not perceived as dangerous, were never satisfied and raised a clamor as they demanded more. In Turkish minds, modern Greeks could not be descendants of ancient ones.

Although the Turkish elite was fast assimilating Western ways and thinking, the rest of the population was not so ready to change, nor were Europeans ready to accept them, a sentiment that continues to this day. Many Western-oriented Turks were no doubt envious of modern Greeks—their former subjects—who were viewed elsewhere as heirs of the founders of Western civilization. Disconnecting modern Greeks from their history was a way for Turks to deal with their envy.

Stories, novels, and plays written between 1909 and 1956 by the well-known Turkish writer Yakup Kadri Karaosmanoğlu shed light on the divided image of the Greek in Turkish literature.[26] Karaosmanoğlu was not only an important literary figure, he was also a politician and personal friend of Atatürk and İnönü. His writings include references to the Greek invasion of Asia Minor and describe irresponsible Greek soldiers who terrorized the citizenry, dishonored women, and killed children. Paradoxically, he compares Atatürk to an ancient Greek god and a meeting in Atatürk's dining room to gatherings held by Socrates.

While their perceptions of the West were split, the founders of modern Turkey were very clear in identifying Islamic fanaticism as the main cause of the Ottoman Empire's demise. They projected unwanted elements onto the royalty (i.e., the sultan), onto religious leaders who were expelled from the new Turkish republic, and onto other traditional and conservative segments of the population. In a sense, many unwanted elements remained *within* the society.

When the Ottomans joined the ranks of losers in World War I, there was so much loss and grief among the Turks of the empire that it was said that walking through the streets of Istanbul one could hear nothing but the sorrowful voices of mothers who had lost their sons during this war and the preceding Balkan Wars. But after the Turkish war of independence, the Turks' idealization of Atatürk and of his vision of modern Turkey kept them from grieving further over the loss of the empire. In the wake of Atatürk's death, symbols of him were erected everywhere. His picture adorned public and private buildings; institutions and landmarks were named after him; schoolchildren began their day by pledging allegiance to him. Most Turks felt adequately compensated for the loss of their empire by having gained something good—a charismatic leader. But the societal divisions continued.

Following the Atatürk and İnönü eras, the split between those who idealized the West and those who shunned secularism and clung to their Ottoman traditions began to produce visible societal effects. It provided fertile ground for the eruption of a bloody left-right dichotomy, mainly among university students, which led to thousands being killed in the 1960s. Though expressed in terms of communism versus nationalism, the struggle was fueled by the original rift, which would also be at the root of the Turkish-PKK (Kurdish Workers' Party) conflict of the late 1980s and 1990s.

Paradoxically, mourning the loss of the empire was stimulated by "gaining" land in Cyprus. The 37 percent of the island that Turks gained in 1974 was not significantly more than the 35 percent they had owned in the former British Cyprus. But it was a great victory compared to the intervening years, 1963–1974, when they had been forced to live in restricted enclaves on only 3 percent of the island. This belated mourning led to a further separation between the heirs of people belonging to a former millet system—this time Cypriot Greeks—and those of conquerors, the former Ottoman Turks or Cypriot Turks. The "togetherness" of Cypriot Turks and Cypriot Greeks had not ended with the Greek and Turkish wars of independence; it came to an end with the physical and psychological division of Cyprus.

In 1960, the Republic of Cyprus was formed as a unified sovereign state. Since the beginning of troubles in 1963, and even after the de facto partition in 1974, the world (except Turkey) has continued to treat the Cypriot-Greek government as the government for the entire island. This does not reflect, however, the reality that the Cypriot republic, as originally envisioned, lasted only three years. Nevertheless, the world has been busy attempting to reunify the island, an idea that psychologically threatens both parties. Large groups that have been together for a long time—for centuries—and then separated have a tendency to hold more stubbornly to rituals that support and maintain their separate identities.

The history of Cyprus and international efforts to resolve the so-called Cyprus problem keep Turks and Greeks (both in Cyprus and in their respective motherlands) on their toes. In such an atmosphere, two uninhabited rocks in the Aegean Sea assume irrational, major importance and can bring two large groups threatened by identity confusion to the verge of war.

—·—

Neither Turks nor Greeks have successfully mourned past losses or resolved previous traumas, nor have they modified their negative images of the other group. The Greeks have made Turkokratia, their shared perception of the conditions of Greek life under the Ottomans, a marker of their present-day identity. This augments a sense of both victimization and entitlement. Attempts at genuine friendships with present-day Turks threaten this marker and create anxiety. The sense of entitlement embodied in the Megali Idea has to be maintained.

After the Greek defeat during the Turkish war of independence, Turks perceived the Greek adherence to the Megali Idea as largely rhetorical and certainly not dangerous. This perception drastically changed when the Greeks attempted to unite the island of Cyprus with the mainland. Their wish to expand their territorial seas, effectively turning the Aegean into a Greek lake, was cause for further alarm. The Greeks' irredentism was answered by the breaking down of the constriction provided for Turks by Misak-i Milli. Now each side would see the other as wishing to expand its territories.

For a long time after Atatürk's death in 1938, his image continued to bolster the modern Turkish spirit. He was literally preserved as well: his body was embalmed and not buried for fifteen years. Muslim tradition requires that a dead body be ritually washed, wrapped in white linen, and placed in a coffin from which it should be removed for interment before the next sunset. But Atatürk's body—like Lazar's for the Serbs—was needed to help the Turks deal with the unfinished business of "working through" the loss of an empire, transforming their political system, and building a new identity. Atatürk became "Immortal Atatürk," until he was finally interred in 1953, which signaled his return to mortal status (by comparison, Lazar's body was not buried for six hundred years, thus postponing Serbs' mourning). By the late 1980s and early 1990s, the Turkish elite, including then Turkish president Turgut Özal, could finally admit that Atatürk no longer held the place of a deity.

Mourning could at last begin. But group mourning of past losses is usually not experienced as sadness and grief. In fact, the average citizen is not aware that a group mourning is in process. It takes its course in societal actions, where its derivatives appear in the review of past affiliations, such as emotional attachment to religious institutions of the Ottoman Empire, and contemplation of how to integrate them in the modern identity.

Derivatives of Turkish mourning can also be found in the unusual government established in Turkey in 1996. For the first time in history, the Republic of Turkey had a conservative Islamic prime minister, Necmettin Erbakan. He began his tenure by forming a coalition with a secular party led by a westernized woman, former prime minister Tansu Çiller. But internal conflict came to the surface in the spring of 1997, when the secular Turkish military chiefs began positioning themselves against Erbakan and his fundamentalist followers.

What Turkey and Greece need are leaders who are psychologically informed enough to be comfortable with ambiguity. Such leaders would realize that while a political rapprochement between the two countries may increase anxiety it will not prove fatal.[27]

Chapter 8

UNWANTED CORPSES IN LATVIA: AN ATTEMPT AT PURIFICATION

After the Greeks won their independence (1821–1829) from the Ottoman Empire and slowly consolidated a new Greek identity combining elements of Hellenism and the heritage of the Byzantine Empire, they created Katharevusa, the neoclassical form of the modern Greek language that excluded many Turkish words. A hundred years later, after the Turks won their war of independence, they began to discard Arabic and Persian words, replacing them with ancient Turkish or Western words. The Greeks and Turks were performing a kind of "purification," the Greeks symbolically cleansing away unwanted aspects of their Ottoman heritage, which they perceived as the "enemy within," and the Turks modifying their former immersion in the Islamic world.

Attempts at purification often occur during postwar restabilization periods, when an ethnic tent has been shaken and must be reinforced. But they may also take place during wars and warlike situations. Performing such purifications, even innocuous-seeming ones that address only the language, can renew antagonisms and create an atmosphere for crisis.

Purification assumed its most malignant form during the seizure of Srebrenica in July 1995, during which seven thousand Muslims perished at the hands of Bosnian Serbs. Sometimes the radio played songs of Serb greatness, with lyrics such as: "Die, you scums, we are the champs. Come out on the terrace and hail the Serb race."[1] A potentially dangerous purification nearly took place in Latvia in 1993 but was averted.

— · —

In 1991, Latvia declared its re-independence from the Soviet Union, as did the two other Baltic states. The word *re-independence* was used since Latvia had been independent between 1918 and 1940 and there were Latvians who, like the U.S. government, refused to recognize Soviet rule. Many considered Soviet Latvia an occupied territory. Although the Soviet government never formally recognized the re-independence of Latvia, the Russian Federation, the principal heir of the Soviet Union, did. Many problems, practical and emotional, remained between Latvia and the Russian Federation.

The "togetherness" under the Soviet regime had changed the ethnic mix in each of the Baltic states. When Latvia regained its independence, only 52 percent of the population living there were Latvians; 34 percent were ethnic Russians, and the rest were Belorussians, Ukrainians, and Poles. In every large Latvian city, including the capital, Riga, there were more Russians than Latvians. One crucial issue after Latvia regained independence was what to do about the large Russian population. Different types of Russians lived in Latvia, as well as in other Baltic republics. There were those who had settled in Latvia long before, had learned the Latvian language, and apparently wanted to join the Latvians in rebuilding the country. Others were "immigrants." These were people who had come to Latvia relatively recently to improve their economic well-being, had stayed in Latvia and created their own communities, but had never bothered to learn the Latvian language since Latvia was then part of the Soviet Union, where everyone was expected to speak Russian.

Still others were "occupants," that is, members of the former Soviet apparatus, armed forces, or the KGB who happened to be in Latvia when the Soviet Union collapsed. The Russian Federation, declaring a housing shortage, seemed not to want them back. Suddenly, these formerly powerful Russians were no longer an official controlling force but a threatening and unwelcome anomaly. While the occupants were the most unwanted, Latvians considered all Russians in Latvia unwanted after re-independence.

Demographics in Latvia affected internal ethnic affairs, international relationships with Russia and other neighboring states, and, inevitably, the highly charged question of national identity. Because defining "who we are now" evoked powerful emotions, the issue of Latvian citizenship for the Russians in Latvia was complex.

In April 1993, Russian (former Soviet) troops were still stationed in independent Latvia. Strong emotions and conscious and unconscious perceptions arising from this enforced togetherness interfered with official diplomatic negotiations intended to forge a new relationship between Latvia and the Russian Federation. Russians accused Latvians of human rights abuses against ethnic Russians. Latvians expressed impatience at the Russians' sluggishness in withdrawing their troops. There was considerable fear that Russia was not ready to relinquish its imperial ambitions.

The first post-re-independence elections for the Latvian parliament (Saeima) were scheduled for June 5 and 6. When CSMHI visited Riga in April, we found that election rhetoric had heightened tensions. Frustration over the continued presence of Russian troops was exacerbated by media reports of a summit meeting in Vancouver between Presidents Bill Clinton and Boris Yeltsin during which the Latvia-based Russians had once again linked troop withdrawal to the treatment of ethnic Russian minorities in the Baltics.

Baltic perceptions were affected by a long history of occupation and subjugation. Successive Nazi and Soviet military invasions had been accompanied by cultural influences from both groups. Many Latvians were formerly Nazi sympathizers; many others embraced communism. In addition to these divided Latvian groups, there were nationalists who considered themselves revolutionary freedom fighters defending their country against both Germans and Russians. The occupation by the Soviet Union had brought with it, among other humiliations, a systematic program of enforced Russification. It had always been a difficult task to maintain a pure Latvian identity in the midst of larger and more powerful nations, and the policy of Russification was even more stifling.

The story of a thoroughfare in Riga records Latvia's history of invasions and how they influenced the Latvian identity. When Latvia was under the Russian Empire, this thoroughfare was called Alexander III Prospect. Between 1918 and 1940, during Latvia's first period of independence, it was renamed Brivibas Iela (Freedom Avenue), but during the Nazi occupation, it became Hitler Straße. After the Soviet "liberation," its name was changed again, this time to Lenin Prospect. Finally, with the recovery of Latvian independence, the road was once more called Freedom Avenue. Compared to the cobbled streets and baroque buildings of Old Riga, it is not a particularly attractive thoroughfare. In 1993, the only splash of color came from huge Pepsi Cola and Philips advertisements, symbolic, perhaps, of yet another invasion.

The new Latvian identity, formed after the country's restored independence, needed to mend the divisions among Latvians. This meant that unwanted elements within individuals, relating to past associations with Nazis and Soviets or disagreements within their own large group, for example, had to be externalized. The Latvia-based Russians were the targets of these externalizations; Latvians considered them more dangerous than they really were.

— · —

Our task in Latvia was to bring together influential representatives from Baltic republics and the Russian Federation for four days of unofficial dialogues. Shared group emotions had the potential to lead to irrational acts that could jeopardize the Baltic republics' relationships with the Russian Federation and the republics' efforts toward democratization. Informal dialogues might allow crucial issues to surface that could not be addressed in official gatherings, and the meetings might inspire new ideas that could lead to a long-term resolution of present conflicts.

A year before, we had met with representatives from Lithuania, Latvia, Estonia, and the Russian Federation in Kaunas, Lithuania. The sounds and sights of the Russian military, including helicopters flying over the conference center, filled the air. At the time, the Russians had not yet sent ambassadors to the Baltic republics. Baltic government officials had to deal directly with Russian military officials stationed in their countries instead of going through Russian diplomatic channels. A key recommendation from the Kaunas meeting was to expedite the establishment of Russian embassies in the Baltic states. The Russian participants took their message to Boris Yeltsin's government.

By the time we met in Riga, Russian ambassadors were already in place in each of the Baltic republics. The new Russian ambassador to Latvia, Alexandre Rannikh, and his first secretary attended the Riga meeting. So did the new Russian ambassador to Estonia, Alexandre Trofimov. They and other high-level Russians from Moscow were able to hear, in an unofficial setting, the concerns of the Baltic republic representatives, including government officials and members of important parliamentary commissions. The meeting had many fascinating moments, one of which illustrates the concept of purification from a psychopolitical angle.

— · —

Two months before we arrived in Riga, a dispatch in the *New York Times* reported that the Latvian parliament had voted "to remove the remains of Soviet Army soldiers" from the Latvian national military cemetery, the Cemetery of Brothers in Arms. A Latvian lawmaker, Yanis Freimanis, was quoted as saying: "Soldiers who served in the Red Army under Stalin's command were deliberately buried there to defile the cemetery."[2] It appeared that the Latvians planned a kind of ethnic cleansing of unwanted corpses from a sacred place. This purification effort, if carried out, might exacerbate the already tense relationship between Latvia and Russia. The Russians, especially military veterans, reacted with rage. The idea of a cleansing would put salt in the wound of having to let go of Latvia. The fact that the Russian troops had not yet withdrawn perhaps induced Latvians to hesitate and modify their original intent, but, still, some form of physical modification to the cemetery was being considered.

Another report, printed in the *American Baltic News* shortly afterward, insisted that Latvians simply wanted to restore the cemetery to its original design: "In the process, the bodies of about 200 Communist leaders and Soviet Army officers [would] need to be relocated to other sites." A delegation of Russian "peace marchers" (or, as we were told later, war veterans) traveled to Latvia to protest the decision but left reassured that nothing objectionable would take place.[3]

Built between 1924 and 1936 at the site of mass burials of Latvian riflemen killed in the battles of 1915, the Cemetery of Brothers in Arms contains the remains of soldiers who perished in World Wars I and II, as well as fighters for independence. It is a beautiful place, a walled park with many large oak and lime trees. On either side of the entrance are heroic figures on horseback, carved in stone. On the sidewalk on one side of the park, between the wall and a busy road, we saw dozens of Latvian women selling flowers to visitors to place on the graves of loved ones or heroes. Inside the park, a stone statue of Mother Latvia nine meters tall looms over simple graves. None of these were to be disturbed by the cemetery "remodeling." The controversial graves were situated near the entrance and belonged to "Soviet officials," who were "out of place" in this national military cemetery. Whatever the truth of the matter, and whatever the real aesthetic or moral justification for restoring the cemetery by disinterring Soviet military men, it was clear that there were understandably strong feelings about the previous sovietization of the Latvian national cemetery and a corresponding wish to undo that "sacrilege," in spite of the likelihood that it would produce a strong reaction from the Russians.

A look at the gravestones under the watchful presence of Mother Latvia made me understand why the desire to purify the cemetery had evolved: they reflect the fragmentation of the Latvian population and its alliances. Walking along the rows of soldiers' gravestones, one can see some marked with a Nazi swastika directly next to others marked with the star of the Soviet Red Army and still others marked simply by a cross or a Star of David—and all are Latvian. These fragments needed to be mended so people under the new Latvian ethnic tent would feel united. This mending would entail the externalization and projection of unwanted elements from the past to create a new togetherness. Latvians had found a reservoir in the undesirable corpses and sought to distance and/or forget them. This was the psychology underlying the Latvians' desire to cleanse the national military cemetery.

One participant at the Riga meeting, Juris Boyars, raised the emotional stakes when he stated that the Russian Mafia, working with Jews, was an obstacle for the new Latvia. Boyars was chairman of the Democratic Labor Party, director of the Institute of International Affairs at the Latvian State University, and a key figure in drafting the new citizenship laws. Although educated in Moscow and married to a Russian, he denied "contamination" by anything Russian. He informed us that his children were pure Latvians, that their Russian blood did not count, much like the Serbs who declared that the children born to raped Muslim women were pure Serbs. It seemed that Boyars wanted to do to the Russians (Soviets) what the latter had done to the Latvians. His remarks were infuriating and humiliating to the Russians, who felt that the Latvians owed them gratitude for helping them defeat the Nazis.

At one point the Russian embassy first secretary, Vladimir Ionkin, shouted at Boyars: "I saved you!" The singular pronoun "I," rather than "we," seemed to make him a spokesperson for his ethnic tent. "You" referred not so much to the Latvian and other Baltic representatives as to Western civilization as a whole. Reaching back in history to find a chosen glory when the Russians had defended Western Europe, he reminded us how, in the fourteenth century, the Russians had stood alone between the Mongols and the West and perceived themselves as defenders of Western culture.

Indeed, in 1241, under the leadership of Genghis Khan's grandson Batu Khan, the Mongols established the so-called Golden Horde at Sarai on the lower Volga. From there they virtually ruled the Russia of that time until 1480. In 1380, however, the Mongols suffered an important setback at the hands of the Russians that marked the beginning of the decline of Mongol power.

The defeat of the Mongols by the Russians in 1380 took place at Kulikovo plains near the Don River. The Russian forces were led by the prince of Moscow, Dimitri (later known as Dimitri Donskoy [of the Don]), and Grand Prince Vladimir. Their enemy, Khan Mamai, was expecting help from Iogalia, the grand prince of Lithuania. But Dimitri defeated the Mongols before Iogalia and his army could even help them.

The battle at Kulikovo plains is a major chosen glory for the Russians. They believe that their success in this battle protected the Western world from subjugation to the Mongols. Had the Lithuanians successfully joined forces with the Mongol horde, the history of Russia and Western Europe, Ionkin suggested, would have been very different. In this mental image of the past, present stereotypes were reversed: the Lithuanians were the villains, and the Russians were the saviors of Western civilization.

The present rejection by Latvians of all things Russian, including the Russian dead, represented in Ionkin's mind a monstrous ingratitude toward those who had "saved" the Latvians, as well as Lithuanians and Estonians and even Western Europe, from the Mongols. It became clear that the Kulikovo battle was an allegory in which Mongols represented a far more recent threat to Western civilization: the Nazis. Many Latvians (and other people from the Baltic states) had allied themselves with these later "Mongols." Now the group sensed one of the psychological needs underlying the wish to remove the unwanted Russians from the Cemetery of Brothers in Arms. The Russians, former enemies of the Nazis, had to be removed in order for the new Latvia to absorb those who had been Nazi sympathizers.

Paradoxically, Ionkin's emotional defense of his people against Baltic ingratitude restored a measure of Baltic self-esteem, for the representative of a big country was noticing and needing recognition from the representatives of so-called little ones. Then Ionkin introduced another symbolic ethnic cleansing into the discussion. General I. D. Chernyakhovski had been commander in chief of the Soviet forces that had liberated Lithuania from the Nazis. After his death at the German front in 1944, a monument honoring him was placed in the center of the Lithuanian capital of Vilnius. With independence, however, the general's statue was moved to his hometown in Ukraine. When Ionkin described how upsetting it had been for him and for other Russians to hear of the removal of the general from his place of triumph, Vladimir Jarmolenko, a member of the Lithuanian parliament and of the parliamentary Commission on Foreign Affairs, reminded him that Chernyakhovski's family had requested this action. But for the Russian, this made no difference.

Clearly the removal of the statue was, for one side, an important step in the liberation of Vilnius from Soviet influence and, for the other side, an act of gross ingratitude for its liberation from the Nazis. We suggested that perhaps each side could try to understand the various emotional investments in the statue. A few hours later, the Lithuanian Jarmolenko spontaneously returned to the topic of General Chernyakhovski: "I felt uncomfortable," he admitted, "sending Chernyakhovski back!" The participants then agreed that Baltic-Russian relations would have been improved had Chernyakhovski stayed in Vilnius and had the graves of the Soviet officials in Riga been shown more respect.

At this point, it was apparent that the participants were ready to accept that the complexities of Baltic-Russian relations were a shared problem. The issue of the unwanted corpses was then reported to the other participants at the meeting, and it was agreed that a moratorium should be imposed on all unilateral changes to cemeteries, memorials, and monuments. Such changes should only be made after consultation with all the parties whose heroes or other dead were involved. The participants decided to take their suggestions to the authorities in their respective countries and explain the meaning of such a moratorium.[4]

Two years later, I was in Riga interviewing Latvians and Russians living in Latvia.[5] In 1993, the beautiful old city had looked like a ghost town. By 1995, renovations and the building of office and hotel space were bringing it back to life. Latvians were pressing for free-market reforms and privatization. Obviously they wanted to join the European economic and security organizations, such as NATO, as soon as possible. But the emotional fragmentation among Latvians remained, and the psychological border between Latvians and Russians living in Latvia seemed even more rigid. There was no mention of the unwanted corpses in the Cemetery of Brothers in Arms. The attempt at purifying the cemetery had fizzled away as the psychodynamics of ethnic relations that had led to it were transferred to efforts at legalizing a gap between the Latvian and Russian communities.

Chapter 9

A PALESTINIAN ORPHANAGE:
RALLYING AROUND A LEADER

An anxious or regressed group clings more stubbornly than usual to its ethnicity, nationality, or religion because these connections provide a netlike support that protects the group from deeper regression or disintegration. It may grow attached to its leader and perceive him or her as the symbol of a large group's identity. An ethnic or national leader, whether a king, dictator, or president, exerts a dominant influence on the followers' rituals with the enemy group, which may range from a preoccupation with minor differences to activities of purification. At a Palestinian orphanage in Tunis that I once visited, attachment to the leader was exaggerated because the children had not only lost their families but had no information about them. Being grouped together in one location reinforced in them certain observable behaviors; the intensity of the children's connections to their ethnic identity made the orphanage a fascinating place to study ethnic bonding and the leader-follower relationship.

In the spring of 1990, I interviewed many of the orphans at Biet Atfal Al-Sommoud (the Home of Children of Steadfastness), a former maternity hospital in a residential district of Tunis.[1] At the time of my visit, the orphanage housed thirty-one boys and twenty-one girls, aged seven to eighteen. They had never known their parents, or if they did, they remembered them only dimly. They had been told that their parents had been killed by Israelis, and they were treated specially, as heroes' children. All of them had been sent to an orphanage in Lebanon and then to one in Syria before being transferred to this one in Tunisia.

When I visited Tunis, the city was filled with tourists, mostly French, drawn by nearby Carthage and its beautiful beaches. Life had the appearance of normality. But within this city also lived a community of Palestinians constantly alert and involved in an ongoing security watch. The Palestine Liberation Organization (PLO) headquarters was based in Tunis at this time, as was Chairman Yassir Arafat, though he lived and slept at different secret locations for security reasons. It was not unusual for Palestinians to call one another in the middle of the night and ask simply, "Are you all right?" Members of Arafat's security forces, driving old, ordinary cars, passed by Palestinian houses, making sure that everything was in order. Palestinians were in constant fear that Israeli commandos would arrive in Tunis at night on a raid to kill this or that person. Indeed, one of Arafat's closest associates had been assassinated in his home not long before my trip to Tunis.

During my visit, I was taken to PLO headquarters. What I found there was striking in its symbolism. The building was literally stripped of furniture. In each office, there was an old desk and chair, with nothing available for visitors to sit on as they waited, sometimes for hours, to complete their business. The reason for the barren appearance was the Palestinians' wish to honor the children in Gaza and on the West Bank who were involved in the Intifada (which was going on at the time of my visit). I was told by a PLO official that they felt it improper for Palestinians here at the headquarters to indulge themselves in luxuries, such as comfortable chairs, while those involved in the Intifada endured hardship.

The Palestinian director of the orphanage belonged to this culture of perpetual alert. She was a pleasant woman in her late thirties, born in Israeli-occupied territories, who at the age of sixteen had been jailed for some months by the Israelis for her activities. Like her orphan charges, she was a latecomer to Tunis. She lived not at the orphanage but in another residential district with her two young children.

The orphanage had a large, walled courtyard with a flagpole bearing a Palestinian flag. On the walls were posters of children involved in the Intifada, as well as pictures of Arafat and other Palestinian leaders. The orphans at Biet Atfal Al-Sommoud were paired by gender, and an older child always roomed with a younger one. Then four or five pairs would create a "family" looked after by an older woman. Except for the physician, all the caretakers who lived at the orphanage were women.

The director's goal was to make a home for these youths, and she encouraged them to make friends outside of the house, even to spend the night with city hosts. My impression was that the children visited mostly Palestinian families and seldom Tunisians. Each orphan received a weekly allowance, and the older children shopped for their own clothing. Many of the children played sports, and all of them traveled by bus to a school for Palestinian children rather than attend Tunisian schools.

I had occasion to observe five children, all very young, who tended to stay together while playing in the courtyard. They had been rescued as infants from the massacres of some two thousand unarmed Palestinian and Lebanese civilians by Israeli-backed phalange Christian militiamen at Sabra and Shatila, refugee camps in West Beirut. Four children had been found in trash cans and one under a bed. Apparently their parents, before they were killed, had hidden the children to save them from being murdered. The children's real identities were unknown. They seemed "normal" when together, but when they were separated for the interview—through an interpreter—each one became agitated and experienced extreme difficulty relating to me and to others. One hallucinated acutely, and another began destroying the furniture. It was evident to me that these children did not have well-established individual identities. Being with others from Sabra and Shatila enabled them to appear normal.

In contrast to these five children was a handsome seventeen-year-old, whom I will call Farouk. He had the strongest self-identity of the children I met. Farouk was five years old and living in Lebanon when he witnessed Israeli soldiers beat his father to death. The next day, his mother, a sister, and a cousin were shot and killed. (These are the facts as Farouk reported them, and I did not feel compelled to verify them, because the interviews were aimed at revealing the subject's experiences of self and images of others, not necessarily the literal truth of the person's history.) "I no longer remember my parents' faces," he claimed, and he described how he often wept when alone, adding, "It is a healthy thing to do." He was the captain of the orphanage's soccer team and was much loved by the other children.

As Farouk spoke with me in excellent English, I noticed his habit of rubbing a big scar on his right foot, visible through his sandals. The scar was the result of a household accident in Lebanon when he was very small. While his grandmother was cooking sweets in a pan on an open fire, he accidentally stepped in the pan and burned his foot. His parents had put ointment on it and tried to soothe his pain.

Farouk linked himself to the image of caring parents through his scar. In a sense his family identification was burned into him like an emblem; as long as the scar persisted, he would have his parents under his skin, giving him strength. He truly believed that his scarred foot was special; it was strong. Indeed, all the other children admired this foot, with which he had scored many goals against opposing soccer teams, all Tunisian.

Farouk was conscious of the meaning of his scar. "I almost feel my parents from within, inside my foot, inside my body," he said. He had made it a ritual to touch his scar after each game of soccer as well as every night before going to sleep. Farouk's symbolic creation of his parents' images and his contact with them were at the root of his positive personal identity.

During the week I spent at Biet Atfal Al-Sommoud, I came to see that all the orphans, from the Sabra and Shatila children to Farouk, clung to their Palestinianness as their shared, second identity. For Farouk, the ethnic (Palestinian) identity was not the dominant one. But for many of the other children and teenagers, ethnic identity dominated personal identity. The maintenance and protection of the group identity were psychological necessities. Farouk saw his future in a civil profession. Many of the other children and youths wanted to be military pilots so they could fly to the land of their ancestors and bomb enemy positions. In Biet Atfal Al-Sommoud the atmosphere was such that "we-ness" appeared everywhere, and often even Farouk and others like him would willingly join in this sense of togetherness.

While studying, playing, eating, watching television, and almost constantly hugging and kissing one another, the orphans gave the initial impression of being in a nonstop love fest. The children were healthy as long as they were Palestinian orphans, patching up one another's personality deficits. A teenage girl with a beautiful voice sang songs of victimization, and her words spoke for all of them as they clustered around her. There was external support for the we-ness as well. The orphans were collectively referred to by their caregivers as "the children of martyrs."

The group with which these children identified extended beyond the boundaries of their orphanage. During my visit, the orphans watched television footage of Intifada children throwing stones at Israeli soldiers in the West Bank and Gaza. While watching them, the orphans would involuntarily mimic the motion of throwing stones, literally identifying with those in the occupied territories, hundreds and hundreds of miles away. Even when they were not watching television but were speaking of the Intifada, their bodies would move in a way that gave one the impression that they were actually fighting their enemies.

The little tent of Biet Atfal Al-Sommoud was placed under the big tent that belonged to all Palestinians, the one in which Palestinian identity itself was under threat. The orphans were exhibiting a literal illustration of Hans Kohn's description of large-group bonding:

Nationalism—our identification with the life and aspirations of uncounted millions whom we shall never know, with a territory which we shall never visit in its entirety—is qualitatively different from the love of family or of home surroundings. It is qualitatively akin to the love of humanity or of the whole earth.[2]

One day at lunch the children wanted me to notice that they had bananas to eat, even though bananas were not grown in Tunisia. These had been sent to them from a place Yassir Arafat had recently traveled to. Chairman Arafat visited Biet Atfal Al-Sommoud frequently and sent the orphans gifts from the places he went. Since none of the routine caretakers at the orphanage were male, Arafat was the children's principal father figure. Those who did not know the names of their natural fathers, at least twenty of the children, carried the last name Arafat. Their names linked them to one another as they rallied around Yassir Arafat, the pole of the Palestinian tent. When Arafat visited the orphanage, the children surrounded the chairman, each trying to touch him.

— · —

In primitive societies, which lack the concealing layer of sophisticated political institutions, the pole of leadership is often clearly visible. In studying two groups of Kagwahiv Indians in Brazil, anthropologist Waud Kracke found a leader—whom he calls Homero—who had a rigid moral code and demanded strict obedience from his followers. In another Kagwahiv settlement, the leader, whom Kracke dubs Jovenil, had a very different personality. Jovenil was sensitive to the needs of his followers and showed a balance between his sensitivities and his firmness. Despite the individual differences in personalities and leadership styles, Kracke detected four common characteristics: both leaders enjoyed power and prestige; neither feared competition; both exhibited strong identifications with their fathers, which reduced their reliance on others; and both held a broad view of the social and political climate of their settlements.[3] What is most important in maintaining leadership is not the personality type of the leader, but his feeling at ease with power, competition, and independence and his possessing a wide-ranging vision of societal processes. Even though his personality (cold or warm, obsessional or grandiose, paranoid or trusting, etc.) will affect his governing style, these four characteristics determine his ability to lead at all.

In some individuals, excessive self-love and feelings of entitlement propel them to seek leadership positions. There are also obsessional people who are absorbed by the conviction of having a moral mission, and this impulse leads them to seek power. As Peter Loewenberg has noted:

Most people derive their pleasures and gratifications from intimate relationships with family, lovers, children, and friends. But for some people, the politicians, those who seek public office, positions on stage in the limelight, the essential need is for external confirmation and rewards of exercising power.[4]

In addition to studying Kagwahiv leaders, Kracke also studied their followers. In both settlements, Kracke noted that to the followers the leaders fulfilled a role analogous to that of parents for a growing child. The followers used the leaders and their images to gratify their emotional needs, to develop self-control, and as models for further maturity. For example, the anthropologist collected followers' dreams and fantasies in which the head man provided a delectable feast and either gratified or frustrated the followers' sexual impulses. Kracke described both Jovenil's and Homero's relationships with their followers as two-way streets: leaders influence followers, and followers' needs shape the leader.

But what Kracke observed in these two Amazon settlements also applies to more advanced societies, though psychological motivations and attitudes are usually hidden from view. According to Professor James MacGregor Burns of Williams College, governing in complicated societies

> does not take place in a vacuum . . . but in the context of the political and psychological forces, rational and irrational, operating through it. The stately procession of ends and means usually [becomes] displaced and deranged in practice. The human materials of executive decision-making [are] not standardized and replicable but unpredictable combinations of enthusiasts, foot-draggers, expediters, empire builders, adjusters, and others who [bring] to bear their own motivations, attitudes, and goals. People respond to unseen ideologies and mythologies, to distant bugle calls and drumbeats. Executive decision-making [is] filled with unanticipated and dysfunctional activities.[5]

Matthew Holden of the University of Virginia considers the basic administrative structure of any sophisticated political organization to be tripartite, where the central elements are the leader, the operating entities that perform administrative work, and what he calls the "entourage" (from the French *entourer*, to surround). According to Holden, U.S. presidents, for example, are usually surrounded by "cronies," that is, people of senior status who are the president's peers, personal friends, and trusted advisers. Ronald Reagan's so-called kitchen cabinet is one example of such an entourage. Another circle of a president's entourage includes what Holden calls the "ambitious young servants" who perform whatever services are required or imagined to be required. They are deeply loyal to the chief executive and follow him with zealous obedience. From the time of Abraham Lincoln to the present, three in ten of the identifiable chief aides to American presidents have been thirty-five years old or younger when they initially assumed their responsibilities. The last group within the president's entourage are the "migratory technocrats," like Henry Kissinger and Zbigniew Brzezinski, who provide special advice and information to the president.[6]

With sophisticated large groups then, there are often layers of government—bureaucracy—between the political leader and his followers. But the leader is the top officer. In interacting with his followers, he continually updates and modifies their shared needs and attitudes, chosen traumas and chosen glories, while consciously and unconsciously assessing his effect on them and their degree of devotion to him. Burns correctly remarked that "a leader who fails to measure his impact on his followers is like a youngster who plays at leading the town parade, but who foolishly continues to 'strut along main street after the procession has turned down a side street to the fairgrounds.' "[7] At the same time, "what the people want is mightily affected by the promises and preachings of politicians."[8] The leader takes a group interest or need, transforms it into an ideology and a program, and then rallies his followers around it. The followers may be transformed in the process, and their situation may improve—or it may not: Charles de Gaulle, for all his pomp and revitalization of the French civil spirit, did relatively little to change the circumstances of the average French citizen.[9]

Since the classic 1922 work of Max Weber, *Wirtschaft und Gesellschaft (Economy and Society)*, many have studied the appearance in times of crisis of "charismatic leaders" whose strengths match the needs of an emotionally bonded group. A group in crisis searches for someone who offers salvation and deliverance and often finds him in a leader whose charisma promises to transform the group's identity.

One example of a charismatic savior who appeared at a time of crisis comes from Turkish history. At the end of World War I, when the Ottoman Empire was defeated, the Turks found a charismatic leader in Mustafa Kemal (Atatürk). The internal world of this leader had, from childhood on, prepared him for his role as savior.

He had been born into a house of death: all but one of his siblings had died before or soon after his birth in 1881, and his father died when Mustafa Kemal was very young. He adapted to his traumatic childhood by developing rescue fantasies and exaggerated self-esteem.[10] As an adult, he displaced the childhood image of his grieving mother onto the Turkish nation in crisis. After the Turks won their war of independence and established modern Turkey in place of the Ottoman Empire, Atatürk embarked on a series of cultural revolutions, which, in turn, changed the Turks' group identity.

Charismatic leaders with exaggerated self-esteem who seek to transform group identity can be either reparative or destructive. Atatürk was a reparative leader. Such a person helps the large-group identity evolve in a positive way by enhancing the previously injured shared self-esteem of his people. But some leaders do not go about the transformation of their group's identity in a constructive way. They too have the goal of bolstering their group but do so by hurting and destroying another group, so that only in comparison do their followers seem better off. Between the two extremes are those whom Abraham Zaleznik terms "consensus leaders."[11] Consensus leaders help their groups to assimilate changes and consolidate new ways of feeling about the now-modified group identity. Fortunately or unfortunately— it depends on how one looks at it—in democratic societies free of external threat, consensus leaders follow one another, eroding their potential influence on group identity.

— · —

The two-way traffic between a leader and his followers may be congested in either direction because of the psychological makeup of the leader or external forces that influence him as well as his followers. Some leaders use political and historical arenas to find or create external solutions for their internal, mostly unconscious, wishes and personal conflicts. For them, wielding power relates closely to their individual needs for survival and adaptation. Instead of mobilizing followers to enhance group self-esteem, such leaders coerce them into responding to the leader's internal needs and believe that by doing so the followers' self-esteem is improved. In other cases, when a large-group tent shakes, the group welcomes a savior whose wishes, conflicts, and mental defenses strongly influence the identity of his followers—for good or for ill.

Chapter 10

ETHNIC TERRORISM AND TERRORISTS: BELONGING BY VIOLENCE

When the word *terrorism* was first used in 1795, it referred to acts of intimidation by a government against its people—terrorism from above. The term derives from French revolutionary statesman Maximilien de Robespierre's 1785–1794 Reign of Terror during the early years of the French Revolution. Robespierre defended governmental terrorism by claiming that the Revolution enacted the despotism of liberty against tyranny. Historically, terrorism from above has far exceeded, in the sheer number of its victims, any other form of terror, and the twentieth century has witnessed the most horrific examples of it: the Holocaust, Stalin's purges, and the killing fields of the Pol Pot regime.

Today, the term *terrorism* refers more often to acts from below that attempt to disrupt, overthrow, or simply express rage against the existing political order. Acts of terrorism from below have existed for at least two thousand years. During the first century A.D., two Jewish groups in Judaea, the Zealots and the Sicarii, resorted to what might be described as ethnic terrorism as they tried to inspire a popular uprising against their Roman occupiers. Between the eleventh and thirteenth centuries, a Shi'ite Muslim sect called the Assassins carried out ideological religious terrorism by assassinating Muslim leaders whom they accused of corrupting true Islam.[1]

Most scholars agree that modern terrorism from below began in the nineteenth century in Russia with the rise of an ideological group that called itself Narodnaya Volya (People's Will). They assassinated czarist officials and attempted to propagate revolution within Russian society.[2] Members of Narodnaya Volya beat themselves as punishment for taking the lives of their victims, despite their obvious hatred of those they killed. Such self-torture and remorse are not part of modern-day terrorism, or at least are not in evidence among today's terrorists.

Some terrorism is motivated by ideological beliefs and revolutionary thoughts. *Ethnic terrorism* refers to situations in which terrorist leaders have excessive attachment to their large-group identity and seek to enhance it through widespread violence and to perpetuate it under improved political conditions, such as some form of autonomy or statehood for the group. Ethnic terrorists legitimize their actions by referring to the dominant ethnic or other large group as an occupying, opposing, colonizing, or foreign force. The Basque liberation organization Euzkadi Ta Azkatasuna (ETA), the Kurdish Workers' Party (Partiya Karkari Kurdistan, PKK), the Liberation Tigers of Tamil Eelam (LTTE), the Irish Republican Army (IRA), the Palestinian Hamas and PLO, and the Lebanese Hezbollah are all examples of ethnic terrorist groups.

Hezbollah, the Party of God—"after a verse in Qur'an: 'Lo! The Party of God, they are victorious' "[3]—is a Shi'ite Islamic fundamentalist group in Lebanon, but its aim is to end the "occupation" of Lebanon by Israel and to create an Islamic state in Lebanon. It was Hezbollah that familiarized the world with suicide bombings in the mid-1980s when it attacked the American embassy and marine barracks in Beirut.

Just before the 1996 election of Benjamin Netanyahu as Israeli prime minister, Sheikh Hassan Nasrallah, secretary-general of Hezbollah, described for *Middle East Insight* how Hezbollah was formed.[4] According to Nasrallah, when the Israelis invaded Lebanon in 1982, a group of Islamist leaders (ulema) met and issued a directive for Islamic groups in the country to dissolve themselves and regroup under one framework—later named Hezbollah—with the aim of fighting the occupation. Nasrallah insisted that Hezbollah was a Lebanese initiative, not an Iranian one, and stated that if there had been no occupation there would be no Hezbollah. The first cell of the organization consisted of nine people. They had no plans other than to resist the occupation, but they knew that it was impossible to confront the enemy "with old conceptions and forms." Islamic cultural clubs already existed in Lebanon, but, as Nasrallah noted, a cultural group was obviously not equipped to confront the occupation: "Could they do so by giving lessons, for instance?"[5] Therefore, a more militant organization was needed. The cell had no adequate weapons. Nasrallah explained: "Naturally, we asked for assistance. From any party. And the duty of the people was to help. From then on relations were begun with Syria and Iran; others were not as responsive for many of them thought that what was going on in Lebanon did not concern them."[6] Since then, Hezbollah has become increasingly structured. It is a "centralized and accountable organization."[7]

The initial cell of an ethnic terrorist group needs financial support for its activities and will solicit help from governments and other organizations that support terrorism. Instrumental to the rise of an ethnic terrorist group is the willingness of those who are *not* actively involved in terrorist activities, but who share the same ethnic background, to express at least covert sympathy for the terrorists and, correspondingly, little compassion for their victims. This makes it easier for the leader to find followers who will join him.

Historically, Shi'ite Muslims in Lebanon lived in rather isolated settlements. When Lebanon became an independent country in 1946, the state was governed by Maronite Christians and Sunni Muslims. According to Martin Kramer, an Israeli expert on terrorism at the Dayan Center in Tel Aviv, Shi'ite Muslims resisted westernization and held on to the fourteen-hundred-year legacy of Shi'ism, "a legacy of martyrdom and suffering, resting upon an ancient grievance: the belief that Islamic history was derailed when political power passed out of the hands of the Prophet Muhammed's family in the seventh century."[8] While initially Shi'ite Muslims were marginalized within the political system, their birthrate surpassed that of non-Shi'ite Arabs in Lebanon. From 1921 to 1956, Lebanon's Shi'ite population rose from 100,000 to 250,000, and by 1995 it had reached 750,000, or about 30 percent of the country's total population.[9] When Hezbollah established itself, members declared that they sought an Islamic government in Lebanon in order to bring peace to their part of the world through preaching Islamic fundamentalism. Islamic fundamentalism in turn attracted a broad cross section of society and overt or covert support for Hezbollah.[10]

But ethnic terrorism exhibits a paradox: despite their tendency to sympathize with acts of violence against the enemy, members of the large group who are not actively involved in terrorism are often caught in the cross fire of terrorism anyway. So strong is the terrorist cell's perceived need to silence opposition and establish unassailable authority within its own ethnic group that a campaign of internally directed terror—toward people of its own ethnicity—is often considered essential to an effective campaign against the other dominant large group. The PLO, for example, has killed members or other Palestinians who are thought to have consorted with Israelis. Fear is generated both to crush internal opposition and to disrupt the enemy. The seemingly arbitrary and random nature of the terrorists' acts of violence intensifies the fear they generate. In fact, however, most acts are carefully selected for shock value and political gain.

In ethnic terrorism, innocent people are victimized in order to verify the victimhood of the terrorists' ethnic group. But since the terrorist acts themselves are so ghastly, the world community cannot help but lose sympathy for the ethnic group's victimhood. Nasrallah's remarks about hostages in Lebanon (seized after the Israeli invasion) serve as a case in point: "Hostages were taken in Lebanon, but because they were American or French or German the whole world was concerned—the world press took great interest. It is unfortunate that the world doesn't recognize that Israel occupies part of Lebanon, and the Israelis hold more than 300 Lebanese—some women, who were taken from their homes."[11] But precisely because hostage taking was such an inhuman and shocking act, the world became more concerned with the fate of the hostages than with verifying the victimhood of the Lebanese.

Ethnic terrorism rarely furthers the proclaimed aims of the ethnic group or of the terrorist group itself, so vast is "the gulf between efficacy and aspiration," notes terrorism expert Loren Lomarsky.[12] In Northern Ireland, on a number of occasions, horrendous terrorist acts have managed to derail a peaceful solution when it appeared to be in sight.[13] Similarly, in 1996, when Israelis and Palestinians were making genuine progress toward peaceful coexistence, Hamas engineered a series of suicide bomb attacks in Israel. For Hamas, terrorism is an end in itself.

But many ethnic terrorist leaders believe that terrorism truly is effective in defeating the occupying or foreign dominant peoples. Nasrallah indicated his belief that the Israeli evacuation from Lebanon without negotiations was due to the success of ethnic terrorism. From 1982 to 1985, with Hezbollah in effect, "the Israelis became unable to walk in Beirut and [on] the mountain roads and [in] the Bekaa and the south. They considered all wadis [valleys] and ravines ambushed. Every can or stone might cover an explosive. It became difficult for the Israeli soldiers, especially the psychological aspects [of the conflict]."[14]

— · —

Despite boasting, ethnic terrorist leaders are cognizant of their limited military and political effectiveness. So what drives them to act as they do? What unconscious motivations are involved here? The late psychologist Jeanne Knutson, who founded the International Society of Political Psychology, was an expert on Northern Irish terrorist leaders and had held hundreds of interviews with them. Knutson found that they had common elements in their personal histories: all had been victims of terror themselves, all had experienced violations of their personal boundaries that damaged or destroyed their faith in personal safety. In a manuscript unfinished at the time of her death, Knutson wrote:

> One never erases the identity of a victim. The first blows make the victim permanently on guard for the next attack by the next victimizer. Even if the latter—a tribe, another ethnic group, or nation—loses power or the ability to mount a credible threat, the victim's fear continues even if diminished. A life-preserving, primitive belief in personal safety has been breached. Once having been terrorized, a victim thus simultaneously grieves over the past and fears the future. At the base, this intense anxiety over future loss is driven by the semiconscious inner knowledge that passivity ensures victim-

ization. The genesis of political violence . . . is the belief that
. . . only continued activity in defense of oneself (one's group)
adequately serves to reduce the threat of further aggression
against oneself.[15]

Terrorist leaders, however, are rarely mentally ill. Many are highly
intelligent with the ability for strategic planning, even if personal identity problems are common among them. Out of the range of possible
responses to identity problems, terrorist leaders tend to shore up their
internal sense of self by seeking the power to hurt and by expressing
their sense of entitlement to power.

On the basis of CSMHI research, it appears that ethnic terrorist
leaders' personal identity problems begin during their developmental
years.[16] Many experience violations of their personal boundaries in
the form of beatings by parents, incest, or other such events. Their
reactions to these personal traumas later dovetail with their victimization by an enemy group or their perception of human rights violations inflicted by members of an "occupying" army. In 1990,
international relations specialist Katherine Kennedy interviewed
twenty-three state-labeled terrorists or self-proclaimed freedom fighters in Northern Ireland. All of them had experienced traumas in their
formative years. One had been beaten by an alcoholic father, another
had been sexually molested. Most had also been humiliated at the
hands of their enemies. One, for example, had been beaten beyond
recognition at age nineteen after being stopped at a border checkpoint.

Early or childhood victimization, of course, need not be physical;
it can include being abandoned by a mother at an early age, disap-
pointment over being let down by loved ones, a deep sense of personal
failure following parental divorce, or rejection by peer groups. Because of flawed personal identities, those who become leaders of terrorist cells use their shared ethnic identity as their primary identity.
In other words, the tent canvas serves as both personal garment and
ethnic tent. In their ethnic identity, they find a second layer of clothing
that compensates for the inadequacy of the first layer. The two layers
become interchangeable. Their psychology is identical with the psychology of many of the Palestinian children whom I interviewed at
Biet Atfal Al-Sommoud.

A trigger from the environment, such as state-sanctioned violence, may be the catalyst that propels the traumatized individual toward terrorism. His conversion to terrorism comes when he believes that passivity will bring further trauma and when he identifies the ethnic garment as his principal tool for dealing with anxiety.[17] Later, he is recognized and verified as an ethnic terrorist by others who support his newly founded internal cohesion. Financial support and praise for his activities from governments and other organizations legitimize his activities and sense of self-worth.

Obviously, not everyone who has personal identity problems and is traumatized starts a terrorist cell. Those who become terrorist leaders or their lieutenants have a psychological need to "kill" the victimized aspects of themselves and the victimizing aspects of their aggressors that they have externalized and projected onto innocent others. As reflected in statements by known terrorists, there are no innocent people. Violence is idealized to enhance self-esteem and as a defensive response to an individual's (or group's) sense of entitlement to revenge.

Similar psychodynamics have been found through clinical studies of those who suffer from what psychoanalysts call "malignant narcissism."[18] Many serial killers are malignant narcissists,[19] who seek "aggressive triumphs," sometimes deadly ones, in order to verify their self-worth.[20] Malignant narcissism occurs on a spectrum, with the propensity toward evil ranging from modest to extreme proportions. Because studies of terrorist leaders are rare, and clinically speaking insufficient, it is difficult to know which type of malignant narcissism they may suffer from. It appears likely, however, that most ethnic terrorist leaders who order the killings of innocent people would not be serial murderers if they were not involved in ethnic terrorism. We are left to assume that when a person wears the cloak of an ethnic tent he receives internal "permission" to plan or execute the killing of innocent people. Since the targets of his violence are symbolized as unwanted and dangerous elements that originated from his internal world, the terrorist does not consciously feel guilty.

In some terrorist organizations, such as Hezbollah, the initial cell was founded by a group of people, rather than by a single individual. If the dynamic of an initial terrorist cell does not involve a single leader, it is possible that the group solves problems of individual guilt that would deter their violent activities by allowing members to share and absorb one another's guilt.

Since wearing the ethnic canvas patches up a sense of self, terrorist leaders appear normal and are capable of carrying out routine tasks. But their personalities exhibit a kind of split. On one side of the split, they are (indirectly) violent killers, but on the other, they show concern for people they love—family members or close friends. Katherine Kennedy recounted an interview with a leader of the Ulster Defense Association who played lovingly with his infant son while boasting of having ordered a bombing two weeks earlier that had killed a mother and her two children. On another occasion, Kennedy interviewed an influential member of the IRA in an unheated office in the middle of winter. The man interrupted his description of personal involvement in terrorist activities to find Kennedy a coat.

The personality of a terrorist leader also illustrates the gulf between the organization's stated goal and activities that prohibit reaching it. Paradoxically, the very fact that a terrorist leader clings so tightly to the terrorist group (to provide a sense of belonging and to substitute for a "missing" personal identity) works against the efficacy of the group's officially stated goals. If his group were to succeed, it would no longer be needed and would eventually dissolve. Since a leader cannot tolerate an identity vacuum, he unconsciously aims for the impossible. Faced with the opportunity to negotiate a settlement with the target group, a terrorist may increase his demands and intensify his violence. Psychiatrist Jerrold Post calls this phenomenon the "threat of success":

> For any group or organization, the highest priority is survival. This is especially true for the terrorist group. To succeed in achieving its espoused cause would threaten the goal of survival. This fact suggests a position of cybernetic balance for the group. It must be successful enough in its terrorist acts and rhetoric of legitimization to attract members and perpetuate itself, but it must not be so successful that it will succeed itself out of business.[21]

The tendency among terrorist leaders not to achieve the officially stated goal is supported by the need for continual externalization of the victimized aspects of his or her personality and the victimizing aspects of others: the aggressors.

— · —

Ethnic terrorist leaders and their lieutenants need determined followers who can be trained to commit violent acts against civilians or other targets. Followers are usually not much older than twenty-five years of age, and, like those who started the cell, have a strong urge to belong.[22] One study of Basque separatist terrorists (ETA) found that the percentage of people of mixed Basque-Spanish parentage within the ETA was proportionally much higher than in the Basque population of Spain as a whole (40 percent versus 8 percent). Since those of mixed Basque-Spanish parentage in the Basque region are generally reviled as half-breeds, the study surmised that the "outcasts" who joined ETA were trying to demonstrate that they truly belonged to their chosen ethnic group.[23]

When the acts of ethnic terrorists shake an ethnic tent, individuals beneath it respond by strengthening their investment in ethnicity, which makes them more susceptible to being recruited by the terrorist group. Inducing fear within their ethnic group is one strategy ethnic terrorist leaders use for finding new followers. When people, especially the young, are afraid or anxious, they tend to identify with the aggressor (in this case the ethnic terrorists) in order to gain a sense of security through association with such power. As the dominant (non-terrorist or occupier) group responds, sometimes severely, to each act of ethnic terrorism, the fear and anxiety of young people in the terrorists' ethnic group increase. This escalation of violence, combined with rage toward the enemy group, propels members of the terrorists' ethnic group to rally around the terrorist leader. The dominant other group is also an aggressor, but identification with this other does not provide a sense of belonging. Retaliation by the dominant group may only intensify the terrorist followers' identification with their own leaders.

— · —

Despite the strong prohibition against suicide in Islam, Lebanese Shi'ites of Hezbollah carried out many suicide bombings between

1983 and 1985, and Hamas Palestinians have continued the trend. After the 1983–1985 incidents, the names of the "martyrs" were publicized, and they were considered fallen heroes and role models for newer recruits. "Hero cards" were printed and distributed to young members of the ethnic group, who collected them the way American children collect baseball cards. The world press, by contrast, emphasized the pathological nature of the terrorists' behavior. According to Martin Kramer, this had "some effect in the Shi'ite streets, where it was rumored that the terrorists who carried out the operations were possibly disturbed, making it necessary for the Islamic Jihad to conceal their identities after the attacks."[24] Nevertheless, Israel's security experts have pieced together information about the identities of many suicide bombers or would-be martyrs.

Terrorist leaders have mastered a variety of techniques to recruit and indoctrinate youths for suicide bombings. Whether intuitively or through experience, they understand the natural psychology of the adolescent passage when boys leave the restrictions of their families behind to seek out new identities as members of a group, gang, sports club, and so on. Typical recruits are unmarried males aged seventeen to twenty-three (sometimes younger). Scouts often choose youths who have been hurt by ethnic conflict: those who have been beaten up or have lost a father or brother in demonstrations; those who have not successfully completed their adolescent transformation and are alienated and without much hope for the future in existing political and economic conditions. The chosen youths are divided into small groups where they collectively read the Qur'an and chant religious scriptures. Terrorists have found passages in the Qur'an to respond to the Islamic prohibition against suicide and killing civilians. They direct recruits to read Qur'anic verses, such as: "Think not of those who are slain in God's way as dead. Nay, they live, finding their sustenance in the presence of their Lord." To create a mystical and religious togetherness and to instill in them a special identity, the leaders instruct the group of new followers to repeat and memorize cryptic passages, such as: "I will be patient until Patience is worn out from patience." The mechanisms that pull together a football team or boy scout troop are similar to those used to create a terrorist group, but in the latter, secrecy binds the recruits. Suicide bombers are instructed not to inform their parents of their mission. Thus, on a conscious level, the parents do not know the fate that awaits their children, though they may unconsciously have some idea of it.

According to fundamentalist Islamic tradition and corresponding cultural norms, most of these teenagers suppress their sexual desires; some even refrain from watching television to avoid sexual temptation. Indoctrination creates a severe—but external—superego, which demands adherence to restricted ways of thinking and behaving. But as a counterweight—or incentive—there is the suggestion of unlimited pleasures in heaven, where their stomachs will be filled with scrumptious food and they will receive the love of houris (angels). After the death of a suicide bomber, members of a terrorist group actually hold a celebration (despite the family members' genuine grief) and speak of a martyr's death as a "wedding." With the examples of those who died before, recruits are given hope and a belief in immortality, as well as assurances that after their demise their parents and siblings will be well taken care of by the terrorist group. In fact, relatives receive compensation.

The recruiting methods used by Hamas for the 1996 suicide bombings were different. Yahye Ayash, a terrorist leader nicknamed the Engineer, had recently been killed by Israelis who sabotaged his mobile phone with plastic explosive. Ayash was the leader of a faction named Izzedin al-Kassem—in honor of a Syrian terrorist killed in a shoot-out with British soldiers in Palestine in the 1930s. Now Ayash's lieutenant, Abu Ahmed, was hell-bent on revenge. Abu Ahmed traveled from Gaza to the West Bank town of Ramallah. According to Israeli intelligence, there were no suicide bombers in Ramallah when Abu Ahmed first arrived.[25] He befriended a young psychology student, Mohammed Abu Wardeh, and began enlisting volunteers, mostly from a refugee camp called Al-Fawwar (boiling pot) on the outskirts of Hebron. The recruits were subjected to a crash course in radical Islam before they were ready to be martyrs. They called themselves the "Ayash brigade" in memory of the deceased Engineer and killed fifty-seven Israelis before they were stopped. Abu Ahmed managed to disappear.

Many individuals who claim leadership in Hamas are in Israeli jails. As a result, Hamas now "consists of a collection of autonomous and highly secretive splinter groups,"[26] making the movement much less predictable. The story of the formation of the Ayash brigade is illustrative of how an original terrorist cell can spread and metastasize. While Hamas is evolving in a decentralized fashion, other terrorist organizations have remained under the control of a leader and his entourage. One such centrally controlled organization is the Kurdistan Workers' Party (PKK).

Chapter 11

FROM VICTIM TO VICTIMIZER: THE LEADER OF THE PKK (KURDISH WORKERS' PARTY)

Direct psychological research on terrorist leaders is nearly impossible; obviously, no terrorist would volunteer to lie on a psychoanalyst's couch or take psychological tests. However, in 1993, one such leader, forty-four-year-old Abdullah Öcalan, discussed his life in great detail.[1] Öcalan, nicknamed Apo, is the leader of Partiya Karkari Kurdistan (Kurdish Workers' Party, known as PKK), a group of Marxist-Leninist dissidents who seek a separate Kurdish state in Turkey.

In 1961, the Turkish constitution allowed the formation of a socialist party, and the Turkish Workers' Party came into being. When elections were held in 1963, the party received only 3 percent of the vote. Nevertheless, a leftist movement grew, and within a few years leftist societies and clubs in Turkey had multiplied; most had revolutionary aspirations. In those days, leftists, whether of Turkish or Kurdish origin, worked together; their focus was on Marxist-Leninist ideology and not on ethnic consciousness. By the early 1970s, divisions ran deep between leftists and rightists, especially among university students; many were killed for their ideologies.

Abdullah Öcalan was a political science student at the University of Ankara during this time and was very much involved in the leftist movement. At one point, he was imprisoned for seven months for illegal leftist activities. Following an amnesty in 1974, Apo and six of his friends decided to initiate their own Marxist-Leninist revolutionary movement. This time, however, the movement would include only Turkish Kurds. Apo left Ankara for southeastern Turkey, where 40 percent of Turkey's nearly twelve million Kurds live as full citizens. Apo and his small group began recruiting followers, and in 1978 they named themselves the PKK. Initially, their actions were targeted against local and politically important Kurdish landlords and leaders. Turkish Kurds could (and still can) be found in all parts of the country and in all professions—as high government officials, businessmen, university professors, artists, and writers, for example. In poorer parts of the southeastern region, although tribal structures were disintegrating, many Kurds still honored tribal customs. They listened to local leaders on such issues as how to vote in elections.

Apo exploited blood feuds, and the PKK killed local Kurdish landlords who did not support his movement. Apo also brought class differences to the population's attention, pitting wealthy landlords against ordinary villagers who worked in the landlords' fields. In the process, he induced great ambivalence among citizens of Kurdish origin not only about their own identity, but about Turks and the government. This was a planned strategy to establish the power of the PKK.

Apo launched his campaign of terror in August 1984. In time, the killings and terrorism escalated. The PKK turned into an openly separatist movement, with the stated aim of establishing a Kurdish state within Turkey and a new Kurdish identity. They committed spectacular and horrifying acts, killing four thousand government troops and collaborators, as well as five thousand Kurdish villagers, women, and children who refused to follow the PKK. Terror reigned. After a while, Kurdish nationalism spread, and many Turkish Kurds voluntarily joined the PKK. Those who did not join nevertheless became more aware of their ethnic backgrounds. Between the mid-1980s and the mid-1990s, about ten thousand PKK activists were also killed as a result of the Turkish government's attempt to suppress the PKK.

There are some twenty to twenty-five million Kurds living in Turkey, Iraq, Iran, Syria, and elsewhere. Saddam Hussein's treatment of Iraqi Kurds and PKK activities in Turkey have brought the plight of the Kurds to the world's attention. But because of the dispersed population and rivalries among leaders, there is not a single, unified Kurdish political movement. Tribal and language differences play no small role in these divisions: Kurds in Iran speak Guran and Laki dialects; in Turkey, they speak Kurmanji and Zaza; in northern Iraq, Kurmanji; and in southern Iraq, Sorani, the only written Kurdish language.

Sovereign nations in the area are also involved in the Kurdish issue, depending on their own national interests. In northern Iraq, for example, one group of Kurds is sponsored by the Iraqis and another by the Iranians. Turkey fights against the PKK while joining the United States and other allies in protecting the Iraqi Kurds. Syria, meanwhile, has given refuge to Apo and has helped train PKK terrorists, in part as a counterresponse to Turkey's potential control of the regional water supply. Turkey has undertaken a $32 billion program to build twenty-two dams and nineteen hydroelectric plants along the Euphrates and Tigris Rivers. Both Syria and Iraq want assurances that Turkey will allow enough water to pass downriver into their countries. As Turkey, Iran, Iraq, and Syria position themselves according to their national interests and become protectors or enemies of this or that group of Kurds, the Kurds themselves in northern Iraq are massacring one another. Internal fragmentation, competition, and greed, exacerbated by external manipulation, have led the various Kurdish groups seeking political identity down a path of violence and chaos. Meanwhile, the terrorism of the PKK, combined with increased Kurdish nationalism, has become a multinational, multimillion-dollar enterprise connected with illegal drug trafficking.

In Turkish, Öcalan's name means "he who takes revenge." Öcalan did not say whether he inherited this as a family name or chose it for himself. Regardless of its source, the name Öcalan makes a fitting title for Apo. In his memoirs, Apo described how citizens of Turkish, Kurdish, Armenian, and Arab origin were all mingled together in a cluster of villages in the Hilvan-Siverek region of Anatolia where he grew up. They worked in the fields and in vineyards and looked after their animals. Marriages between people of different ethnic backgrounds were acceptable, and whether parents called their children Turks or Kurds was not of great importance. Apo's maternal grandmother, who sometimes appeared in his memoirs as more nurturing to young Apo than his own mother, was Turkish. "For me, my [ethnic] roots are not important," Apo claimed.[2] Recalling that in this region of Anatolia bloodlines were crisscrossed, he added: "I did not start the Kurdish peoples' struggle because I am a Kurd but because I am a socialist."[3]

Apo came from a very poor family. His mother had no education but was strong willed, and she dominated her husband. She did not like to associate with other villagers, and other women stayed away from her. She criticized and devalued her husband daily in front of their children. Local custom dictated that a wife should serve her husband his meals, but Apo's mother would often start a fight with her husband and throw his food on the floor. "Every day, my mother fought with neighbors, with my father, and with me," Apo recalled.[4]

Apo's father was the weakest, palest person in the village. As an adult, Apo wondered why his father was a nobody in the village, why other villagers had a low opinion of him. Apo suspected that his father was not supported by the members of his own tribe: "Not even his [the father's] relatives took him seriously, and he was hurt by them. It was as if he did not exist, he was gone."[5]

In order to get away from the daily unpleasantness at home, young Abdullah would escape to a nearby mountaintop. His father also visited the same spot. The older man, the laughingstock of the village, continuously felt humiliated, frustrated, and angry, but he was too passive to assert himself or express his rage openly in the village. So he would go up the mountain, scream his heart out, and curse the other villagers. When he saw young Abdullah there too, he would urge the boy to do the same. Abdullah would not follow his father's urging. He was instead filled with a sense of shame.

Abdullah's father encouraged his son to be aggressive—in a sense, to do things that the older man could not. He could not earn enough money for bread to feed his family properly, and encouraged Abdullah: "Bread is a rabbit, you be a greyhound and catch the rabbit."[6] He wished his son would grow up to reverse his own passivity and feelings of humiliation. "Abdullah has a sign of a conqueror on his forehead," he would say. "Wherever he goes he will conquer."[7]

Abdullah's mother also incited him. One childhood memory he recalled vividly:

I remember it as if it were happening now: I was fighting with kids in the village, and they cracked my head open [the skin was cut]. I returned home sobbing and saying that I had been beaten up. Of course, by crying, I expected my mother to protect and defend me. As soon as I came home, instead of protecting me my mother said to me: "Go and take revenge or I will not allow you to enter this house." She insisted that I do this. Even though it was forced on me this first time, my tendency for action [toward taking revenge] had started. I began to be an attacker; I cracked the heads of many children.[8]

In order to be accepted by his mother, little Abdullah turned to violence. "I looked for some love in my mother, but I couldn't find it. In order to receive love, I had to be molded as she wished me to be."[9] He remained "a child" so he could hold out the hope of one day truly obtaining his mother's love by hurting others; by the same action, he would reverse his father's humiliation. As an adult, Apo continued to live with "the excitement of a child who is seven to ten years old. I do not accept being a grown-up, I don't care how [anyone] interprets this."[10]

Öcalan described two sides of his personality as a child. The first was related to following his parents' direct and indirect orders to be rebellious, cruel, and revengeful.[11] He was the oldest son in the house and had a feeling that, because he had a weak father, he should be the one to protect his family's honor through violence. The villagers said it was very unfortunate for Abdullah's family to have such a son. They called him "the one who goes to the mountain alone," "the lonely one," or "the one who has cut off the rope" (a Turkish saying implying that one is unable to control one's impulses or abide by social norms).[12] Abdullah's second personality trait was not so austere. Deep down, he knew that he was frightened and shy, filled with humiliation and hunger for love. He remembered: "In reality, I had timidity and shamefulness in me, these still continue [in adulthood]. But, at the same time, I possess boldness."[13]

His shyness, his feelings of shame and being unloved appear to stem in part from the villagers' treatment of his parents and from his own perception of his parents' humiliation. His self-proclaimed boldness was a defensive measure against a devalued core. Both of his parents encouraged him to maintain and demonstrate this aggressive strategy, implying that if he were the attacker he would not be attacked and humiliated. As a result, young Abdullah developed fame in the village as a snake killer. Whenever a villager saw a snake, "the first person they would call was me."[14]

Abdullah was actually afraid of snakes, but he had to hide his fear from others. He was determined to be the boy everyone would call to kill snakes. He killed them using the same weapons he used against other children—stones.

While Abdullah was not liked by other children, he learned how to manipulate them. "My favorite was to find a child and take him to the mountains for a day. I would tell him, 'Let's go kill a snake, catch birds, or find an eagle nest.' "[15] He formed a secret club with other boys to fight against village traditions but offered no further details except to say that establishing secret organizations began early in his childhood. He also daydreamed a great deal about religious heroes and their battles. Through these daydreams, he felt a sense of omnipotence: "From my early life on, I had a drive to excel."[16]

There was no school in his village, and for five years Abdullah had to walk an hour each way in all kinds of weather to the elementary school in a neighboring village. Finding no positive role models at home, little Abdullah attached himself to his elementary school teacher who taught him to speak fluent Turkish. (As an adult, Apo only speaks Turkish and does not know Kurdish.) Throughout his education, he continued to seek attention from his teachers, and most of them liked him.

Apo's memoirs mention two sisters and two brothers. During his childhood, his older sister, Havva, was sold and married to a man from another village. He recalled how some unknown men from a village two or three days' walk away arrived at his home bearing a few sacks of wheat and a little money (it was a custom to pay the would-be bride's father so that he would allow his daughter to be married) and took Havva away.

Havva had been a mother substitute for him. When she was taken away, "I recall having a sense of regret, . . . [thinking] if I were a revolutionary, then I would not let this happen. They would not be able to take her away. She went away and had daughters. I thought that I would be able to save one of my nieces [from the same fate], . . . but, since I left the region, I do not know what happened to her. Perhaps she was sold too."[17]

The loss of Havva was traumatic. Apo spoke of disliking men with traditional-villager macho images and long twisted mustaches, even though as an adult, he wears a mustache. In his "childhood dreams,"[18] Abdullah had a sense of revulsion as he wondered about sexual intercourse without love. His sister's departure may have been one reason for Apo's sexual ambivalence. Another could have been his mother's rejection of him and the fact that his father was not a good male role model. As a child, Abdullah felt more comfortable around girls; as an adult, he associated himself with Mahatma Gandhi, who had "extreme control" over his sexuality.[19]

— · —

A turning point in Abdullah's psychic life occurred during adolescence. He referred to it as his "first rebellion."[20] Abdullah was fighting with Osman, his younger brother, whom he did not like. They were in a vineyard, and Abdullah chased Osman and threw stones at him. Osman ran home and told their father about the fight. The older man came out of the house and began throwing stones at Abdullah, cursing him. Abdullah fought back. "Again, all the villagers came out to be spectators of the fight between me and my father. . . . I was hurt, I was in a difficult position, I was very, very angry."[21]

The incident led Abdullah to steal ten Turkish liras from his father, which, for a poor villager, was a lot of money.

> As soon as I took the money I left the village. . . . Of course this was a bold move. I was a ten- or twelve-year-old child who had not had a chance to develop. What is important is the bravery of a child who decides to get up and walk to [a nearby] city. It is true that this was a rebellion. There was a great deal of rage and daring to rebel! After three steps, I turned toward the village and looked [at it]. "I will not return to you," I said. This was important! I went over a hill, I turned toward the village once more. "I have the courage to leave you," I re-

peated. I would not return. I was angry up to my throat [a Turkish saying that implies being full of extreme rage]. The separation created in me waves of opposite feelings. Of course, I was tied to the village, however I had definitely decided to leave it. I continued to walk and found a [new] village. Actually, I was walking with difficulty, to pass through this [new] village was as difficult as climbing up a mountain. I passed this village. . . . I reached Karamerza. Let me add here that I was a very timid child.[22]

He was afraid of his unfamiliar surroundings, and walked on to the town of Nizip, where his sister had a house. The second day he found a job as a field hand. He worked two days, until his hands were swollen from cutting wheat, and earned ten Turkish liras. "What I want to say is that this was an important rebellion, predominantly against the authority of a father, and to earn money with one's own labors."[23]

During an individual's passage through adolescence, there is an unconscious review of childhood attachments to others, which leads to a "second individuation" when an individual's personality organization crystallizes.[24] Normally, this second individuation allows an adolescent to free himself somewhat from the images of his parents so he can adaptively expand his relationships to the world at large. The extent to which this occurs, however, depends on how well the child has resolved earlier developmental tasks. Apo arrived at adolescence with continuing internal problems pertaining to his parents and siblings, and the dichotomy between his two major character traits was clearly troublesome to him. His description of leaving his village reflects his attempts at a second individuation and his "revisiting" parental images. By saying that his escape from his village was a rebellion against the authority of his father, he is acknowledging that the physical separation from the village and the psychological rejection of his father were intertwined. His description of his journey also indicates an attempt to resolve his dependence on his mother, though he is visibly unsure of whether he should let go of his attachment to home: he stops to look back at his village/mother one last time. In the end, he arrives at the house of a mother substitute, his sister.

While Apo succeeded in completing the physical separation, all indications are that he could not effect a psychological break. The two types of separation are not parallel. Normally during adolescence, an individual modifies existing character traits and incorporates them into a revised personality structure. Because of his unresolved conflicts, Apo could only crystallize his existing character traits, which went on to form, without modification, his postadolescent personality. His internal world remained fragmented. On the one hand, he remained as dependent on his family—and as enraged—as he had been in childhood. On the other hand, he retained his defensive boldness. Since he had managed at least physically to separate himself from the village, he held on to his independence (or one might say pseudo-independence) and bravery even more stubbornly so the hungry-for-love-yet-angry-child part of him would be kept under control.

"I am a very complex person," said Apo.[25] He exaggerates his defensive, powerful self (in psychoanalytic terms, *grandiose self*) and claims that he no longer needs anyone. On some level, however, he cannot fully maintain such independence, for he is conscious of the child within him.

Sometimes they say, "He (Apo) thinks of himself as a prophet." I too sometimes compare the evolution of modern religion to the evolution of the PKK. But there is no need to consider myself a prophet because, today, everything is done through science. But, there is a similarity—an interesting similarity! In reality, having a desert personality reflects nothingness. [Apo here refers to the desert community from which the prophet Muhammad emerged.] The emergence of the prophet Muhammad is like the explosion of a volcano. The Prophet emerged at a time when female offspring were buried alive in the desert. . . .

You will notice that [the prophet's activities] are similar to [PKK activities]. Looking from this angle, I value holding on to the prophet's positive characteristics . . . to speak like a prophet is important for me. Why would it be bad to be like a prophet?[26]

The desert community from which the prophet Muhammad arose is akin to the "loveless" environment of Apo's childhood. By comparing himself to Muhammad, he betrays his own desire to escape a poor and troubled childhood and emerge as an omnipotent force so the injuries he suffered as a child can be obliterated.

Apo's chronicle provides little information about his life in Nizip. He stayed with relatives, went to secondary school, and continued to encounter difficulties there. His Turkish grandmother looked after him like a good "governess."[27] In order to bolster a grandiose sense of self, he identified with religious figures who were engaged in battles. If his feelings of omnipotence helped assuage the dependent side of his personality, the aggressive nature of this omnipotence allowed him, unconsciously, to hold out hope of receiving the love of parents who had made it clear to him that they would accept him only if he were vengeful. Abdullah wanted to enter a military school in Turkey or attend a religious university, Al-Azhar, in Cairo. Instead, he ended up as a political science student in Ankara, where he became deeply involved in leftist movements during his early twenties.

Apo said very little about the seven months he spent in jail when he was a leftist student. He made a passing remark about being briefly tortured by a corporal and four soldiers, and I can only assume that this event and his imprisonment in general dovetailed with the humiliation that lingered from his childhood and contributed to his transformation into an ethnic terrorist leader.

In spite of his superficial boldness, a sense of omnipotence, and his search for leadership roles, he remained very much a child. "I do not have feelings in me indicating that [I wish] to be a grown-up, . . . to have children or to be a father," he confessed.[28] Nevertheless, he married Kesire sometime after his imprisonment. Not surprisingly, his marriage was a troubled one; he felt that his wife perceived him as an ordinary peasant while she boasted of her own established Kurdish family background. She pressured him to choose between her and the party, between her and his friends. The marriage lasted about ten years. As Apo described it: "I escaped from marriage, and I am still escaping from it."[29]

As leader of the PKK, Apo recruited thousands of young Kurdish women as guerrillas and instructed them to stay pure. "How can you tolerate having a huge man on top of you? . . . I am not really putting myself in the place of a woman, but now and then I imagine how one shares one's life with such men. Obviously, I find this ugly. I do not wish to contaminate myself with something that is ugly. I am trying to remain clean."[30] The cold environment of his childhood, rejection by his mother, and the presence of a humiliated father all contributed to a disgust with heterosexuality and the evolution of the psychodynamics of latent homosexuality. Elsewhere in his memoirs, he added, "To have a mate is not a bad thing, but how to manage it is an internal battle for me. . . . [Other men] may wish to be fathers and be proud of it, but I am puzzled by this. Let fathers pardon me, I am still a forty-four-year-old child."[31]

— · —

Apo had an impossible task: to deal with both sides of his fragmented internal world, he had to serve two masters at the same time. Throughout his life, he tried various ways of dealing with this dilemma. He had killed snakes even though he feared them in order to gain the respect of the villagers and distinguish himself from his "coward" father. He identified with religious crusaders to compensate for his identification with a humiliated father. He rebelled against his parents while he needed them but was also willing to mold himself as they wished him to be. Apo was like the person who hits others over the head while demanding their love, respect, and validation. His grandiose self required aggressive triumphs, and these were realized through terrorist activities. He perceived the existing Kurdish identity as "nothing,"[32] or as an oppressed child, and thereby identified with it. In turn, he tried to help it. "The Kurd will grow up with me," he said.[33] For Apo, the Kurdish identity—like his own—would start from "ground zero,"[34] and "new" Kurdishness and "new" Apo would have no ties to the traditions of feudal Kurdishness and Apo's victimized, childhood self.

So as leader of the PKK, Apo could order the destruction and killing of ordinary villagers—including women and children—many of Kurdish origin. These people represented his own unloved childhood self, and since they were "nothing," he had no need to feel guilty for destroying them. Instead, he felt entitled to get rid of them so the new Kurds (and, by extension, Apo himself) could renew their existence in a purified form. Angry Kurds would replace devalued ones. In fact, many Kurds heard this message and, presumably without knowing their leader's personal motivations, joined Apo.

Apo himself was acutely aware of the connection between his own and his group's identity issues:

> What is this [new] Kurdish type? What will I be? How will I fit into society's mold? That is, how will I answer the identity questions? I am forty-four years old, but I am in this business with the excitement of a child. I am not in a hurry; I am busy every second. I am trying to bring about a new [Kurdish] type that is beautiful, just, egalitarian, free, hard-working, environmentally conscious, and—though you may think that I idealize greatly—at the threshold of heaven.[35]

He makes no reference to the destructive methodology he uses to create the new Apo/Kurd. But his methodology implies that one has to pass through hell before coming to the threshold of heaven.

If by killing off "traditional" Kurds he is also killing off his childhood self, by assassinating government officials, government troops, and local landlords, he is wreaking revenge on the parents who did not love him. In addressing the state, he used words he might have invoked to address his coward of a father: "To the state, to that great chief, I say, 'If you have a drop of courage, if you understand humanity as much as the tip of a needle, come and let us sit down and talk.' There is no man in Turkey, however,"[36] implying that in his mind there are no strong male figures in Turkey; they are all cowards like his father.

Apo wants to push Turkey to be worthy of him, as if he were looking for the strong father who, according to his unconscious belief, will be pleased with Apo's aggressiveness. Paradoxically, the reality of severe government retaliation against the PKK must have been gratifying to Apo's unconscious expectations, in turn perpetuating a vicious circle of violence between government forces and Apo's followers.

Through terrorism, Apo could gratify his rage toward his parents, villagers who laughed at his family, the brother with whom he fought, and the jailers who treated him badly. By being aggressive, he tried to fulfill his father's defensive prophecy that he would become a conqueror. By his atrocities, he also tried to earn the love of his mother, who had told him that only if he were vengeful would she accept him. "This battle that I am conducting is for love," he said.[37] His terrorist activities parallel the acts of his childhood when he took children to the mountains. As a child, Abdullah had told his captives that they would have a good time and be rewarded by food (birds Abdullah caught); as leader of the PKK, he sent young people to the mountains—by kidnapping and coercion if necessary—to become his followers, too. He told them that they would be rewarded with the ideal of new Kurdishness.

Nowhere did Apo express remorse or sadness for the horror and loss of human lives caused by the PKK. Instead, he idealized the terror. "Our beauty queen is war, we definitely can point at the beauty of war . . . war is fire. Whatever you throw into fire burns, but in spite of this, our god is a fire god."[38] Surprisingly, Apo admitted to a phobia of firearms and sharp cutting tools like knives, yet he has perfected "the theory and practice of war." He recognized this incongruity ("How do you explain this?"),[39] which suggests his own puzzlement about the extremes to which he feels he has been driven. But he is unable constructively to channel the feelings of rage that characterize his divided self.

Chapter 12

_____

TOTEM AND TABOO IN ROMANIA: THE INTERNALIZATION OF A "DEAD" LEADER AND RESTABILIZATION OF AN ETHNIC TENT

The story of Abdullah Öcalan's internal world illustrates how the two-way street of leader-follower interactions can become congested by urgent and disturbing messages from the leader. That a leader is able significantly to influence a large group's identity is a clear indication that the followers have internalized his image. Once this happens, the followers may find it difficult to change their identification with such a leader, even long after he disappears. In Romania, the influence of Nicolae Ceauşescu continued to have far-reaching effects years after his execution.

Ceauşescu ruled Romania with an iron hand from 1965 until a bloody revolution toppled his government in December 1989. With the execution of Ceauşescu and his wife, Elena, on Christmas Day 1989, the communist regime in Romania gave way to the beginnings of a kind of democracy. Romanians were jubilant to be rid of the Ceauşescus, but the disappearance of the dictator did not mean the discontinuation of his effect. For many years after his death, Ceauşescu continued to have an impact on the efforts of Romanians to restabilize their shaken ethnic tent.

A despotic leader, Ceauşescu was the Communist Party chief, head of state, commander in chief of the army, chairman of the Economic Council, and the architect of a "new" Bucharest. He was the proverbial dreaded father figure, whom people hated but from whom it was difficult to detach themselves. Many Romanians were connected to Ceauşescu through membership in the Communist Party. The reasons for their having joined the party varied: some had joined just to get ahead, others out of conviction, and still others out of patriotism after the Soviet invasion of Czechoslovakia in 1968 convinced them that Romania would be next.[1] In addition to these practical attachments to his political agenda, Romanians were emotionally drawn to Ceauşescu because of his aura of power.

Attachment and hatred sound mutually exclusive, but, of course, ambivalence is a key factor in almost any relationship. Abused lovers are often reluctant to detach themselves from their partners despite continued suffering. A follower may long for escape but find leaving impossible because of a dependence that amounts to bonding with the aggressor. In the case of the Romanians, their attachment—albeit conflicted—to Ceauşescu's image made mourning him and his wife difficult.

Mourning was further complicated because the response to the loss of the Ceauşescus was condensed with responses to the loss of others who died during the Christmas Revolution. All of the dead from the revolution in Bucharest lie buried outside the walls of the Romanian National Cemetery in this capital city—both revolutionaries and Ceauşescu supporters. A sign proclaims revolutionaries and defenders alike "Heroes of the Revolution." The mix of rebels and villains in the same location makes mourning them complicated because, no matter what the mourner's sympathies, the burial place is contaminated with "bad" dead buried alongside the "heroes."

— · —

It is interesting to look at post-Ceauşescu Romania in light of Freud's psychoanalytic reconstruction of the unrecorded history of primitive man. In *Totem and Taboo,* Freud suggests, based on a variety of anthropological sources, that long ago primitive people lived in small tribes led by despotic leaders. With his unlimited power, the leader or father considered all the women of the tribe his exclusive property. If the young men, or sons, expressed jealousy, they were killed, castrated, or excommunicated. Their fate unbearable, the young men joined forces, killed the father, and ate him. But the father's influence would not disappear. In death, he became more powerful. By eating the leader, the sons had satisfied their hate. But because of their secret love for their father, they also felt guilty for killing him. In fact, the guilty feelings led them to renounce what they had set out to accomplish through his murder: because of their guilt, they could not have sex with the women of the tribe.

Haunted by the ghost of their father, the sons replaced him with a symbolic representation of a horrible and strong animal, a totem. It absorbed the sons' ambivalence, the simultaneous hate and love they were experiencing for their dead father. Since the ghost of their father lived on in the totem, however, the sons were still not free of his influence.

While some primitive cultures resorted to human sacrifices and cannibalism to free themselves of a totem's influence, others developed rituals in which consumption of a symbolic animal (the totemic animal) was strictly forbidden on all occasions except special festivals, during which it was ritually killed and communally eaten, thus allowing all to disclaim responsibility for its death. The sacrificed animal was then mourned by the entire clan, and an uninhibited celebration followed. (The ritual mourning performed in primitive totem festivals does not accomplish the same ends as a gradual and effective work of mourning in which loss eventually is accepted and internal adjustments are made.) The totem was used to maintain two powerful prohibitions—one against killing the totem animal (patricide) and the other against having sexual relations with women of the same clan (incest). The simultaneous hate for and attachment to the leader and the act of eating him led to a troublesome identification with the father.

Whether or not Freud's reconstruction of the beginning of human history is literally true, certain psychological truths emerge from *Totem and Taboo* and have an almost uncanny relevance to events in Romania. The fact that the Ceauşescus were killed on the sacred day of Christ's birth makes the act a ritual killing, and killing on a day that celebrates a birth points to a degree of ambivalence about the killings themselves. While few today would openly suggest that Romania was better off under Ceauşescu, Romanians allowed him to live on in many ways—most importantly, through the actions and policies of the leadership that followed his death. The new leadership served as a kind of totem. To understand how and why Ceauşescu exerted such influence, we must look first at his personal background and context in history.

— · —

Nicolae Ceauşescu was born about a hundred miles west of Bucharest to a poor, large peasant family. After only a few years of formal education, he left his family at the age of eleven, moved to Bucharest, and in his teens became an ideological communist. He was jailed for his communist activities, but by 1948 Romania was a people's republic, and Ceauşescu was welcomed with open arms. He rose to power in 1965 as the pace of industrialism was increasing. The West perceived him as an independent communist who would not give in completely to the Soviets and conveniently overlooked the fact that he was a despot. Unfortunately, when Charles de Gaulle and Richard Nixon went to Romania in 1968 and 1969, respectively, they did not dismiss the myth of Ceauşescu as a trustworthy communist. In reality, however, Ceauşescu was grossly violating human rights, and he became increasingly paranoid as he got older. Beginning in the 1960s, he banned contraception and abortion for women with fewer than four children so more Romanians might live to carry out his grandiose plans.[2] Later, to quell dissent, he ruled that typewriters had to be registered with the police so the sources of anti-Ceauşescu correspondence could be identified.

Robert Cullen reported that Ceauşescu hired tasters to make sure his food was not poisoned, that he would cleanse his hands with alcohol after greeting strangers, and that he installed radiation detectors in his offices and homes. Even the children who were selected to present flowers on public occasions "were sent to hospitals, examined, and certified free of infection before they were permitted to proffer their cheeks for his kiss."[3]

In the 1980s, Ceauşescu announced a plan to raze eight thousand of Romania's thirteen thousand rural communities. While ostensibly his goal was to build a better Romania, these actions were also clearly targeted to destroy Hungarian settlements, although some Romanians and other minorities would also be affected. Of Romania's 23 million people, 2.2 million are ethnically Hungarian,[4] the majority of whom live in Transylvania, an area that throughout history has been claimed by both Hungary and Romania. Ceauşescu's renewal projects only exacerbated ethnic problems with Romania's Hungarian community.

While the objective of "systematizing" rural Romania was never fully carried out, large parts of Bucharest were leveled in order to build new structures that confirmed the superiority of Romanian culture and its Roman lineage. In 1985, a fifth of historic Bucharest was bulldozed. Over nine thousand homes, one cathedral, and more than a dozen churches, most of which had been built during or before the nineteenth century, were destroyed. In their place, Ceauşescu ordered the building of Casa Poporului (House of the People) and the three-kilometer-long Avenue of Socialist Victory. After the Pentagon, Casa Poporului is the largest building in the world.

A substantial portion of Romania's limited resources was devoted to turning Bucharest into "the first socialist capital for the new socialist man." Before his death, Ceauşescu visited Casa Poporului several times each month. He called it "my house" and routinely ordered major alterations. In the late 1980s, a crew of twenty thousand worked on the project around the clock. But Ceauşescu never lived to see the completion of Casa Poporului and the Avenue of Socialist Victory. After his death, the white, four-tiered structure was renamed Parliament House and the avenue, Bulevardul Unirii (Unity Avenue).

— · —

That the Romanian revolution was sudden and came as a surprise did not mean there was no resistance to the regime before December 1989. A leading personality of the revolution went on to become one of the most outspoken critics of the post-Ceauşescu Romanian government.

In 1986, Bishop Lázló Tökés, an ethnic Hungarian and a Reformed (Calvinist) minister, was "temporarily reassigned" from a location in northern Transylvania to a church in downtown Timişoara, a city in southern Transylvania with a mixed population. His tenure there was supposed to end on December 15, 1989, at which time he was expected to return to his former parish. Tökés got into trouble, however, when he allowed students to recite nationalistic poetry in church.

Some months later, he was urged by the government to relocate to another church instead of returning to his home parish or face suspension from the ministry.

The congregation, which liked the young and charismatic minister, rose to his defense and demanded that he remain in Timişoara. Upon notice of his eviction, two hundred congregation members came to guard him on December 15, 1989. Things were bound to come to a showdown. As in similar power plays that were occurring in communist-dominated countries throughout Europe, Tökés courted the press and played the role of spokesperson for the Hungarians in Romania. The people of Timişoara, including Romanians, flocked to the scene to show their support.

The next day, a group of Timişoarans marched to Communist Party headquarters and destroyed it. One witness said that the crowd "went crazy as if everyone was under hypnosis." National songs were sung that called on Romanians to awaken, and shouts of "Down with Ceauşescu!" were heard. That Ceauşescu had previously managed to suppress such volatile emotion was a testament to the oppressive police state he ran. On December 17, his forces fired on and killed some hundred demonstrators. Two days later, a general strike was called, and the people of Timişoara filled the streets. With phone lines and roads now cut off from other parts of Romania, Timişoara residents had no idea what was happening in other regions. The government-run news media casually referred to the events in Timişoara as "ethnic disturbances." How the revolution spread to Bucharest and elsewhere is not clear.[5]

On December 20, Ceauşescu made a television address in which he blamed hooligans, irredentists (meaning Hungarians), and foreign espionage agents for the events in Timişoara. A demonstration was then arranged to show support for Ceauşescu, who, accompanied by his wife and the members of his Political Executive Committee, appeared at a rally in Bucharest to the cheers of the crowd. But something unusual happened. Some people began shouting, *"Ceauşescu dictatorul!"* (Ceauşescu the dictator!). The streets were soon filled with young people, and suddenly the revolution in Bucharest had begun in earnest.

In March 1993, I was in Romania as part of a team of Americans investigating the Romanian-Hungarian conflict.[6] I interviewed a woman who had been shopping in downtown Bucharest on December 21, 1989, when she encountered a crowd near the university made up mostly of young adults. Until then, she had not been aware of any revolt. Another woman recalled being in an open café having coffee and seeing only a grandmotherly woman taking a girl to her violin lesson, a man walking his dog, and a line of people waiting to buy bread. But history was in the making. The next day, she came to a barricade and witnessed the deaths of eight people, and that night she watched the revolution on television.

On the morning of December 22, seventy-one-year-old Ceauşescu, with Elena, narrowly escaped from the Central Committee building by helicopter as hundreds of demonstrators seized the party headquarters. Disaffected party members such as Ion Iliescu (who would become Romania's next leader) and Martian Dan, along with dissidents such as Radu Filipescu and Mircea Dimescu, took over the Romanian television station, announced the formation of the National Salvation Front (NSF), and presented themselves as the new leaders of the country. But apparently there was no previously organized coup or widespread mobilization of dissidents in Bucharest. How Iliescu and his friends managed to usurp power also remains a mystery.

According to one story, the dictator and his wife were simply turned over to NSF representatives by General Victor Atanasie Stanculescu, who that morning had been asked to guard the Central Committee building (Stanculescu would later be named Romania's minister of defense).[7] Whatever the truth of the matter, upon their capture, an NSF spokesman promised a public trial. Three days later, it was announced that the Ceauşescus had been executed. They had been tried for nine hours and sentenced to death by a military tribunal. Heavily edited videotapes of the trial, execution by firing squad, and the crumpled dead bodies of the Ceauşescus were released for Romanians and the whole world to see. On the tapes, Stanculescu can be recognized in the courtroom. The corpses were buried in unmarked graves.

— · —

Romanians rejoiced over the removal of the dreadful leader, but after the initial excitement, most eventually felt that little had really changed. Many considered the NSF merely an anti-Ceauşescu faction within the Romanian Communist Party and saw the new regime as simply the replacement of one group of communists with another. This perception further eroded the belief that a real revolution had occurred.[8] Few were tried during President Iliescu's term for the atrocious crimes committed during Ceauşescu's regime. Members of the Securitate and those who had committed vicious human rights violations were still key players in the government. Most Romanians, in one way or another, felt shame for their previous affiliations with Ceauşescu or for their former fear of him. Even fundamentally decent people suffered guilt for having benefited from being "good" communists, or having joined the party and marched in Ceauşescu's parades, or having cooperated with the Securitate. Romanians were aware that, while other Eastern European countries had had significant dissident movements, theirs had barely existed—Gabriel Andreescu and Radu Filipescu notwithstanding.

Romanians never fully realized that with the end of Nicolae Ceauşescu his "sons" had not only murdered but also "eaten" him. Having ruled Romanians for over two decades, Ceauşescu had become a part of them. With his death, a part of each Romanian also died, but their shame for being associated with him and their hidden guilt for "killing" him had to be denied. Yet through their identification with him, they also kept the dictator alive.

In *Totem and Taboo*, Freud wrote that one of the most puzzling, but at the same time instructive, developments in complicated mourning is a prohibition against uttering the name of the dead person. Freud surmised that openly referring to the dead person by name unconsciously invited his ghost's return. During my 1993 visit to Romania, I noted an apparently tacit prohibition against mentioning Ceauşescu's name—it was as if he had never existed. When I mentioned this fact, the response consisted either of satisfaction over the dictator's death or, more often, a comment along the lines of "I don't want to remember." When I asked a few individuals if they ever had dreams of the Ceauşescus or the revolution, their shock at this question was in effect a rebuke.

Having heard about their courage, I looked forward to meeting former dissidents of Ceauşescu's regime in Bucharest. I was quite surprised, however, by their despondent demeanor. Instead of heroes, they seemed more like ghosts. They were barely able to describe their imprisonment and the physical abuse they suffered. One dissident kept referring to himself as "you"—as if his former "dissident self" were a separate person. Without an oppressive and brutal environment to justify it, his dissident self could no longer be maintained.

After the revolution, a home that had belonged to Ceauşescu's youngest son, Nicu, was appropriated by some of the revolutionaries for use as an office.[9] A stockpile of cigarettes and liquor was found in the attic. Objects that had secretly belonged to the aggressor now belonged to them; they consumed their quarry as if taking in aspects of Ceauşescu himself. But like the sons who could not have intercourse with the women of the tribe once they had killed and eaten the father, these heroes, because of their unconscious identification with Ceauşescu, could not enjoy their victory.

In June 1990, nationalists launched a weekly publication called *România Mare* (Great Romania), a reference to the traditional rallying cry of Romanian nationalists for centuries before Ceauşescu. In a short time, the paper acquired "the largest circulation of any Romanian weekly newspaper." Articles in *România Mare* succeeded in keeping Ceauşescu "alive" through an undisguised nostalgia for his regime. In 1991, it praised "General Iulian Vlad, Ceauşescu's last head of the Securitate, for his intellectualism and patriotism."[10] A year later, the founders of this weekly newspaper established a political party of the same name. Their efforts to rehabilitate Ceauşescu's Securitate were bolstered in 1993 when six novels by former intelligence officer Pavel Corut sold out almost immediately at a time when few could afford such a luxury, and two more in the series were already in press. In one of them, Bishop Tökés is portrayed as a Hungarian agent. As Michael Shafir, a senior researcher from Radio Free Europe Research Institute, quotes Corut: " 'Hungarian revisionists . . . ate the flesh of Romanians killed in December 1989,' an obvious allusion to an ancient anti-Hungarian, nationalistic cliché that makes all Magyars out to be savages."[11]

In the aftermath of the Ceauşescus' demise, Romania was riven by clashes of opinion. When students in Bucharest began to question the policies of Iliescu and his colleagues, coal miners from the Jiu Valley came to the capital to support the NSF, shouting, "Death to the intellectuals!" In September 1991, the coal miners returned to protest the NSF, but it managed to remain the ruling party. Although almost 15 percent of the vote in the September 1992 election went to radical nationalist parties who were decidedly more pro-Ceauşescu than the NSF, Iliescu succeeded in winning.

But a mere two years later, on the very day after the United States granted Romania most-favored-nation trading status, Iliescu sent his minister of culture to a town near Bucharest to attend a ceremony commemorating Marshal Ion Antonescu. On the one hand, Romania was trying to break with its totalitarian past. On the other hand, it was clinging to Antonescu, the most infamous dictator in its history: an ally of Hitler, a figurehead of the fascist Iron Guard, a man responsible for the deaths of some 250,000 Jews and 20,000 Gypsies who, like Ceauşescu, was finally executed.

— · —

After the 1989 Christmas Revolution, Hungarians living in Transylvania were able to form, with lightning speed, a broad-based political organization, the Democratic Alliance of Hungarians in Romania (HUDR). While careful to pledge its loyalty to the Romanian state, HUDR focused on the creation of a Ministry of Minorities, the introduction of mandatory bilingualism in Transylvania, and the development of an educational system in Hungarian that included the reestablishment of an independent Hungarian university in Transylvania. This frightened Romanians into thinking that the Hungarians might demand too much. The Romanian fear of a Hungarian uprising may have contributed to the need to keep Ceauşescu's image alive, especially in Transylvania.

Bishop Tökés loudly expressed the sentiments of Hungarians. He had become a symbol for many Hungarians living in Romania. But he also fulfilled an unconscious Romanian desire: Tökés served as a target that allowed Romanians to focus on the Hungarian threat instead of the more complicated work of mourning and adapting to the drastic changes after Ceauşescu's death. As an insightful Romanian told me: "Tökés provides a continuity of conservatism in my country."

In response to the creation of HUDR, Uniunea Vatra Românească (Romanian Hearth Union) quickly emerged in Transylvania. Vatra was founded in Tîrgu-Mureş in February 1990, by the artist Radu Ceontea, and initially gained a strong following throughout Romania. Vatra drew its power from the Romanian belief that Transylvania belonged solely to Romanians and from its spirited defense of the Romanian language; it also exploited Romanians' fears of Hungarians. Ceontea's personal prejudice against Hungarians seemed intertwined with Vatra's aims; his father had instilled in him an almost intuitive mistrust of Hungarians.[12] In 1991, he was elected chairman of the National Unity Party (PUNR), and the next year, PUNR emerged as a political force in Transylvania. But Gheorghe Funar, who modeled himself after Ceauşescu, took over chairmanship of this party, ousting Ceontea.[13]

On March 19, 1990, five thousand Romanian and Hungarian demonstrators faced off in Cluj-Napoca, the principal city of Transylvania. On the same day in the ethnically mixed city of Tîrgu-Mureş, the first violent ethnic clash occurred, leaving eight dead and hundreds wounded. Government security forces quelled the violence, and a commission was appointed to investigate the incident. The commission's findings were not released until January 16, 1991, and only then because publishing them had been made a condition of Romania's obtaining observer status in the Council of Europe and becoming eligible for European Community assistance. In a television interview, the chairman of the inquiry commission called it a "theoretical study,"[14] even though the potential for ethnic violence in Transylvania was great.

By 1993, Bucharest newspapers were reporting Bishop Tökés's accusation that ethnic cleansing was occurring in Romania. According to Tökés, the government was purifying Transylvania by oppressing and even expatriating the Hungarian minority. Tökés pointed out that, before the migration of more Romanians to the area, only a few decades earlier, the city of Cluj had been predominantly Hungarian (and called Kolozsvár). He and like-minded Hungarian leaders accused the Romanian government of making life difficult for Hungarians in Transylvania and submitted public charges against the government-appointed chief of Romanian television. They also accused Funar, who was the mayor of Cluj-Napoca, of making demagogic anti-Hungarian statements and fanning the fires of hatred by dwelling on the "Hungarian threat" posed by "antinational forces."[15] Editorialists and many other Romanian political figures condemned Tökés as a temperamental troublemaker and liar. By denying that ethnic problems existed, they only exacerbated them.

Hungarians are now less than one-third of the population of Cluj-Napoca. This transformation is due to restrictions in the past decade on the public use of the Hungarian language, severe limitations on opportunities for bilingual education at the high school and college level, few job opportunities for Hungarians, and a Romanian settlement policy.

In the center of Cluj is a statue of King Mátyás Hunyadi (a city native and the king of Hungary from 1458 to 1490). The statue is a reminder of the city's Austro-Hungarian past, but it became the focus of Hungarian-Romanian tensions in the fall of 1992 when Funar announced that a Romanian nationalistic inscription would be added to it.[16]

When I visited Cluj in March 1993, Adrian Marino, a former dissident now in his early seventies, told me that he still received threatening letters accusing him of being a Hungarian-lover. Marino's fighting spirit was sustained through his opposition to Funar and those like him, whom he saw as extensions of Ceauşescu. He suspected that some form of the Securitate was still in operation and that they were the ones sending him letters that accused him of complicity with Hungarians and treason against Romania.

Perhaps influenced by the events in nearby Bosnia-Herzegovina, Europeans have tried to serve as buffers against malignant developments in Transylvania. The devastating ethnic conflicts in Bosnia-Herzegovina may also have played a role in restricting ultranationalist Romanian forces from pressing their goals, for there is nothing like a big fire in the neighborhood to make people more cautious and careful about starting one themselves.

— · —

A wall encloses Romania's National Cemetery. Outside its main gate, in a small area marked "Heroes of the Revolution," lie buried the casualties of the December 1989 revolution. From December 21 to December 23, some 400 people died in Bucharest. Many others died elsewhere throughout the country, although reports vary on the total number of casualties. One government report gives a national count of 689, while other findings suggest more than 1,000, but only Bucharest's 400 dead have been memorialized as heroes of the revolution.

I visited the place with an engineer whose father had been a diplomat during the Ceaușescu regime. She had even gone to school with the Ceaușescus' youngest son, Nicu. "I am not ashamed of having been a member of the Communist Party during my student days at the university," she said, as if I would have blamed her. Communism was a good idea, she maintained, but one that did not work well in practice. One can't attribute Romania's problems solely to the Ceaușescus; "the system" itself was at fault. Unlike the dissidents and intellectuals who opposed Ceaușescu, there were some Romanians who did not hold an exclusively negative view of him. "He did good things and kept Romania's identity from becoming totally submerged under Soviet power," my companion explained.

The white marble gravestones that mark the resting places of the heroes are all the same, except for the carved names and photographs of the deceased. On the side of one of the grave markers, challenging the perfect symmetry and sterility of the rows, someone had erected a large metal sign questioning the death of the young woman lying there. Because both Securitate government personnel and anti-Ceaușescu demonstrators are buried here, the ambiguity as to who, precisely, are the heroes makes real mourning impossible, rendering the cemetery of the Heroes of the Revolution an ineffectual memorial.

While we walked between the grave markers, my engineer friend recounted how she had seen a student shot to death in front of the Bucharest television station, a young man who seemed to be only nineteen years old. Perhaps he was under one of these tombstones, lost in the midst. She spoke of him so casually that she seemed to have forgotten him. But as soon as we proceeded through the gate into the National Cemetery, her mood changed. Once more, she was the proud Romanian.

In contrast to the cemetery of the Heroes of the Revolution, the Romanian National Cemetery, like the renowned Novodevichiye Cemetery in Moscow, expresses the history, the culture, the soul of its people. Its graves are not sterile and impersonal like those of the heroes of the revolution.

Though alone in the cemetery, we noticed the deep footprints of an earlier visitor who apparently had come to clear the heavy snow from the grave of the poet Mihail Eminescu (1850–1889), exposing colorful flowers, red berries, and green leaves. Eminescu, a widely translated Romantic poet, had elevated Romanian literature to one of its highest points. He was a symbol of pre-communist Romania, when Bucharest was considered the Paris of Eastern Europe. The clearing of the snow was a very poignant and revealing gesture. Blanketing everything, the snow seemed to me to symbolize the collective desire to keep things hidden, to cover the unsolvable struggle and trauma Romanians had experienced in regard to communism, the Ceauşescus, the revolution, and the heroes.

My companion began to read a poem inscribed on Eminescu's tombstone without bothering to translate it into English. Then she pointed out graves of other noteworthy poets and writers. "The perception of Western countries that we are gypsies is not correct!" she said, identifying with an idealized past that was dissociated from Nicolae Ceauşescu. Not content with my promise to read Eminescu's poems when I returned home, she insisted we find an English translation of his work in a bookstore. We quickly left the National Cemetery and went from one shop to another, but unfortunately we could not find a translation, and I felt as cut off from Romania's written heritage as Romanians themselves must have when the state library was destroyed during the revolution.[17]

As we walked around Bucharest, my friend asked me if I would like to see her old home. She was making an effort, perhaps unconsciously, to return to and review her past. In a way, her walking along with a psychoanalyst whom she thought might understand her internal struggle indicated her willingness to confront her feelings about Romania, to let go of her own and her family's attachment to the family of the former dictator. This was something that Romanians, collectively, could not yet achieve. We had walked a mile or so when we came to the television station with its tall tower. In a garden in front stood a lonely grave marker made of carved wood. I suddenly realized that it might belong to the nineteen-year-old student whose death she had witnessed there; perhaps she had brought me here for the purpose of mourning him at last. As she stood silently, I sensed her sadness and saw that she could no longer maintain her denial of what had happened.

Ceauşescu's neighborhood was on the other side of the television station. One of the least run-down sections of Bucharest, it boasted single-family homes and walled gardens. A few children played in the snow not far from a house that had apparently burned down during the revolution. Some buildings were bullet-ridden. The current serenity lay in sharp contrast to the events of a few years earlier.

—·—

At dinner the next evening, I sat between Vasile Popovici, a representative of the Democratic Convention in the parliament, and Mariana Celac, a city planner. Popovici sported a well-trimmed beard and wore a scarlet jacket. With his bright blue eyes, he looked like an actor playing a prince. Celac was wearing a simple black suit and no makeup, as ascetic as a nun. With the orchestra playing, a vocalist singing, and the waiter bringing more and more delicious food, we might have been in the capital of a free Western European country, socializing without a care in the world. In this atmosphere, it was difficult to sense any pain in my companions' adjustment to post-Ceauşescu Romania.

But then Celac described to me her great frustration in planning a memorial for the heroes of the revolution. As a consultant to this project, Celac had supported a plan to model the monument after a small but emotionally and religiously significant church that had been destroyed by Ceauşescu. She believed this would be an appropriate gesture for those who had died. She was surprised, however, that a majority on the planning committee rejected the idea, choosing instead a design of massive proportions that reflected the grandiosity and nationalism of Ceauşescu's trademark style. It seemed as though Ceauşescu lived on within the collective mind of the committee. Why else would it even consider such an inappropriate and paradoxical means to honor those killed in overthrowing him?

—·—

When I returned to Bucharest a little over a year later in May 1994, few physical changes had taken place, and renovations in public places were rare. In light of this, the decision to finish Ceauşescu's gigantic palace (to house the parliament and the supreme court) was revealing. Rather than reassessing present realities, the government was going ahead and completing the former Casa Poporului as planned by Ceauşescu. But there was also little change in the composition of the government. Funar was still the mayor of Cluj-Napoca. Only the design for the memorial to honor the heroes of the revolution had altered; now a more modest monument was to be built.

More encouraging signs came from Liviu Luca, president of the trade union Petrom, who described the relationship between Romanian and Hungarian union members as harmonious. Luca had a healthy vision of the future. He was also keenly aware of the Romanian preoccupation with finding a new large-group identity in the post-communist and post-Ceauşescu period. He told us the story of Pula.

Pula was the name given during the Ceauşescu regime to a fictitious persona who became the subject of shared jokes and, as such, a symbol of national character in his own right. A typical buffoon, he was an impotent, humiliated coward (in Romanian, *pula* is a vulgar term for penis). In one story, Pula goes to a political meeting, opens his briefcase, pulls out a revolver, and aims it at Ceauşescu. He shoots and shoots, but in their enthusiasm, the encouraging crowd pushes Pula to and fro, causing him to miss the target repeatedly in a pathetically comic manner.

Pula represented Romanians under the communist regime. Because they were afraid of expressing their cynicism of the regime, their collective fear was transformed, through hate for the former dictator, into comic pathos. Before the revolution, feelings of humiliation and shame seemed to dominate those who participated in the regime and the social interaction demanded by it. However, when the Ceauşescus were killed, so too was Pula; his existence depended on theirs. According to Luca, Romanians were still searching for a new identity, a modified ethnic tent.

— · —

Perhaps it is easier for us to imagine reluctance to let go of a lost good leader than a bad one. Americans, with the help of the media, continue to honor the anniversaries of John F. Kennedy and Martin

Luther King Jr., two good leaders. But why hold on to bad leaders after they are gone? The answer lies in the psychological phenomenon of identification with the aggressor. When we fear someone a great deal but perceive him as omnipotent, one way of dealing with our anxiety in relation to him or his image is to internalize his image and make it part of us. When this occurs at the collective level, the result is a paradoxical situation such as the one in Romania, where the dreaded person was hated but also needed as part of the national identity. Examination of this phenomenon also helps us to understand similar paradoxes, such as why neo-Nazi groups in Germany have kept aspects of Hitler alive and why there are many in Russia who look back with nostalgia to the reign of Stalin.

From his meager beginnings, Ceauşescu, in true Stalinist fashion, succeeded in creating a cult of personality. In a country that had been historically occupied and ruled for centuries by outsider empires, Ceauşescu's chauvinism and hypernationalism appealed to many Romanians. With quick shifts from passivity to brutality, from sentimentality to indestructibility, he had become an untouchable leader. Toward the end of his dictatorship, people seemed to hate Elena more than they hated Nicolae, but since they were perceived as a team, presenting both female and male sides of leadership, they were regarded as a "total parent." Untouchable charismatic leaders, psychoanalytic studies show, combine for their followers both feminine and masculine qualities.[18] Furthermore, they confuse the followers and make them dependent on the pole of the ethnic tent through their sudden personality changes. Seen from the vantage point of a Westerner, the Ceauşescu cult had elements of pathology, but according to Trond Gilberg, an expert on Romanian history, this personality cult "nevertheless is consistent with the Romanian historical tradition, in which the 'Domn,' or leader, lived in oriental splendor and claimed control over all aspects of people's lives. . . . Once again, history intrudes firmly and decisively upon the making of the 'new' political and ethical order."[19]

As in Freud's reconstruction of human history, a totem had been created in Romania in place of the killed father figure. Funar and other ultranationalists, and perhaps even the government itself, exerted a totemlike influence over the Romanian people, blurring the dividing line between pre- and post-Ceauşescu Romania. In many ways, especially on the surface and outside of Bucharest, it looked like business as usual. Many former Communist Party leaders reformed themselves and remained in power. As described earlier, the plans for a monument to the heroes of the revolution suggested the presence of unresolved emotional complications in which the good intention to honor the dead was contaminated with an unconscious resolve to keep aspects of Ceauşescu alive.

During my two visits to Romania, Ceauşescu's presence seemed like a ghostly hand still pulling strings long after his death. Of course, no one would expect miracles after only a few transitional years—the confusion and anxiety I observed were to be expected.[20] A positive sign that the Ceauşescus' images could be dealt with in a more realistic fashion was the removal of their corpses from unmarked graves and their reburial in marked graves by the time of my second visit to Bucharest. Reburial helped make their deaths more real since there was now a concrete place where they were known to rest. That place could also be an occasion for atonement. "We do not need to treat them like dogs," one person said. Some people have visited the new burial site and lit candles there in memory of the fallen leaders, but in all likelihood, as time passes fewer Romanians will visit the graves. Whether they do or not, knowing that the Ceauşescus have a specific burial place will help Romanians mourn their loss.

The most interesting sign that mourning over Ceauşescu could be initiated came from a film titled *The Conjugal Bed*, written and directed by Mircea Danelive. Hidden and shared social processes often find direct expression in art forms, as if the artists in a society become spokespersons of what may be called "hidden transcripts."[21] These are the shared ideas and messages that are usually concealed by society and often contrast with the "public transcripts" expressed openly. While Romanians in general deny their involvement with the Ceauşescu regime, or express only pleasure over the death of the dictator and his wife, artists like Danelive have pointed out a continued, unconscious preoccupation with Ceauşescu.

The Conjugal Bed, an absurd comedy, "is full of shadows of the deposed dictator; it even takes as a motif the helicopter that spirited him away during his overthrow, which is evoked by copters, rotors, and even the pinwheels sold on the street by a former secret police-man."[22] But the film centers on Vasile, who wants his wife, Carolina, to have an abortion, a clear contrast to the strict pro-life policies of Ceauşescu's Romania. While the couple do not have enough money to pay for the abortion, in the long run it would cost less money than feeding another child. Vasile finds a copy of one of Ceauşescu's books, which he learns may have significant resale value because it is thought to contain Ceauşescu's Swiss bank account number. One simply needed to decode the secretly written numbers to gain access to his hidden wealth. The leader, Danelive suggests, remains powerful even after death. In his own way, Vasile is a confused Pula whose obtuse rage reflects that of society and is a key element in accepting that a change or loss has occurred, an important marker of the work of mourning.

Similar examples were evident in the Soviet Union when peres-troika and glasnost allowed the artistic expression of issues previously censored. For example, in the Gorbachev era, a Soviet motion picture directed by Tengiz Abuladze and titled *Pokjaniyeaka, Monanieba (Repentance*, 1987), set in a mythical town, symbolically dealt with the Stalin era through the depiction of a villain with obvious character-istics of Stalin. The character representing Stalin dies and is buried, but his body is dug up (symbolically brought back to life) only to be buried again. This repetition reflects the difficulty in accepting the death of a dictator as well as the normal psychology of mourning, where we let the dead "die" in a gradual fashion.

— · —

The Romanians in power would rather forget their past, sweep it neatly under the carpet, and integrate quickly into Europe, the North Atlantic Treaty Organization, and the European Community. But some prob-lems, whether buried or denied, can remain flammable, and if they ignite, they may set the carpet covering them on fire and burn down the house, as happened in the former Yugoslavia.

Romania was formally admitted to the Council of Europe as a full member, despite objections from the Hungarian minority, on October 7, 1993. Two days later in Strasbourg, where the council held its summit, President Iliescu stressed Romania's commitment to democracy and reform, though many members of the council and even some Romanians were skeptical of the government's intentions. An article in the Bucharest newspaper *Severin* stated that Romania's government could no longer behave like "a pupil whose main concern is to cheat his teacher. . . . We still look upon the Council of Europe as an adversary or a political rival, not as a family into which we are accepted with all rights and obligations."[23] Nonetheless, President Iliescu made politically correct moves, such as acknowledging the Romanian role in the extermination of Jews during the Nazi period.[24] Prospects for Romania's integration with Western economic and defense structures remained good as long as Romania could put its own economic house in order.

— . —

In the fall of 1995, President Ion Iliescu came to the United States to meet with President Bill Clinton. When he appeared at the National Press Club in Washington, D.C., it was clear that belonging to a brotherhood of democratic states was helping him in his transformation toward political maturity in Romania. He reported on the increased availability of newspapers in his country and the establishment of private local television stations. Speaking in correct but heavily accented English, he demonstrated his nationalistic feelings and his pride in being Romanian when he referred to Romania as the center of Europe. He grew excited, however, when questioned about Hungarians living in Romania and demanded understanding from the audience for his sensitivity on this issue. As luck would have it, a fire alarm suddenly sounded, interrupting Iliescu. Momentarily panicked, he asked, "Is it the police?" and then regained his composure.

One year later, under pressure from the European Union, Romania signed a treaty with Hungary that confirmed existing borders. Later that fall, Iliescu was up for reelection. In an interview with *New York Times* journalist Jane Perlez, Silviu Brucan, a Romanian ambassador to Washington during the 1950s, offered views from the inside. Brucan's remarks confirmed the perception that Romanians feared change and seemed willing to suffer severe poverty (in 1996, the average pay in Romania was about a hundred dollars a month).[25] Iliescu had done little to dismantle the centralized economy, and Romania's health care system was regarded as the worst in central Europe; few attempts had been made to improve it since the Ceauşescu era. Brucan suggested that the reluctance of Iliescu and his entourage to change the old systems stemmed from the leadership's communist background. Perhaps so, but I believe that this paralysis in Romania at a time when drastic changes were taking place in other eastern European countries (e.g., Poland, Hungary, Slovakia) was also due to an inability to mourn. Iliescu, his party, and probably many members of the society at large continued to cling to the "lost" Romania.

Iliescu lost the presidential election to Emil Constantinescu, a fifty-five-year-old geology professor who had never before held elected office. Constantinescu's inauguration was held in Casa Poporului. In his speech, the new president said, "It is our duty not to destroy or bury the past, but to make this building a noble place by transforming a palace born as a symbol of dictatorship into a symbol of democracy."[26] It is not yet clear whether Constantinescu will succeed in creating a new Romanian identity free from the ghost of Ceauşescu.

Chapter 13

EXPERIMENT IN ESTONIA:
"UNOFFICIAL DIPLOMACY" AT WORK

Two irreducible and interrelated principles exist in the psychology of large groups. First, one group cannot be the same as its neighbor (the other). Second, a psychological border must be maintained between the identities of neighboring large groups. Reliance on these two principles becomes more pronounced when stress and anxiety increase. At such times, rituals to maintain the two principles gain in prominence: exaggerating major differences, elevating minor differences to significant proportions, utilizing shared symbolic inanimate objects, reactivating dormant chosen traumas and glories, and experiencing physical borders as psychological skins. Meanwhile, political leaders are driven to be spokespersons of these rituals as they consciously and unconsciously monitor, inflame, or contain them.

Wars, expectations of victimization, economic collapse, and the death of a leader generate stress and anxiety for the large group, as do revolutions and shifts from one political culture to a new one. Revolutions and political shifts, like the birth of a nation, produce their own shared mental representations. Such representations remain within the collective mind of the group and may be transmitted from one generation to the next. If there are elements of a mental representation that continue to provoke anxiety, they most likely will, in somewhat modified forms, remain embedded in the next generation's experience of itself or others.

The revolution in Estonia had a complex impact on Estonians' identity, one that differed significantly from what was happening in Romania, though the two transitions occurred at roughly the same time. In addition to elation and pride, Estonia's bloodless break from the Soviet Union paradoxically was accompanied by anxiety about maintaining a "pure" Estonian identity. Whereas Romania traced its heritage to Rome and could then extend this continuity into the future, the history of Estonia offered less support to the maintenance of group identity.

Estonia, the northernmost of the three Baltic states, covers a territory of 45,215 square kilometers—approximately the size of Denmark or of New Hampshire and Vermont combined. Slightly more than 1.5 million people live in Estonia; 61.5 percent are ethnically Estonian, 30.3 percent are Russian, and the remainder have Ukrainian, Belarussian, Scandinavian, or other roots. Little is known about the first inhabitants of Estonia, although Finnish-Estonian tribes, originating in central Asia, had founded settlements and a patriarchal society by 1500 B.C., establishing the basis of Estonia's Finno-Ugric language. Since the Middle Ages, Estonia has been part of numerous empires and spheres of influence. Vikings overran the territory in the ninth century. Germanic knights invaded in the twelfth century to Christianize the region, and their descendants retained local power as feudal barons for many centuries. The Danes also exerted control over parts of Estonia, as did the Hanseatic League, although rule passed to Sweden in 1561, and then to Russia in 1710. Estonian independence was declared in 1918, ending Russian imperial rule, but it lasted only until 1940, when Estonia was "conquered" by the Soviet Union.

How the relatively tiny population of Estonians maintained its identity throughout centuries of foreign domination is nearly a miracle. While Estonian culture managed to persist over the years in some form, it began to be articulated in earnest as ethnicity or nationhood through the efforts of Estonian intellectuals in the nineteenth century. Especially influential was Friedrich Kreutzwald (1803–1882), who wrote *Kalevipoeg*, the classic Estonian saga in which he re-created the mythological beginnings of the large group. Now having concrete evidence of a common past, the term *Eesti rahvas* (Estonian people) began to evolve into a visible and felt identity.

The growing sense of we-ness in Estonia found an echo in an

unusual shared reservoir: the singing of folk songs. Singing patriotic songs often plays a part in large-group rituals, and singing became a way of strengthening the bonds between members of the group who now called themselves Eesti rahvas. The first Estonian national song festival was held in 1869 in Viljandi and was followed by others approximately every five years.[1] The importance of the song festivals increased rapidly; by 1894, fifty thousand Estonians were gathering to sing and listen.

The sense of togetherness created by the song festivals helped to define what was Estonian and what was not. Initiatives emerged to purify the folk music and standardize the Estonian language so as to eliminate foreign influences, such as German, which continued to be spoken in parts of Estonia throughout the Swedish and Russian eras. New Russification policies barely slowed down the Estonians' drive to solidify their national identity, which emphasized reading and other intellectual activities. For the Estonians to be intellectually superior to their occupiers was like a booster for their large-group identity; it was their chosen glory, in place of a military one. By 1897, 96 percent of Estonians could read, and Estonia became the most literate region of the Russian empire.

In spite of attempts at revolution in 1905, Estonians were still under Russian rule when World War I started in 1914. Initially, Estonia was on the periphery of the war, but a force of some hundred thousand Estonians was eventually mobilized as part of the Russian military. Twelve thousand Estonians were killed. In 1917, Estonians feared a German invasion, especially after the German capture of Riga in neighboring Latvia. In the fall of 1917, Germany captured the Estonian islands west of the mainland and began advancing on Tallinn, Estonia's capital, in February 1918. Russia, in the grip of its 1918 revolution, offered little resistance. Estonian leader Konstantin Päts and his underground National Council declared Estonia's independence and granted equal rights to all residents of Estonia regardless of their ethnicity in November 1918. The German forces entered Tallinn, ending Russian (now Bolshevik) power. Torn between Germans and Russians, and aided by the British, Finns, and others, Estonians won their war of independence in 1920 and began to live as citizens of an independent republic. But in 1939, the Soviets signed the secret

Molotov-Ribbentrop pact with Nazi Germany, agreeing to partition Poland in exchange for control of the Baltics. Soviet forces soon secured military bases in Estonia and incorporated it into the USSR in 1940.

When Nazi forces invaded the Soviet Union in 1941, the Molotov-Ribbentrop pact was broken, and Estonia again became a battleground between Germans and Russians. In 1941, approximately 60,000 people (6 percent of the Estonian population) were deported, sent to prison camps, or drafted into the Soviet military.[2] Those deported included intellectuals, farmers, military personnel, and religious leaders. By 1944, Soviet control over Estonia was solidified. Estonians were divided according to their previous alliances to Soviets or Nazis or their resistance to both. By 1949, only about 775,000 Estonians out of a prewar population of 1,134,000 remained.[3] As the Estonian population dwindled, Soviets encouraged ethnic Russians to settle in Estonia.

In Soviet Estonia, the impetus to restore independence evolved slowly but steadily in the atmosphere created by glasnost and perestroika. Unlike Romania's rebellion against a dreaded and powerful leader, Estonia directed its revolution against an occupying nation, the Soviet Union. Because Estonian leadership was not oppressive and remained in tune with people's desire for independence, there was no bloody political struggle in Estonia as it broke away from the USSR. The bloodless revolution that led to Estonia's re-independence is aptly known as the Singing Revolution because of its roots in an all-day rally at the 1988 song festival grounds in Tallinn, as well as to the symbolic importance of folk songs in Estonians' sense of we-ness.[4]

When independence was again established, Estonians found themselves facing many practical and psychological issues. Most problematic was the continued presence of thousands of former Soviet troops in Estonia and the existence of hundreds of military installations where Estonians were forbidden to go. Every third resident was an ethnic Russian, whether they were among those who had lived in Estonia for generations or had come during the occupation.[5] Other disputes centered around the demarcation and administration of the new border with Russia and the transfer of property previously under communist control. There were numerous questions about who could become a citizen. Furthermore, Estonians feared that Russians now living in Estonia could ignite a fifth column preparing the eventual return of Russian domination. Organized crime associated with several ethnic Mafias was another threat to Estonians' control over their country.

In addition, the Russian government was exerting pressure on Estonia by complaining of human rights violations against Russians living there based on what were perceived as excessively stringent and ambiguous citizenship requirements.[6] The Estonian government had established, as part of the criteria for citizenship, a difficult language examination, which was not standardized and reportedly included arcane questions. Since most Russians living in Estonia did not speak the Estonian language and test administrators were likely to hold negative emotions for their former oppressors, the examination was considered unfair.[7] According to some accounts, even those who had a good command of the difficult Estonian language did not pass the exam. After so many years of subjugation by other powers, the newly free Estonians associated Russians with Soviets and feared another invasion, especially while former Soviet troops remained in Estonia and the aggressive rhetoric from ultranationalists, such as Vladimir Zhirinovsky, supported a hard line in the Baltic.[8]

— · —

Looking at the complex problems of independent Estonia through a psychoanalytic lens may be useful in illuminating unconscious but potentially troublesome elements. But such an endeavor invariably raises questions. Are there ways to investigate these elements and modify them so that they no longer disturb the large group and future generations? Are there ways to apply psychoanalytically informed insights to political, legal, economic, and social changes in a country shaping a new identity? Lastly, how can institutions be built so that they absorb the psychological insights and serve as an antidote to regressions in the large group and in the interaction of leaders and followers?

To address such questions, the Center for the Study of Mind and Human Interaction collaborated with The Carter Center in Atlanta,

Georgia, on a multiyear project in Estonia.[9] When we began to study the situation in April 1994, three years after Estonia had regained its independence, we found Estonians very quiet, reserved, and cautious; few would express their thoughts and feelings openly. Living under Soviet domination for fifty years had clearly affected them. After a certain degree of trust had been established with a stranger, some Estonians would express their rage toward Russians in psychosomatic ways, such as through facial expressions, but otherwise they did not articulate it.[10]

When Estonians asked themselves, "Who are we now and where are we going?" all they could fall back on was that they had somehow managed to survive through the millennium under various masters. During the Soviet period, the history of Estonia was rewritten in a Soviet version, and Estonia's fledgling heroes and myths were replaced by Soviet ones. Russian became the language of the song festivals until glasnost and perestroika, when Estonian was tolerated as well.

As Peeter Tulviste, a psychologist and rector at Tartu University, put it: "Imagine your child coming home from the kindergarten and telling you that Lenin is the father of all Soviet children, or giving you the news that radio, telephone and most other things had been invented by Russians, or that it is only during the Soviet rule that children have been given the opportunity to attend school in Estonia."[11] Yet little recourse was available since Estonian parents, fearing punishment, would hesitate to comment on their children's accounts from school.

But inevitably the children learned a second, banned history of Estonia. A child, upon coming across a picture of a parent's sibling, might say, "Mother, I didn't know that you had a brother." The mother might then report that her brother was in Siberia, to which the child would ask, "What does he do in Siberia?" The intergenerational transmission of a historical grievance was at work. Despite parental caution, the child learned that tens of thousands of Estonians were exiled by Stalin. Ironically, as Tulviste observed: "The forbidden fruit is sweet and the public lie mobilizes curiosity among those who realize that there is something to be discovered."[12] Estonians under the Soviet regime had their own version of history, even though there were few opportunities to debate or openly discuss such events and issues.

When the "forbidden fruit" was no longer prohibited, the internalization of the anxiety of previous decades, caused by the suppression of ethnic or nationalistic sentiments, lingered on.

—·—

The Russian population living in Estonia held a different mental representation of the drastic changes in Estonia in the early 1990s. This group ranged from those who had settled in Estonia long before, such as the Old Believers who came to the Lake Peipsi region four hundred years earlier, to the newcomers, who had lived in Estonia since the end of World War II, to the "occupants," the technocrats and former military personnel who had lived in Estonia for only a short time before independence was restored. For most of the Russian population and especially the occupants, sons and daughters of a powerful empire who would probably not be offered citizenship by the Estonian government, the world had turned upside down overnight. One day they were the superiors and the next, second-class residents and stranded refugees.

In contrast to the generalized anxiety evident among Estonians, humiliation prevailed among Russians in Estonia. The drastic turn of events was difficult to accept, causing many to deny the reality of their circumstances. Their countrymen in Russia would take action to help them! When the assistance they fantasized did not come, it was initially very difficult or impossible for Russians to consider submitting to Estonians, whom they perceived as members of a small and inconsequential country. Far easier was it to hold on to the image of being members of a great power, which in turn increased the resistance of Russians in Estonia to learning the Estonian language and conforming to Estonian culture.

The continued presence of Russians in Estonia was complicated by conditions in Russia, whose citizens and leaders constituted the third actor in this drama of revolution and change. The Russian authorities claimed that there were no facilities in Russia to house the troops stationed in the Baltics, nor were there jobs or housing available for the former Soviet technicians and administrators if they returned to Russia from the Baltics. Beneath the physical problems of an influx of Baltic refugees were fears that this group might be a source of both military and public unrest at a volatile time in Russia. Estonians, on the other hand, believed that, given the poor and uncertain conditions in Russia, an increasing number of Russians would remain in Estonia, where life promised to be better, but their allegiance would remain with Moscow.

These problems also involved an interesting dynamic. For many Russians living elsewhere in the Soviet Union, the Baltic region had been a land of Western mystery and intrigue: they were regarded as *sovetskaya* or *russkaya zagrantiza*, Soviet or Russian foreign countries. These were lands of romanticism connected with the European Baltic Sea and direct access to the West. Many of Russia's intelligentsia had chosen to vacation in the Baltic resorts where heavy pollution was not readily observable. A summer trip to Baltic seaside towns to some extent was a substitute for a forbidden trip to the Western world. Finnish television was available in some regions, creating an illusion of contact with the cosmopolitan West. Russians also believed they could taste more intellectual and spiritual freedom there since Estonia had a long tradition of academic excellence and religious tolerance. The esteem that Russians had for the more European Estonians was also echoed by the Estonians themselves, who had maintained and defended their group identity and cohesion by believing in their intellectual superiority over the "oppressors."

Some of the Estonian mystique was associated with Tartu University, founded in 1632 when Estonia was under Swedish control. After war forced it to close, the university was reopened as the Kayserliche Universität zu Dorpat by Russian czar Alexander I, the only German-language university in the Russian Empire. In 1919, with Estonian independence, it was renamed the Tartu Ülikool, and although it became a Soviet institution after 1944, it continued to be linked to Western European education. Thus, Russians of the Soviet era considered Tartu a kind of mecca for young Russian intellectuals. Attending Tartu University or following the writings of some of its prominent professors was for many students an accepted means of identifying with and expressing liberal and enlightened ideologies.[13]

Support for freedom in Estonia and the other Baltic republics did exist among Russian intellectuals. Yet this support typically went only as far as freedom from the dictatorship of the Communist Party, not for complete independence and sovereignty. After Estonian independence, those Russians who had considered Estonians compatriots in their battle to overthrow communism were sometimes angered and humiliated when they were lumped together with and generalized into evil Soviet oppressors. Though they had once fought on the same side, they were now considered the enemy by Estonians. Others in Russia, especially hard-liners, felt contempt toward Estonians (as well as Latvians and Lithuanians) since they seemed ungrateful for the Soviet Union's defeat of Nazi forces in the Baltic and the services and technology the USSR had provided since World War II.

The Russians were also upset with Estonia's claim to an additional forty-five kilometers of territory, based on provisions of the Tartu Peace Treaty (1920), along Estonia's eastern border. For Estonians, if the terms of the Tartu treaty were recognized by the Russians, then the Soviet era could be conceived as the unwanted occupation of a free country and a link could be created between the previous and current periods of independence. The Russians, however, perceived the desire to change the existing border as twisting the knife already in Russia's back and an unreasonable demand characteristic of Estonia's postindependence policy.[14]

Given this intertwined conglomeration of real issues and psychological impediments, the dialogue among Estonians, Russians living in Estonia, and Russians from Russia promised to be quite challenging but instrumental in shedding light on large-group psychology. Such dialogues were also necessary for practical purposes. After the Soviet empire collapsed, there were few friendly official efforts to resolve problems between Russians and Estonians, and each side was concerned about ultranationalist sentiments expressed by the other. These surface problems were then fueled by underlying emotions, ranging from anxiety to humiliation, from elation to a wish for revenge. The threat of confrontation and even bloodshed was possible.

An opportunity needed to be created for influential representatives from the conflicted groups at least to talk with and get to know one another. Our initial objective was to reduce the spread of poisonous emotions by sponsoring a series of dialogues among influential representatives of Estonia, Russia, and Russian speakers in Estonia. The meetings took place three times a year for three years.[15]

— · —

One way of diagnosing the emotional state of large groups is by visiting hot spots with them, observing their behavior, listening to their remarks. These are locations such as national cemeteries, memorials, museums, or monuments that became invested with strong emotions because of past or current political, military, or historical conditions. Perhaps I exaggerate a little when I say that collecting this kind of data is to large-group psychology what listening to a patient's dreams is in the psychoanalysis of an individual. A patient's dreams provide access to his unconscious, while visiting hot spots serves a similar function in revealing what otherwise might remain hidden or unexpressed in an intergroup dialogue.

In the spring of 1994, the former Soviet nuclear submarine base at Paldiski, Estonia, was such a hot spot. Paldiski is located on the Gulf of Finland, about twenty-five miles west of the Estonian capital, Tallinn. At the time of our visit, the heavily fortified base had been mostly shut down, and only a few vessels in need of repair remained at the once busy facility. The nuclear reactor was still in operation, guarded by a small detail of Russian soldiers, and some inactive military personnel remained in the barracks. Prior to independence, Estonian access to the base had been prohibited. In April 1994, during our first meeting, a tour of the base was arranged for the American team and the Russian and Estonian participants.

As we entered Paldiski by bus, the base resembled a huge garbage dump. What was once one of the Soviet Union's most sophisticated naval bases now looked as if it had been devastated by a tornado. Russians walked around the compound in a ghostlike daze. Our bus was met by an Estonian history teacher from a nearby town who served as our guide. Later, two Russian military officers in civilian clothes from Paldiski offered to join us to give additional information about the base. A verbal battle between the guide and the officers soon erupted. The Estonian insisted that the two Russians were not welcome since Estonia was once more an independent country and Paldiski now belonged to Estonians. The Russian officers left in disgust.

As we toured the base, our guide listed one after another the historical grievances of Estonia; the Russians provided facts that sup-

BALTIC REPUBLICS, 1994

FINLAND

Helsinki

St. Petersburg

Narva

Tallinn

Stockholm

ESTONIA

RUSSIA

Baltic Sea

Parnu

Tartu

SWEDEN

Riga

LATVIA

LITHUANIA

Kaliningrad

Kaunas

RUSSIA

Vilnius

Gdansk

Minsk

POLAND

BELARUS

0 Miles   50   100   150
0 Kilometers   50   100

UKRAINE

© 1997 Jeffrey L. Ward

ported notions of their own superiority and their efforts to protect the ungrateful Estonians. On the surface, the issue of Paldiski centered around who should be responsible for cleaning up the base. The Russians behaved as if to say, "Since we, the sons and daughters of a large and powerful country, are forced to dismantle our military might and retreat from Paldiski, we will leave behind our waste and hope that you ungrateful Estonians drown in it. At least we will force you to clean up our mess." This sentiment existed above and beyond the fact that there may not have been sufficient funds or time to complete an orderly withdrawal.

I also heard in the Estonians' remarks a subtext to their position of being in no hurry to clean up the mess themselves, though they also claimed that they lacked the funds to do so. Comments from the Estonians reflected both their wish to elicit sympathy from the American group for their victimization under Soviet rule and their unconscious resistance to changing their identity as victims. As long as Paldiski remained a dump, the Estonians had a concrete symbol of the suffering and injustice they felt they were subjected to by the USSR. It is a psychological truth that there is a degree of resistance to any drastic change, even when such a change promises a better life. Changes in identity, whether of an individual or a group, provoke the strongest resistance. The visit to Paldiski allowed the facilitating team to experience firsthand some of the dominant emotions and identity issues of the opposing groups that would appear as resistance to change during the psychopolitical dialogues that were about to begin.[16]

— · —

These psychopolitical discussions are not academic gatherings; they do not involve the presentation of scholarly papers, nor are they a onetime event. Instead, they involve an open-ended process. A typical meeting runs over four consecutive days. As with the Arab-Israeli dialogues, the main work is done in small groups of about twelve participants led by at least two members of the facilitating team.[17]

It is the task of the small-group facilitators to create a psychologically safe environment for discussion.[18] This is accomplished first and foremost through the facilitators' neutrality. Neutrality does not mean that the facilitator must be oblivious to the impact of participants' emotions. Instead, he should remain curious about the feelings expressed and events described so that each participant's curiosity is piqued. The point is to elicit a variety of responses in an atmosphere that encourages the modification of one's own rigidly held view. Examining an issue in a flexible way helps rehumanize an opponent with a different opinion. The background of safety is further enhanced when the facilitators absorb the emotions that surface when members of opposing groups trade historical grievances.

Throughout the meeting, facilitators watch for and monitor developments that threaten the participants' group identities and the psychological border between them. Two examples of such threats are when antagonists perceive one another as too similar to maintain the difference of their identities and when one group acts as a spokesperson for the other. I prefer to think of the former as an aspect of the accordion phenomenon.

In our Estonian dialogues, we saw the accordion squeeze together when the Russian and Estonian participants in one small group blamed the extremists in their respective camps for the problematic relations between their countries. Finding a common enemy enabled the participants from each side to come together—they appeared to be friendly and agreeable, hiding their aggression through its displacement onto extremists. This illusory closeness, however, threatens the principle that a group must not be the same as its opponent and must maintain a psychological border between its identity and that of the other. By explaining this phenomenon, the facilitator removes the illusory togetherness and the hidden anxiety that can create resistance to continuing the dialogue.

The facilitating group also intervenes when one group becomes the spokesperson for the opponent group. In one small group, Russians began to make long statements about how Estonians feel, think, or react, what they believe in, and so on, instead of talking about their own views. A facilitator then interceded and clarified for the group that what Russians were saying about Estonians might be what they wished or feared the Estonians would think or do. The Russians' projective behavior may have been realistic, yet it may also have been far-fetched and inaccurate. If the Russians let Estonians speak for themselves, then they might be able to modify their faulty perceptions and tame their projections. Facilitators asked the Russians to allow the Estonians to report about their own feelings, thoughts, and actions so that the Russians could perceive a reality that was not colored by fantasized and projected expectations. Generally, this kind of intervention also stops the illusory merging of large-group identities, lessens the anxiety, and creates a safe background for realistic discussion.

— · —

Discussion among participants often begins with a specific real-world problem, with the aim of reaching a logical solution for it. At one small-group meeting, a Russian diplomat suggested that Estonians implement a "green card" system for those living in Estonia who were not citizens, that is, Russians. He stated that this system must not be arbitrary, but the privilege of a green card should be determined by an impartial organization, such as a court. The number of aliens in Estonia would thereby be greatly reduced. An Estonian participant (a former cabinet member) replied that there were many people living in Estonia whom she would not want to become permanent residents or citizens, such as Mafia members and illegal immigrants, and she would rather see them expelled. Another Estonian participant then discussed the eleven known Mafia organizations operating in Tallinn, which included one Estonian organization as well as some Estonians in other groups. To combat this problem, he suggested close cooperation between Estonian and Russian law-enforcement agencies to limit Mafia activities and control their trafficking across the Estonia-Russia border, which was not patrolled effectively.

The lawlessness of the Mafia and the numbers of illegal immigrants crossing Estonia's borders were certainly real and significant problems. The threat to Estonia's borders was felt on a personal level among Estonians. If the physical borders of Estonia were shaky, the group and individual identity of Estonians would be unstable, too. Estonian members of the small group therefore sought to elude this issue by citing facts and figures, discussing the use of Interpol to combat organized crime, and suggesting that Estonians be trained to patrol the border and that known Mafia criminals be put on trial and deported. Facts, figures, and other technical information were of course necessary to the discussion, but obsessive preoccupation with them hid more important problems that caused the Russians and Estonians to disagree at every turn and impede real progress. One facilitator remarked: "The Mafia is both a real problem and a psychological one, since criminals cannot be easily identified. Is it possible that Estonians are suspicious of *anyone* who is not a citizen?" A Russian from Narva on the Estonian-Russian border, who was now legally without a country, noted with evident pain that ordinary people like himself could easily be confused with a person in the Mafia for many superficial reasons. How would criminals be differentiated from other people? Would Estonians want to deport him as well?

Beneath the practical level of what to do with the non-Estonian population living in Estonia were issues of maintaining both a physical and psychological demarcation between Estonians and Russians. At a purely emotional level, one solution for the Estonians was evident but not verbally expressed: eliminate the foreign elements altogether—deport or exile them, imprison them, marginalize them, somehow purge or "exterminate" them. This would satisfy the Estonian desire for revenge against their enemy and remove any real or fantasized threat posed by these unwanted elements. But it was a highly impractical solution, if nonetheless desired. The Estonians would seem too much like their former Soviet enemies, who used the same tactics to eliminate political rivals and threats and to dominate countries such as Estonia. Once these sentiments were out in the open, the pressure of repressing them—because they were unacceptable—was removed. The Estonian participants' anxiety associated with their secret wish to inflict revenge was diminished so that they could now discuss practical issues in a more logical way.

Another suggestion was for Estonia to establish a closed border so no unwanted elements could enter the country. But creating a wall around Estonia was also a Soviet type of solution that had psychological links to the old iron curtain. If Estonia envisioned itself as an emerging European country, open borders must be maintained, even if they also allowed a flood of non-Estonians—especially Russians—and criminals associated with the Mafia.

Similar concerns surfaced in an ongoing conflict over demarcating the border with Russia. Many Estonians supported defining the eastern border according to the Tartu Peace Treaty, thereby extending the existing border eastward by approximately forty kilometers; maps were printed in Estonia indicating both the current border and the border as it "should be," forty-five kilometers farther east. The Estonians wanted this boundary because it would increase their territory, create a larger buffer or divider between Estonia and Russia, and reaffirm Estonia's previous period of independence. The Tartu Treaty border would also substantially increase the number of Russian speakers in Estonia, since they were the primary inhabitants of the disputed area, thereby incorporating more unwanted people within Estonia's perimeters.

Assimilation or integration were the only realistic alternatives for Russians in Estonia. Yet in early meetings this dilemma was either fraught with so much emotion that it could hardly be contained or buried in unending technical discussions. On one hand, assimilation would mean an influx of more "enemy blood" that could weaken the Estonian identity. "If more Russian blood mixes with our own," one Estonian remarked, "in spite of having our own country, we would not stay as Estonian as we are now. We will be contaminated. . . . We will be mixed-blooded."[19]

The other option—the integration of Russians—could also corrupt Estonian identity, for Estonians perceived Russians as aggressors who would make the Estonian way of life more Russian. In a discussion on the possibility of integrating Russian and Estonian children in kindergarten, Estonians recounted that they had heard of situations in which the aggressiveness of even a few Russian children in an Estonian kindergarten class would result in all the children behaving in a Russian way and in Estonian children learning Russian instead of Russian children learning Estonian.

Practical and pragmatic progress on numerous issues between Estonians and Russians was contaminated by the Estonians' fear of disappearing. This was their shared and anxiety-provoking unconscious fantasy, based on the perception of Estonia's history, both recent and ancient. Such sentiments find an echo in the work of the renowned Estonian poet and former parliamentarian Jaan Kaplinski, who in "No History of the Estonian People" writes:

> Yes, we have no history
> There can be no history of the Estonian people

> We are unhistorical, *unhistorisch*, and what we have
> is at best unhistory.[20]

During the Soviet era, many Estonians had been exiled or killed, others had been forced to Russify, and some had fled to other countries in Europe or to the United States, where their identity as Estonians had been under constant threat. The most recent Soviet domination was only another chapter in the same story of Estonia's struggle for survival in which Soviets replaced Russians, Germans, Swedes, and Danes. To this history were added the facts that the birthrate among Estonians was very low, and rates of alcoholism and suicide were high. Though the Estonians had been victorious in again attaining independence, this and other positive developments were overshadowed by the lingering burden of the mental representation of their history and both conscious and mostly unconscious fears of obliteration. Estonians even feared that the Soviet invasion would be replaced by the economic and cultural invasion of Western Europe and the United States.

The Estonians' fear of disappearing and the need to defend their identity from foreign threats were pervasive.[21] The tragic sinking of the ferry *Estonia* in September 1994, shortly before one of our workshops, was a traumatic symbol of these complex issues. For some Estonians, it was a sign of their inferiority to Europeans and caused them to question their ability to survive on their own. Would the state of Estonia sink and disappear as well? The loss of hundreds of lives brought mass sorrow and grief, but at a different level it also brought (unspoken) humiliation that ran counter to the reality of Estonia's economic vitality and its incorporation into European political and trade organizations.

The understanding gained during the dialogues regarding the border and citizenship issues did not change legal, economic, political, and demographic realities. It simply helped to remove the emotional venom and irrationality that can easily sidetrack effective communication and adaptive, realistic discussion.

—·—

Being in the same room with the enemy spontaneously triggers the telling of ethnically and nationally related personal stories. At first, these stories are often charged with emotions and reflect a large group's historical grievances and an "us" and "them" kind of psychology. The exchange of personal stories also allows participants to see how individual identities are intertwined with large-group identities and to recognize which events have led to their specific ethnic or national investments. Participants are encouraged to listen to the stories of others and to discuss them, opening the door for empathic understanding.

One Estonian's story was as follows:

> When I was four years old, my family and some Soviet officers were "integrated." In our apartment, we were forced to live in one room so that the Soviet officers could live in all of the other rooms. Furthermore, the new inhabitants of our home did not even bother to learn Estonian to communicate with us but wanted us to learn Russian and adopt the Russian culture. They brought their wives and children also, but they would not learn Estonian either.

In this story, issues of us and them, victim and victimizer, are clear. Yet the next day, this same Estonian recalled a story his mother had told him about how, as a small girl, she would visit a Russian military hospital (during World War I) and make socks for the Russian soldiers. Ambivalence had (re)entered this Estonian's perception of the other group. In fact, such ambivalence was a good sign because it replaced the rigid splitting between us and them. He pointed out that in folklore Germans were the historical enemy of Estonia, not Russians, and suggested that Estonians needed self-analysis in order to tame their perceptions of Russians.

When a conflict becomes a shared conflict, the small group may create symbols and/or metaphors that represent important aspects of it. The participants begin to play with this metaphor, to kick it around like a ball.[22] The metaphor, like a toy, captures the attention of the participants and transforms diffuse emotions and blurred reality into a more concrete understanding of the problem. The toy connects the participants, allowing them to share in the game while at the same time addressing a critical issue.

In one small group, former Estonian president Arnold Rüütel told a personal story. As the head of Estonia, he had negotiated with the Soviets for the recognition of Estonian independence. He had been called to Moscow to meet with Mikhail Gorbachev, but when he arrived for his scheduled appointment, he had been forced to wait for two hours. In telling his story, Rüütel seemed upset, most likely because Gorbachev had appeared insensitive to his position and disrespectful of the significance of Estonia and its president.

When Rüütel had finished his story, Yuri Voevoda (then vice chairman of the Committee on CIS Affairs and Relations with Compatriots of the Russian State Duma) wanted everyone to know that he had been opposed to the communist government and that the Russian Federation should not be perceived as an extension of the Soviet Union. He equated Russia to an enormous elephant, albeit a friendly one. He said that, although Russia was a large state that included extremists, such as Zhirinovsky, there was no real reason for Estonians to fear Russia. Another participant added that, if Russia were an elephant, then Estonia was a rabbit. This was followed by a game in which the participants discussed the ramifications of a relationship between an elephant and a rabbit: such a relationship would be difficult since, even if they were friends, the rabbit could not help but fear being stepped on by the elephant. In fact, if the rabbit were too friendly and trusting, he could become careless and not realize he was about to be inadvertently crushed.

The Russians then understood that it was a psychological necessity for the Estonians to remain wary and not accept Russians' gestures of peace and friendship. The Estonians were elevated from being ungrateful to being cautious and became, to the Russians, more acceptable as human beings. The Estonians understood how difficult it was to change from perceiving the elephant as fearsome to perceiving it as friendly, for the degree of danger associated with both types of elephants was, psychologically speaking, the same. In fact, if they continued to see the elephant as dangerous, they would remain cautious and thus lessen their anxiety.

The participants returned to these metaphors in subsequent meetings. An Estonian noted: "If Russia is an elephant, then Russian speakers in Estonia are like elephant eggs in the rabbit's nest—they could hatch and destroy the rabbit and his home, or the parent elephant could come to protect them if it thought they were threatened." One Russian living in Estonia took the metaphor even further: "First the elephant was the Soviet Union, then it was the Russian army that was still in Estonia, and now it is the Russian pensioners. The Russian presence in Estonia is now much smaller, mostly old men, yet still these fears persist. Next it will be something else that is the scapegoat." Another Russian added that using the metaphor of an elephant to describe Russians had an undeserved negative connotation: "Russia is not stupid and big and clumsy. We will not step on the rabbit. We all suffered under the Soviet system [he had been imprisoned during Soviet rule]. We have too much in common, so why make so much out of our differences?"

Nevertheless, even in the negative use of this game, the serious issue of citizenship for Russian speakers in Estonia was symbolically contained. When anxiety-provoking feelings are represented by symbolic objects and named, they become less threatening. One can better tolerate an enemy who is defined and in the open than an unknown enemy lurking in the shadows.

While each psychopolitical dialogue has its own story that evolves over the four-day meeting period, the series of meetings has its own progression from one gathering to the next.[23] The series progression can be described phenomenologically. Harold Saunders, for example, sees five stages in dialogues to change conflictual relationships: deciding to engage in dialogue; mapping the relationships; probing the dynamics of the relationships to generate the will to change; designing scenarios to change relationships; and putting scenarios into action.[24]

By the end of 1995, participants had reached Saunders's fourth stage, due to the process facilitated by the American group and to political shifts in the Estonian-Russian relationship. The Russian military presence in Estonia had now been completely removed, easing fears of another occupation. The potential for chaos had substantially decreased, and many forms of international assistance had consequently been reduced or terminated. Despite this positive prognosis, problems related to citizenship, integration, education, crime, economic and political development, bureaucratic reform, security, and other issues continued to be pervasive and difficult to resolve.[25] Approximately 350,000 noncitizens, most of them Russian speakers, still lived in Estonia, and true progress on their status remained slow.[26] In the psychopolitical meetings, the paralyzing anxiety that characterized earlier meetings was no longer evident. Representatives of each of the three groups, Estonians, Russians in Estonia, and Russians, were now able to express their anger more openly, which suggested that repressed emotions would no longer have malignant consequences.

The reality that there would be a population of others in Estonia did not elicit the same fears of contamination or disappearing; Estonians seemed to accept the inevitable integration of foreign communities. Participants from Russia made it clear that Russians in Estonia must work out their future directly with Estonians—Russia could not decide it for them. Yet according to one Moscow participant, Russians who were learning Estonian and planning to remain in Estonia were perceived as traitors. Such sentiments were echoed in the Russian press. Some participants from Russia wanted to deny Russians in Estonia a good life and to hear them say that they still preferred their mother (Russia) to their stepmother (Estonia). As for Russians living in Estonia, one participant from Narva, still a noncitizen, declared in late 1995 that he was not as much a victim as he had once thought. His teenage daughter had learned Estonian and passed the language exam for citizenship.

That this participant's daughter was in fact attempting to integrate and had in this sense surpassed her father led the facilitating team to turn its attention toward the future of Estonia rather than the present and past. We wanted to see if in fact the younger generation of Estonians and Russians in Estonia were adapting more quickly and positively to change. Four Estonian and four Estonian-Russian university students were therefore invited to join the dialogue. The students entered the process firmly believing that they were different and more progressive than their parents' generation.

Their participation in small-group dialogues, as well as in meetings alone with the facilitators, revealed that, although they did differ from the older generation, they also held many of the same attitudes that rigidified borders and differences between the two groups. The students' recognition of their stereotypical perceptions of each other, and their unconscious role as spokespersons for the previous generations, deeply pained them. They earnestly tried, in a more open and useful fashion than the older generation, to explore how and why they held such views. The older participants witnessed the emotional exchanges among members of the younger group, and many were truly influenced by what they heard.

Outside of the dialogue, impasses still existed on the path to a new social, political, economic, and psychological order, even within small farming and fishing communities. Understanding new concepts, making decisions, and organizing groups and individuals at the local level remained highly problematic. This led to uncertainty, feelings of helplessness, and the potential for conflict.

In the third year of the Estonia project, three Estonian locales were selected as sites for community projects to help build democratic institutions: Mustamäe, a suburb of Tallinn; Klooga, a small village twenty-five miles from Tallinn; and Mustvee, a town on Lake Peipsi, which lies on the border of Estonia and Russia. In each location, the population was roughly half Estonian and half Russian, and each had its unique problems that reflected the diversity of issues involved in relations between Estonians and Russians living in Estonia.[27] We wanted to serve as a catalyst as each community developed democratic and adaptive ways to deal with problems and to provide an antidote to possible tensions in multiethnic communities.

Mustamäe is a typical city suburb of Estonia's capital where sophisticated dialogue regarding cultural diversity and democracy had already begun. The participants were focusing on integration and other issues of Estonian and Estonian-Russian kindergartens.

The situation was very different in Klooga, a run-down locality near a defunct Soviet military installation. Estonians in Klooga were generally newcomers who had moved into former military accommodations, while the Russians, mostly noncitizens, were primarily young women with children who had been left behind after the base was shut down. The whereabouts of many of the husbands was unknown. No true sense of community existed here, ethnic divisions were severe, and many public services, such as law enforcement, garbage collection, and a steady supply of heat from the dilapidated plant, were lacking. The aim in Klooga was to encourage development of community without fueling interethnic conflicts.

In Mustvee, a rural town dependent on fishing and farming, Estonians and Russians have coexisted peacefully for generations. The Russians are mostly Old Believers, members of an Orthodox sect that settled in the area over four hundred years ago. Many residents can speak both Russian and Estonian. During the Soviet period, central control made life simple and predictable: a truck would come to collect the fish caught in Lake Peipsi and the onions and cucumbers grown on nearby farms and take them to Saint Petersburg. With independence, Mustvee lost its primary market, and Soviet authorities no longer made the decisions, which was unsettling the once calm relationship between Estonians and Russians. Here, our aim was to help the villagers revitalize their economy cooperatively.

At each of the three locations, the psychological internalization of Soviet culture was evident, but it was most obvious in Mustvee. When twenty Estonians and twenty Russians (mostly Old Believers) began to gather regularly to discuss developing a community project, participants tended to give speeches instead of engaging in a genuine dialogue with others. While one person stood up and spoke, other participants would talk among themselves, ignoring the person speaking. In the end, they expected someone in authority to make the decisions for them. But what they really needed was to learn how to make independent decisions and reach a consensus.

When Mustvee was being considered for participation in this project, its new Estonian mayor was particularly interested. As it happened, he was in the process of choosing where to buy new sewer pipes for the town. Weighing issues of cost and quality to arrive at a decision on his own without orders from a Soviet official was like having a new toy to play with; it was an exciting experience.[28]

— · —

The Estonia project is the only experiment I know of in the systematic and long-term application of psychoanalytic large-group psychology using an interdisciplinary facilitating team. The total cost for our six years of direct, regular involvement in Estonia will be approximately $3 million. If "preventive medicine" were not administered in an ethnic conflict and it escalated into violence, the cost, in both human and financial terms, would be far greater than that expended in Estonia. As the death toll and the cost of relief efforts in places such as the Great Lakes region of Africa, the Balkans, Transcaucasia, and other areas continue to grow, alternative means of effectively averting potential conflicts must be explored.[29]

AFTERWORD: PSYCHOANALYSIS
AND DIPLOMACY

In studying large-group psychology near the end of the twentieth century, I have turned to psychoanalytic ideas that first took root in the beginning of this century, augmented by my observations as a clinician. When presenting theoretical concepts, I have focused only on those that help to explain my observations and have deliberately avoided expanding on theory distant or less relevant to these observations. The metaphor of an ethnic tent, used throughout this book, is not a psychoanalytic construction—it simply illustrates an idea. I have depended on psychoanalytic concepts to describe the different components of the tent and their evolution.

I am aware that much more has to be done to support or modify the findings reported here. Almost all of my data come from locations around the globe where group emotions have been inflamed or where there have been struggles to adjust to political and historical change. We will learn a great deal more when we study neighboring groups in peaceful relationships. How do the mental representations of chosen traumas or chosen glories become dormant so that they do not inflame large-group sentiments? How do members of a group adaptively mourn past losses and changes so that they do not induce feelings of anger, humiliation, and the desire for revenge? How does the preoccupation with minor differences between neighbors become playful, and how can major differences be accepted without being contaminated with racism? These are significant questions, and answers to them can give us clues for designing programs for peaceful coexistence.

Living under a totalitarian regime does not allow the expression of ethnic sentiments that can lead to political instability. Achieving peaceful coexistence between ethnic groups through oppression by a central power is only a pseudo-solution to the problem, and in my view the price paid for it is too high. Sometimes, the personality of a leader can defuse potentially violent ethnic tensions—Nelson Mandela and the transformation of South Africa come to mind. But in other situations, positive changes in an economy, combined with a general weariness of conflict, can create an atmosphere ripe for compromise and reconciliation. In the first part of this century, there was ethnic tension in South Tirol between German speakers and Italian speakers. After the 1950s, this maladaptive ethnic consciousness disappeared, at least for several decades, as the economy improved greatly and the Italian leadership decided to leave the German speakers alone.[1] It would be useful to study these nonviolent, successful changes through psychopolitical diagnostic work to see if there were additional, but hidden, elements for a positive outcome.

As the diplomatic culture becomes more receptive to nongovernmental conflict resolution efforts around the world, facilitators should be wary of trying to accelerate reconciliation between former enemies. In recent years, the concept of an aggressor's apologizing and asking for forgiveness has gained burgeoning interest, especially since Mikhail Gorbachev's apology for the Soviet role in the Katrin forest massacres in Poland.

The idea of a group or its leader asking for forgiveness from another group or its leader may be a potentially powerful gesture if the groundwork has truly been laid. Forgiveness is possible only when the group that suffered has done a significant amount of mourning. The focus should be on helping with the work of mourning and not on the single (seemingly magical) act of asking forgiveness. Stubborn large-group conflicts cannot be solved by an instant-coffee approach.

In the end, unofficial attempts at large-group conflict resolution can only go so far. There comes a time when agreements between opposing parties have to be officially recognized. As co-chairman of the Commission on Global Governance, Sir Shridath Ramphal and his colleagues at the United Nations are busy considering an amendment to the UN charter that would allow the UN, on humanitarian grounds, to intervene in appropriate cases of domestic crises within sovereign states. This would permit the global community legally to intervene in many ethnic issues.

In June 1995, when Ramphal gave the second Global Security Lecture at Cambridge University, England, he noted that five years after the end of the cold war and the release from many of the compulsions of the nuclear arms race, the world was:

> ... more tense, more fragile, more unstable, and its people more fearful and uncertain. Humanity remains an endangered species, even though the manner of our going may be less with a bang than with a whimper. On the eve of a new century and a new millennium, we probably have less reason for assurance than our ancestors had in 1900, or even the year 1000, that we are passing on to future generations the right to life. . . .
>
> That we urgently need a new universal ethic of survival and a reordering of global priorities appears no longer to be in doubt.[2]

Ramphal went on to state that there can be no global security without the ascendancy of rule of law worldwide: "Few would dispute this, but a large shadow falls between acknowledgment and performance."[3]

The psychoanalytic study of the psychology of large groups can do much to illuminate this large, shadowy area. Better understanding and application of these ideas may help unveil those irrational and stubborn factors that lead to violence so that they can be dealt with more effectively, so that we can bring our worst enemies—our shared identity conflicts and anxieties—from darkness into light.

ACKNOWLEDGMENTS

I wish to express sincere appreciation to all my colleagues at the Center for the Study of Mind and Human Interaction (CSMHI) at the University of Virginia for supporting me in writing this book. Founded in 1987, CSMHI is an interdisciplinary think tank that studies the psychology of large groups and applies its findings to issues such as ethnic tension, terrorism, societal trauma, and national and international conflict. Its faculty and board include experts in psychoanalysis, psychiatry, diplomacy, history, political science, and environmental policy.

In particular, I am indebted to Joy Boissevain, program director at CSMHI. Without her tireless efforts, I would not have been able to complete this project. I also wish to thank Carole Hamilton; Bruce Edwards, managing editor of CSMHI's quarterly journal, *Mind and Human Interaction*; Kelly Hale, my administrative assistant; and Clare Aukofer, CSMHI's communications consultant, for their editorial help. Yuri Urbanovich, formerly on the faculty of the Diplomatic Academy in Moscow and currently international scholar at CSMHI, was always available for consultation on the Soviet Union and Russia, and I thank him for this.

I wish to give particular thanks to Norman Itzkowitz, professor of Near Eastern studies at Princeton University and CSMHI advisory board member. Chapter 7, "Two Rocks in the Aegean Sea: Turks and Greeks in Conflict" is based on studies we did together, which were published in two volumes: *The Immortal Atatürk: A Psychobiography* (1984) and *Turks and Greeks: Neighbours in Conflict* (1994). Professor Itzkowitz was the one who first brought to my attention oedipal issues pertaining to the Ottoman Turkish sultan, Mehmet II. He also kindly read Chapter 4, "Ancient Fuel for a Modern Inferno: Time Collapse in Bosnia-Herzegovina" for historical accuracy. I also thank Mehmet Suphi, a historian from Istanbul, Turkey, for consultations.

An earlier version of Chapter 12, "Totem and Taboo in Romania: The Internalization of a 'Dead' Leader and Restabilization of an Ethnic Tent," was published in the journal *Mind and Human Interaction* (1995) and received the 1996 L. Bryce Boyer Award from the Society for Psychological Anthropology of the American Anthropological Association. This much appreciated recognition prompted me to update the work on Romania for inclusion in this book. I also wish to thank Harry G. Barnes Jr., former U.S. ambassador to Romania, for his review of this chapter and for his helpful suggestions.

Many of the studies described in this book were possible because of my association with CSMHI. The center, in turn, could not have existed without the continuing support of the University of Virginia's School of Medicine and generous grants from several sources, including The Pew Charitable Trusts, the William and Flora Hewlett Foundation, the U.S. Institute of Peace, and the International Research and Exchanges Board. I wish most especially to thank the Massey Foundation, which believed in the uniqueness of CSMHI and whose continuing support has been essential for the center's growth.

Theresa Park, of Sanford J. Greenburger Associates, my literary agent, was the first to believe that *Bloodlines* should be written and encouraged me during its preparation. John Glusman, vice president and executive editor of Farrar, Straus and Giroux, gave me valuable suggestions to make my writing more accessible to a wider public. I thank both of them.

NOTES

PREFACE

1. Smutnoye Vremya covers a period that began with the death of Ivan the Terrible and ended with the selection of Czar Mikhail Fedorovich to the Russian throne. It was characterized by struggles within the Russian nobility, foreign incursions, economic crises, and chronic instability.
2. Nagorno-Karabakh had been carved out of Armenia in 1922 and awarded to Azerbaijan when the region became part of the Soviet Union. Nakhichevan, a largely Muslim region between Iran and Armenia, also was given to Azerbaijan, though it too did not border it. When Armenia and Azerbaijan became separate Soviet republics in 1936, these unusual territorial pockets remained.
3. After Moldova became an independent republic, a political solution to its ethnic troubles was reached. See Lebedeva, "Psychological Aspects of Ethnic Conflict."
4. M. Baklanov, "Moscow, August 1991," *Sputnik*, special supplement (October 1991), p. 4.
5. Between 1918 and 1940, Estonia, Latvia, and Lithuania were independent countries. They were subsequently occupied by Soviet forces and incorporated into the USSR.
6. During the Stalin era, nearly two hundred thousand Crimean Tartars were deported in cattle trains to Uzbekistan in central Asia. Many of them died along the way or in trying to survive in this desolate area. Chechens, Ingush, Kalmyks, Karachai, and Balkars had also been deported from other areas. In a secret speech in 1956, Nikita Khrushchev exposed the atrocities committed

during the Stalin era (see Khrushchev, *Khrushchev Remembers*) and allowed the survivors to return home—excluding the Tartars, because the Crimea was an important strategic location for the communists. In 1987, Mikhail Gorbachev responded to Tartar demonstrations in Moscow and granted permission for Tartars to return to the Crimea. On the surface, the problem had been solved, but even though mass relocations had already begun, the Tartars used this opportunity to air the pain of their Stalin-era trauma.

7. Itzkowitz, "Ottomanization of the Soviet Union," p. 15.
8. This report comes from International Committee of the Red Cross, *ICRC 1993: Emergency Appeals* (Geneva), December 1992, p. 87.
9. Human Rights Watch, *Georgia/Abkhazia: Violation of the Laws of War and Russia's Role in the Conflict* (New York: Human Rights Watch, 1995), p. 25.
10. State Department, *Country Reports on Human Rights Practices* (Washington, D.C.: GPO, 1994), p. 887–891. See also MacFarlane, Minear, and Shenfield, *Armed Conflict in Georgia*, p. 26.
11. S. J. Hedges, P. Cary, R. Knight, P. Glastris, D. Hawkins, and D. Pasternak, "Will Justice Be Done?" a special report in *U.S. News & World Report*, 25 December 1995–1 January 1996, p. 50. See also Allen, *Rape Warfare*.
12. Nnoli, *Ethnic Conflict in Africa*, p. 7.
13. Ibid., p. 8.
14. Ibid.
15. Ibid.
16. Horowitz states that "Nigerian evidence shows that federalism can either exacerbate or mitigate ethnic conflict. Much depends on the number of component states in a federation, their boundaries and ethnic composition" (*Ethnic Groups in Conflict*, p. 603).
17. Des Forges, "Burundi."
18. Malkki, *Purity and Exile*, pp. 21–22.
19. A. de Swaan, "Widening Circles of Disidentification: On the Psycho- and Socio-Genesis of the Hatred of Distant Strangers: Reflections on Rwanda" (paper presented at Civilization and Its Enduring Discontents: Violence and Aggression in Psychoanalytic and Anthropological Perspective, Bellagio, Italy, 4 September 1996).
20. See Wallensteen and Axell, "Major Armed Conflicts," pp. 12 and 81; Margareta Sollenberg and Peter Wallensteen, "Major Armed Conflicts," p. 15; and International Negotiation Network, *The Carter Center State of the World Conflict Reports, 1994–1995*, p. 6, and *1995–1996*, pp. 12–13 (Atlanta, Ga.: The Carter Center). The year 1996 started with seventy-one armed conflicts around the globe; not all of them were major, however.
21. H. D. S. Greenway, "Roots of Ethnic Conflict," *Boston Globe*, 13 December 1992, p. 42.
22. Some rules and regulations governing modern diplomacy go back as far as the fifteenth century, when diplomatic representation became increasingly insti-

tutionalized and permanent missions between sovereign political groups were established.

23. For example, during the cold war era, various deterrence theories evolved that almost exclusively relied on rational considerations. The main idea was the formulation of a threat designed to stop the enemy from carrying out aggressive acts. The physical ability to carry out the threat was then demonstrated, and the threat was thereby clearly communicated. These deterrence theories specifically referred to the bipolar zeitgeist of the potentiality of a full-scale nuclear war between the United States and the Soviet Union in which there could be no winners. What is interesting from the science of diplomacy standpoint is that deterrence was regarded as more than a theory, as if the logical examination and measurement of deterrence could be as exact as the laws of physics. Each side's tanks, troops, ships, submarines, and missiles were counted, compared, and balanced against the other's. Theory and reality were used interchangeably.

Many political analysts agree that the threat of mutually assured destruction (MAD) encouraged rational decision making and thereby prevented the Soviets and Americans from using their nuclear arsenals. Then in 1973, Egyptian president Anwar el-Sadat behaved contrary to the assumptions of deterrence theories and chose to go to war with Israel, despite knowing that the Egyptian air force could not effectively challenge the Israelis in an all-out war. Why wasn't he deterred?

The war between Argentina and Britain over the Falkland Islands also illustrated the failure of deterrence theories to prevent war. Though the British clearly possessed military superiority and their leader, Prime Minister Margaret Thatcher, was outspokenly resolved to defend British territory, the Argentineans, initially at least, rallied around the defiant claims of President Leopoldo Galtieri, who would later resign in defeat.

The precepts of deterrence theories did not adequately explain either the 1973 Egyptian-Israeli war or the Falkland Island conflict, prompting a reevaluation of this scientific approach. In the early 1980s, new sources were sought to explain faulty decision making, among them cognitive psychology. Political scientists began a wholesale borrowing of cognitive psychology concepts, and some insights helped to explain the irrational behavior of supposedly rational states. There were no efforts to turn to psychoanalysis to supplement the understanding of the irrational policies or to understand the emotions linked with historical events.

24. Arndt, "New Diplomacy in the Post-Imperial World," p. 144.
25. Horowitz, *Ethnic Groups in Conflict*, p. 140.

1

1. De Vos, "Ethnic Pluralism: Conflict and Accommodation," p. 9.
2. Ibid.
3. Stein, "International and Group Milieu of Ethnicity."

4. R. Cohen, "Ethnicity Problems and Focus on Anthropology."

5. Cole, *People of Malaysia*; and Shapiro, *Jewish People: A Biological History*.

6. For further examination of this topic, see Thomson et al., "Psychology of Western European Neo-Racism."

7. Commission on Human Rights Sub-commission on Prevention of Discrimination and Protection of Minorities. Economic and Social Council. United Nations E/CN.4/Sub. 2/1992/11, 14 July 1992.

8. Committee of International Relations, *Us and Them: The Psychology of Ethnonationalism*, p. 20.

9. Gittler, "Defining an Ethnic Minority," p. 6. See also Peterson, "Concepts of Ethnicity," p. 234.

10. Peterson, "Concepts of Ethnicity," p. 234.

11. Loewenberg, *Fantasy and Reality in History*, p. 196.

12. Ibid. George Orwell in a 1945 essay distinguished nationalism from patriotism. For him, patriotism was a "devotion to a particular place and a particular way of life, which one believes to be the best in the world but has no wish to force upon other people. [It] is of its nature defensive, both militarily and culturally" ("Notes on Nationalism," p. 362). Seeing patriotism as a normal phenomenon, Orwell went on to describe nationalism as malignant: nationalism is patriotism turned sour and includes "power hunger tempered by self-deception" (p. 367).

13. Chasseguet-Smirgel, "Blood and Nation," p. 31.

14. Howell, "Tragedy, Trauma . . . and Triumph," p. 116.

15. Loewenberg, *Fantasy and Reality in History*, p. 196.

16. Ibid., p. 198.

17. E. H. Erikson, "Ontogeny of Ritualization," p. 606.

18. Boyer, "On Man's Need to Have Enemies."

19. Murphy, "Intergroup Hostility and Social Cohesion."

20. Auden, "The Sea and the Mirror," p. 36.

21. S. Freud, *Group Psychology and the Analysis of the Ego*; Le Bon, *The Crowd*.

22. The human mind develops in stages from infancy on. Every stage has its repertoire of mental tools to deal with the individual's internal and external worlds. When faced with threats, an individual may revert at least partly to using mental mechanisms from an earlier stage. This is called *regression*. Groups, too, can regress.

23. S. Freud, "Why War?" pp. 203–215.

24. Mitscherlich, "Psychoanalysis and Aggression of Large Groups," p. 164.

2

1. Anwar el-Sadat was not the first modern political leader to have identified the psychological basis of international conflicts. In 1974, the Turkish government sent armed forces to the island of Cyprus, effectively dividing it into two sections, northern Turkish and southern Greek, in an effort to protect Cypriot Turks living on the island. In light of the existing Turkish-Greek problems, the

Turkish prime minister at that time, Bülent Ecevit, gave a speech in 1979 in which he spoke of the fact that most of the problems between the Greeks and Turks were psychological. While Ecevit's remarks did not initiate psychological studies of international relationships, Sadat's standing in the world arena, and in the United States in particular, sparked interest in the subject.

2. Regularly joining the American psychiatrists were two diplomats: Joseph Montville, who is now director of the Preventive Diplomacy Program at the Center for Strategic and International Studies in Washington, D.C., and Harold Saunders, a former assistant secretary of state for Near Eastern and South Asian Affairs (1978–1981). Saunders had accompanied Henry Kissinger during his shuttles between Jerusalem and Cairo and had attended the Camp David meetings in 1978 when Jimmy Carter, Menachem Begin, and Anwar el-Sadat met to formulate the Camp David Accords.

3. Psychoanalysts often notice that an emotion experienced by a patient activates closely related old memories that can feed this emotion. This can also be seen in normal people. (See Eissler, "Defects of Ego Structure"; Peto, "On Affect Control"; and V. D. Volkan, *Primitive Internalized Object Relations*, pp. 172–173.)

3

1. Pollock, *Mourning-Liberation Process*, vol. 1, pp. 3, 145; vol. 2, pp. 5, 51.
2. S. Freud, "Mourning and Melancholia," p. 244.
3. Tähkä, "Dealing with Object Loss."
4. V. D. Volkan, *Linking Objects and Linking Phenomena*, pp. 101–6; and Volkan and Zintl, *Life after Loss*, pp. 71–84.
5. The Vietnam War Memorial was designed by twenty-one-year-old Maya Ying Lin, while she was an undergraduate student of architecture at Yale University. When her plan for the monument was made public, some did not like the design and argued that "the monument is below ground, denoting shame" or that "it is black, a color of shame" (Scruggs, *To Heal a Nation*, p. 82). Nevertheless, the project was completed and the black granite wall took on a life of its own. Lin wanted the veterans and visitors to see their own reflections in the stone as they read the names of the dead and missing. This symbolically joined them with the dead. In 1992, Kurt Volkan, senior editor of *Middle East Insight*, wrote:

> As a reflection of death, the memorial allows the living to fuse with the dead, through sight and touch. As a reflection of the psychodynamics of mourning, Lin's creativity resulted in a ritual that is soothing in itself; visitors symbolically repeat the mourning process, and thus master it, every time they come and go, touch the stone and leave. . . . This Wall can be as personal as a mother crying for her lost son, or as public as a nation weeping for a past history that has yet to be resolved.
> ("Vietnam War Memorial," pp. 76–77)

6. K. T. Erikson, "Loss of Communality at Buffalo Creek," pp. 302–325.
7. Lifton and Olson, "Human Meaning of Total Disaster."
8. Williams and Parkes, "Psychosocial Effects of Disaster."
9. D. A. Maurer, "A Long Road to Rebuilding Hope: Missionary Collects Supplies for Navajo," *The Daily Progress* (Charlottesville, Va.), 18 June 1992.
10. After the liberation of Kuwait from the Iraqi occupation, in an interview with me in 1993, a Kuwaiti father clearly was bothered by his guilt for not having been able to protect his children from fear during the occupation. He felt ashamed that some Iraqi soldiers had humiliated him in front of his children.
11. Volkan and Ast, *Spectrum des Narziβmus*, pp. 103–150.
12. On November 25, 1995, Israel's channel 2 television station reported on the decades-long negligence in dealing with the trauma undergone by Holocaust survivors after their arrival in Israel. The report especially focused on the victims' experiences in mental hospitals.
13. Moses and Cohen, "An Israeli View," p. 130.
14. Ibid.
15. Many Orthodox Jews prefer to define themselves in relation to the lost Temple of Jerusalem rather than to the Holocaust, and Israelis of African origin sometimes report that they are less affected by the Holocaust than are other Jews.
16. Loewenberg, "Psychological Reality of Nationalism," p. 7.
17. Kakar, *Colors of Violence*, p. 5.
18. Ibid., p. 10.
19. Ibid, p. 131.
20. Harris, "Reading the Mask."

4

1. Karadžić and Mladić also spoke of Marshal Tito's funeral at length. President Carter had sent his mother, Lillian Carter, to the funeral, and her presence had been viewed very positively. The discussion also focused on World War I and on more recent history that directly related to the events in Bosnia-Herzegovina.
2. The people in the former Yugoslavia—Serbs, Montenegrins, Slovenes, and Bosnian Muslims—are all southern Slavs and thus share the same blood. It is their histories and religious differences that distinguish them as various ethnic groups.
3. Vulliamy, *Season in Hell*, p. 157.
4. "Television was a key element, perhaps *the* key element, fanning the flames of the Serbo-Croatian war that has swallowed up postwar Yugoslavia. . . . The regimes in both Belgrade and Zagreb . . . exercised total control over radio and television and gained public support by serving the populace a diet of lies, inventions, and propaganda, sometimes horrifying, sometimes sentimental" (Parin, "Open Wounds," p. 41).
5. In the JNA, 12 percent of the officers were Croats, but the Croats were 22.1

percent of the total population in 1991. Only 2.4 percent of the army officers were Muslims, although Muslims were 8.4 percent of the total population of the former Yugoslavia in 1991 (Cirić, "From Partisans to Security Service").

6. In today's world of electronic communication and media, we have wide access to knowledge of events and people around the globe, and this surfeit of information can lead us to believe that cross-cultural communication no longer poses difficulties. This is not always true. I have close former-Soviet friends who, even years after their departure from the Soviet system, retain drastically different perceptions and thinking patterns from their American friends. The communist worldview seems to live on in these former Soviets. Sometimes they give preference to central authority over individual initiative, as if they would still like to be told what to do. They will continually check and recheck with the authorities to obtain approval for their actions, when by U.S. standards their concern is quite unnecessary.

7. Such factors exist today, but they are pushed into the shadows by other motivations pertaining to the complicated thinking and planning required of leaders of modern states. Generally, the checks and balances of today's sophisticated political systems overshadow the personal interests of those in power.

8. Itzkowitz, *Ottoman Empire and Islamic Tradition*, p. 16.

9. Volkan and Itzkowitz, *Turks and Greeks: Neighbours in Conflict*, p. 60.

10. R. Lewis, *Everyday Life in Ottoman Turkey*, p. 13.

11. Another ally of Prince Lazar was Ban Tvrtko, who ruled the Bosnian region. Before the battle at Kosovo Polje, Tvrtko had arranged his own coronation as king of Serbia, Bosnia, the Pomorze, and the western lands and was also recognized as king by the Hungarians. In spite of Trvtko's attempt to establish himself as heir of the Nemanjic dynasty, Prince Lazar had remained friendly with him. While Tvrtko himself did not come to Kosovo Polje, he sent some men to fight against the Turks.

12. Thanks to the work of Emmert (*Serbian Golgotha*), there are now, in English, detailed accounts of various versions of the "historical truth" of the Battle of Kosovo.

13. Some of the sources Emmert (ibid.) mentions estimate that Murat I came to Kosovo Polje with over a hundred thousand men and Lazar had assembled an army of over seventy thousand men. Kinross, a historian, insists, however, that the Ottoman army was inferior in number (see *Ottoman Centuries*, p. 58).

14. Serb sources did not mention the name of the assassin until 1497, when he was identified as Miloš Kobilić. Different chronicles throughout the centuries, however, have suggested others, including Prince Lazar himself, as the assassin. Some Turkish accounts state that after the Turks won the battle the seventy-year-old Murat was left momentarily unguarded on the battlefield and killed by a wounded Serb soldier. Recent historians, however, accept Miloš as the assassin.

15. If this account is correct, it explains the Ottoman custom, after the Battle of

Kosovo, to have a subject's arms held behind him when he approached to kiss the right foot of a sultan.

16. After he was proclaimed the new Ottoman sultan, Bayezit ordered the strangulation of his other surviving brother and thus initiated a practice of imperial fratricide. At the time, a passage was found in the Qur'an to sanction the practice. It was felt that it would prevent the new empire from being fragmented. The family feuds and intrigues among European Christian rulers in medieval times did not exist at the same level or quality within the Ottoman ruling family since the Ottomans had found a solution for sibling rivalry.

17. F. Tınç, "Türbedar Kadının Rüyası" (The dream of the grave-watching woman), *Hürriyet*, 7 June 1996, p. 4.

18. Parin, "Open Wounds," p. 43.

19. Marković, "The Secret of Kosovo," p. 111. Eighteen years before the Battle of Kosovo, Turks had defeated Serbs on the Maritsa River. Many Christians were already under their influence in the Balkans, and some of them joined Murat's forces against Prince Lazar's army. Most historians consider the Serbian defeat on the Maritsa crucial in eventually sealing the Serbs' fate. In spite of this, the Battle of Kosovo became a chosen trauma and the battle on the Maritsa River did not.

20. The song recounted here comes from Marković, "The Secret of Kosovo," p. 114. For other Serb songs, see Pennington and Levi, *Marko the Prince*; and Zimmerman, *Serbian Folk Poetry*.

21. This account comes from Emmert, *Serbian Golgotha*.

22. This story slowly evolved and took its present form in *Il regno degli Slavi* (1601), by Marvo Orbini, as reported by Emmert, *Serbian Golgotha*, p. 106.

23. The lithograph, titled *The Feast of the Prince*, is by Adam Stefanović and dated 1870.

24. Marković, "The Secret of Kosovo," p. 116.

25. Earlier, in 1804, Karageorge, or Black George, led a serious uprising of Serbs against the Ottomans. In the end, Karageorge was defeated by the Turks, and later he too was identified as a religious figure and hailed as a messiah.

26. From *Vojincki Glasnik*, 28 June 1932, cited in Emmert, *Serbian Golgotha*, pp. 133–134.

27. J. Cvijić, *Balkansko Polustrvo I juznosevenske zemle* (Belgrade, 1986), reported in Emmert, *Serbian Golgotha*, p. 135.

28. Bohlen, *A Witness to History*. The archduke, after having been informed of the insensitivity of his timing, was actually in the process of leaving Sarajevo when he and his wife were shot.

29. Vulliamy, *Season in Hell*.

30. Kaplan, *Balkan Ghosts*, p. 38.

31. Emmert, *Serbian Golgotha*, appendix.

32. Kaplan, *Balkan Ghosts*, p. 39.

33. Vulliamy, *Season in Hell*, p. 51.

34. "Shared paranoid disorder spreads very quickly, reaching large masses in times of economic or political crisis and collective tension, when their [the group's] critical consciousness is reduced and their realistic observation of reality is obscured" (M. Jakovljevic, "Psychiatric Perspectives of the War against Croatia," *Croatian Medical Journal* 2 [1992], p. 43, quoted in Parin, "Open Wounds," p. 50).

35. S. Sullivan, "To His Hometown, Serb Karadžić Is a Local Hero Who Made Good," *Washington Post*, 21 April 1996, p. A20.

36. Allen, *Rape Warfare*, p. 80.

37. S. Kinzer, "The Nightmare's Roots: The Dream World Called Serbia," *New York Times*, 16 May 1993, p. 2. See also L. J. Cohen, *Broken Bonds*.

38. S. Power, "The World of Radovan Karadžić," *U.S. News and World Report*, 24 July 1995.

39. K. B. Deklava and J. M. Post, "Poet of Death: The World of Dr. Radovan Karadžić" (paper presented at the annual meeting of the International Society of Political Psychology, Washington, D.C., 4–10 July 1995).

40. Vulliamy, *Season in Hell*.

41. Deklava and Post, "Poet of Death."

42. Ibid.

43. Ibid.

44. Personal communication with Norman Itzkowitz. See also Fine, "Medieval and Ottoman Roots of Modern Bosnian Society."

45. Hatiboğlu, *Bosna'ya Farklı bir bakış*.

46. The conflict of 1992–1995 is not the first instance of ethnic cleansing of Bosnian Muslims. Incidents of ethnic cleansing in some areas of the former Yugoslavia began in the last quarter of the nineteenth century with Bosnia's change of status and continued through the two Balkan Wars. The Muslim population of that time was reduced by approximately 25 percent due to a combination of ethnic cleansing and flight into the Ottoman Empire to avoid more of the same.

47. S. Toros, *Milliyet*, 25 September 1995, p. 12.

48. Seifert, "War and Rape, a Preliminary Analysis," p. 63. Seifert also cites statistics showing that civilian losses frequently exceed military losses in armed conflicts; specifically, according to a 1989 UNICEF report, 90 percent of war victims since World War II have been civilians, mostly women and children. Gutman (*Witness to Genocide*, p. 78) reports Serbs' demanding that community figures desecrate mosques by performing such acts there as making the sign of the cross, eating pork, and having sexual intercourse with young girls (i.e., virgins) while the rounded-up community members witnessed the desecration. If the community leader refused, he was taken away and presumably killed.

49. Itzkowitz, *Ottoman Empire and Islamic Tradition*, p. 50.

50. Lazarovich-Hrebelianovich and Calhoun, *Serbian People*, vol. 1, p. 322.

51. Gutman, *Witness to Genocide*, p. x.

52. Hatiboğlu, *Bosna'ya farklı bir bakış.*

53. Gutman, *Witness to Genocide*, p. x.

54. Ibid.

55. Aired on March 12, 1996.

56. B. Allen, *Rape Warfare*, p. 87.

57. The expression of unconscious fantasies of multiplying the ranks of a threatened society has been observed elsewhere. In 1975, Williams and Parkes reported an increase in birthrate in the Welsh village Aberfan for the five years following the engulfment there of 116 children and 28 adults by an avalanche of coal slurry. They attribute this rise mainly to "a process of biosocial regeneration by couples who had not themselves lost a child" ("Psychosocial Effects of Disaster," p. 304). The inhabitants of Aberfan experienced not a riot or war but a natural disaster. Nevertheless, this study shows the wish to multiply the population following a threat to a community. Most likely the adults were *not* conscious of their desire to increase the village population. The Williams and Parkes study also helps in understanding the preoccupation of Cypriot Turks with the fertility of the birds they raised in cages as a shared hobby during their confinement between 1963 and 1968. In India when the Hindus perceived the Muslim population was growing rapidly, they feared that such an increase would use up economic resources. Accordingly, it became a threat. In turn, the fantasy to multiply their own ranks developed. One piece of communalist graffiti advocating an increase in family sizes addresses Hindu women: "Have the next child right away, and an occasional one only after the eighth one" (Mazumdar, "For Rama and Hindutva," p. 7).

58. Stiglmayer, "Rapes of Bosnia-Herzegovina," p. 88.

59. According to Allcock, "The Kosovo stories portray the Serbs as a kind of chosen people" ("Kosovo: The Heavenly and the Earthly Crown," p. 169).

60. In addition to bad economic conditions in Yugoslavia, Milošević's personality, I suggest, has played a role in the sequence of events. Because of the suicide of both of Milošević's parents, he most likely could no longer trust parent figures. There are indications that as a consequence he depended more extensively on his domineering wife, Mirjana, as if she were also a mother figure, while at the same time he remained cautious, for fear of being betrayed and humiliated again. It is said that Mirjana was the only girlfriend he ever had. After Milošević became president, Mirjana's diary, published in the magazine *Duga*, hints that he had an affair with a Serbian TV anchorwoman, but the couple subsequently reconciled (reported in S. Sullivan and T. Sonenshine, "All in the Family," *Newsweek*, 16 December 1996, pp. 38–39). Most of the time, Milošević keeps to himself and has perhaps suffered episodic depression.

61. J. Promfret, "Serbia's Elastic Man," *Washington Post*, 28 December 1996, pp. C1, C3.

5

1. Some adults, especially men, require the presence of an inanimate object, such as a shoe, in order to perform sexual intercourse. The shoe or other fetishistic object has to be available to be seen, touched, and smelled. The meaning of an adult's fetish is understood by focusing on the individual's castration anxiety. If a boy fails to negotiate the Oedipus complex during childhood and continues, mostly unconsciously, to hold on to the fear that he will be punished by his father for his incestuous desires, as an adult he will resort to a variety of means to deal with this continuing fear of castration. One of the paths he might take is to become a fetishist. In this case, the fetishistic object unconsciously symbolizes an extra phallus, indeed a phallus that even women could have. Thus, while he knows that it is not realistic, he unconsciously holds on to a belief that everyone has a phallus. This means that no one, including himself, is castrated, and he can be sexually potent. While he had made earlier references to the unconscious meaning of the fetish, S. Freud fully focused on this topic in "Fetishism."

2. Winnicott explored the function of transitional objects in 1953 in "Transitional Objects and Transitional Phenomena."

3. A child who used a fan as a magical inanimate object is described by Mahler (*On Human Symbiosis*, p. 202). There are also adult forms of such inanimate objects, especially among schizophrenics.

4. I first described suitable reservoirs (or targets) of externalization in June 1985 during my presidential address to the International Society of Political Psychology. See also V. D. Volkan, *The Need to Have Enemies and Allies*, pp. 31, 74.

5. Emde, "Positive Emotions for Psychoanalytic Theory."

6. Emde and Harmon, "Endogenous and Exogenous Smiling Systems."

7. See S. Freud, *The Origins of Psychoanalysis* and *Three Essays on the Theory of Sexuality*, pp. 179–183.

8. S. Freud, *Group Psychology and the Analysis of the Ego*, p. 105.

9. There are other types of identifications involving a more mature child and his or her more complicated relationships with others. For example, identification with an aggressor, a concept first described by A. Freud ("The Ego and the Mechanisms of Defense"), explains why a four-year-old child keeps punching holes in a doll by using a sharp object the day after visiting a physician's office and receiving an injection in his arm. Here, the child turns being submissive to the physician into a state of being active and in control. Nevertheless, it is primarily the early ego identifications that play a role in developing the foundation of the child's identity.

10. There are, however, individuals who fail to integrate their remaining black and white fragments and who then exhibit problems with the organization of their personalities for the rest of their lives. As adults, they remain unintegrated, as

if they were two separate people, truly demonstrating a division similar to that of Dr. Jekyll and Mr. Hyde.

If everything goes normally, when a child reaches thirty-six months of age, he also becomes capable of perceiving other people in his surroundings, such as his mother, as integrated individuals. Prior to this time, he could not fully comprehend that a loving mother and a frustrating mother were the same person; the mother was either good or bad. A realistic mother, who is sometimes good and sometimes bad, is established in the child's mind after his integrative capacities fully evolve.

11. Once, however, in 1926, in an address to the Society of B'nai B'rith in Vienna, S. Freud spoke of its emotional forces:

> What bound me to Jewry was (I am ashamed to admit) neither faith nor national pride, for I had always been an unbeliever and was brought up without any religion though not without respect for what are called the "ethical" standards of human civilization. . . . [But] plenty of other things remained overt to make the attraction of Jewry and Jews irresistible—many obscure emotional forces, which were the more powerful the less they could be expressed in words, as well as a clear consciousness of inner identity, the safe privacy of a common mental construction. ("Address to the Society of B'nai B'rith," p. 273)

12. E. H. Erikson, "The Problem of Ego Identification," p. 113.
13. Ibid., p. 57.
14. Blos, *Adolescent Passage*, p. 171.
15. In Glass, *Private Terror/Public Life*, p. 35.
16. This is also true in relation to the integration of good and bad object (other) relations. See Kernberg, *Borderline Conditions and Pathological Narcissism;* and V. D. Volkan, *Primitive Internalized Object Relations.*
17. In psychoanalysis, the term *projection* has various meanings. For clarity, in this book I use the term *externalization* to refer to the projection of unintegrated self and object elements onto other people or things and the term *projection* to refer to putting unwanted impulses, thoughts, or feelings "out there."
18. W. Nathaniel Howell was nearing the end of his tenure as U.S. ambassador to Kuwait when the invasion occurred. He and his staff of seven refused to evacuate the embassy in Kuwait City despite repeated threats by the Iraqis. Three years later, Ambassador Howell (now retired) and his wife, Margie, a former psychiatric nurse/mediator, led a group from CSMHI to study the societal effects of the Iraqi invasion on the Kuwaitis (Howell, "Tragedy, Trauma . . . and Triumph" and " 'The Evil That Men Do . . . ' "; see also Saathoff, "In the Halls of Mirrors" and "Kuwait's Children").
19. Gregory Saathoff, personal communication, 1996. Cars also figured importantly to the trapped U.S. citizens and staff at the American embassy during the invasion. Even though they had thoroughly disabled all of the compound ve-

hicles by commandeering parts to keep other essential motors running, they squandered valuable water to wash the derelict cars, as a "declaration of non-dependence" to the watching, amazed Iraqi soldiers (See Bodine, "Saddam's Siege of Embassy Kuwait," p. 124).

20. V. D. Volkan, *Cyprus—War and Adaptation*, p. 91.
21. Lind, "Dream as Simple Wish-Fulfillment."
22. Myers and Yochelson, "Color Denial in the Negro." See also Vitols, Walters, and Keeler, "Hallucinations and Delusions."
23. Manning, "Cultural and Value Factors."
24. Grier and Cobbs, *Black Rage*; Pinderhughes, "Origins of Racism"; and Wilkerson, "Destructiveness of Myths."
25. Grier and Cobbs, *Black Rage*, p. 129.
26. Apprey, "African-American Experience."

6

1. V. D. Volkan, *The Need to Have Enemies and Allies*, p. 246.
2. Pinderhughes, "Paired Differential Bonding." See also Committee of International Relations, *Us and Them*.
3. Jacobson, *Self and the Object World*; Mahler, *On Human Symbiosis*; and Kernberg, *Borderline Conditions and Pathological Narcissism*.
4. Spitz, *First Year of Life*, pp. 150–162.
5. Parens, *Development of Aggression in Early Life*.
6. M. M. Suárez-Orozco, "Immigrants and Refugees in the Post-National Space" (paper presented at Civilization and Its Enduring Discontents: Violence and Aggression in Psychoanalytic and Anthropological Perspective, Bellagio, Italy, 4 September 1996).
7. During the Bush administration, militarization of the U.S.-Mexico border was considered necessary for the war on drugs. In 1994, Proposition 187 was approved by voters in California. This proposition aims to bar illegal immigrants from various publicly funded services, including nonemergency medical care and public schooling for illegal children. (As of 1997, the proposition was under litigation in federal and state courts.)

    In January 1996, President Bill Clinton signed legislation that increased the Immigration and Naturalization Service budget from the $2.1 billion provided in 1995 to $2.6 billion. A major part of this money was to be used for border enforcement and detention of illegal aliens.
8. V. D. Volkan, *Cyprus—War and Adaptation*, p. 98.
9. Stein, "On Professional Allegiance in the Study of Political Psychology," p. 248.
10. S. Freud, "Taboo of Virginity," p. 199.
11. S. Freud, *Group Psychology and the Analysis of the Ego*.
12. Ibid. Freud also mentioned this topic in *The Future of an Illusion*.
13. Horowitz, *Ethnic Groups in Conflict*.

14. Kakar, *Colors of Violence*, p. 165.
15. Butler, "Yugoslavia Mon Amour," p. 123.
16. Ibid.
17. Brenner, *The Mind in Conflict*, p. 123.
18. Sandler and A. Freud, "Discussions in the Hampstead Index of the Ego and the Mechanisms of Defence." On dehumanization, see Bernard, Ottenberg, and Redl, "Dehumanization: A Composite Psychological Defense in Relation to Modern War."
19. Kubie, "Outgoing of Racial Prejudice."
20. A. de Swaan, "Widening Circles of Disidentification: On the Psycho- and Socio-Genesis of the Hatred of Distant Strangers; Reflections on Rwanda" (paper presented at Civilization and Its Enduring Discontents: Violence and Aggression in Psychoanalytic and Anthropological Perspective, Bellagio, Italy, 4 September 1996).
21. "Khomeini's Dark Vision," *Boston Globe*, 28 January 1985, p. 14.
22. Loewenberg, *Fantasy and Reality in History*, p. 167.
23. War as therapy is mentioned by Fornari, *Psychoanalysis of War*.

7

1. The Turks claimed that the name of these rocks did not appear in the documents signed at the 1923 Lausanne Treaty at the end of the Turkish war of independence. Therefore, they suggested that the rocks were not put under Greek sovereignty.
2. In 1995, Richard C. Holbrooke brokered a peace settlement among Serbs, Croats, and Bosnian Muslims, embodied in the Dayton Agreement.
3. Some historians consider the battle of Malazgirt a more important event in Byzantine history than the fall of Constantinople. This is not so from a psychological point of view, since the Byzantine Empire continued to exist after the battle of Malazgirt. Thus, the mental representation of the fall of Constantinople, which toppled the Byzantine Empire, became the main chosen trauma for Greeks.
4. Itzkowitz, *Ottoman Empire and Islamic Tradition*, p. 59.
5. Mango, "Greece and Turkey: Unfriendly Allies."
6. Herzfeld, *Ours Once More*.
7. Baggally, *Greek Historical Folksongs*, p. 84.
8. Ibid., pp. 92–93.
9. R. Lewis, *Everyday Life in Ottoman Turkey*, p. 181.
10. Herzfeld, *Ours Once More*.
11. Ibid., p. 32.
12. Evlambios, *Amaranth: The Roses of Hellas Reborn.*
13. Zamblios, "Modern Greek Language" and *Whence the Vulgar and Traghoudho?*; and Politis, "Khelidhonisma" and *Introductory Lecture for Class in Hellenic Mythology.*
14. Kazantzakis, *Report to Greco*, p. 68.

15. Herzfeld, *Ours Once More*, p. 119.
16. Young, *Greek Passion*.
17. Schwoebel, *Shadow of the Crescent*.
18. Ibid.
19. Volkan and Itzkowitz, " 'Istanbul, Not Constantinople.' "
20. Blos, *Adolescent Passage*, p. 179.
21. Adıvar, *Osmanlı Türklerinde İlim*.
22. von Hammer-Purgstall, *Histoire de l'empire Ottoman*, 18 vols.
23. Kinross, *Ottoman Centuries*.
24. Volkan and Itzkowitz extensively studied the symbolism attached to Istanbul in *Immortal Atatürk*, pp. 268–276. Tevfik Fikret, a renowned Turkish poet of the twentieth century, called Istanbul "the incestuous figure of the era" in his poem *Sis* (Fog, 1902). Talat Halman, a contemporary Turkish poet, also described Istanbul as a prostitute in his poem "Istanbul" (in *A Last Lullaby*, pp. 8–9).
25. Volkan and Itzkowitz, *Turks and Greeks* (p. 68) and " 'Istanbul, Not Constantinople.' "
26. Millas, "Türk edebiyatında Yunan imajı."
27. On September 22, 1996, general elections took place in Greece. Among the topics debated by the competing political parties and their candidates was the tension over the Kardak/Imia rocks. Costas Simitis was elected prime minister to secure his position as heir of the late Andreas Papandreou. It appeared that Simitis would take a more flexible approach to the continuing conflict with Turkey than did Papandreou. Public opinion in both countries continued to resist a rapprochement.

8

1. J. Pomfret, "For Ousted Bosnians, a Trail of Tears," *Washington Post*, 14 July 1995, p. A26.
2. "Lativians to Remove the Remains of Soldiers of Red Army," *New York Times*, 3 February 1993.
3. "Latvia to Rebuild National Cemetery to Past Condition," *American Baltic News*, April 1993.
4. For further information about this meeting, see Volkan and Harris, "Vaccinating the Political Process." See also R. Cullen, "Cleansing Ethnic Hatred," *Atlantic Monthly*, August 1993, pp. 30–36, for his account of the meeting.
5. I was accompanied by Joyce Neu, associate director of the Conflict Resolution Program at The Carter Center, and by Yuri Urbanovich, international scholar at CSMHI and formerly associate professor at the Soviet Foreign Ministry's Diplomatic Academy in Moscow.

9

1. As'ad Masri, a Palestinian-American psychiatrist, and Nuha Abudabbeh, a Palestinian-American psychologist, accompanied me on this trip.

2. Kohn, *Idea of Nationalism*, p. 9.
3. Kracke, *Force and Persuasion: Leadership in an Amazon Society*.
4. Loewenberg, *Fantasy and Reality in History*, p. 10.
5. Burns, *Leadership*, p. 379.
6. M. Holden, "Bargaining and Command in the Administrative Process: Chief Executives and the Executive Entourage" (paper presented at the Institute of Government, University of Virginia, April 1984). See also Holden, "Bargaining and Command by Heads of U.S. Government Departments."
7. Burns, *Leadership*, p. 427.
8. Ibid., p. 425.
9. Ibid., p. 37.
10. There were other traumatic childhood events too. Volkan and Itzkowitz wrote a psychoanalytic biography of this leader titled *Immortal Atatürk*. What is reported here is based on our extensive study of Atatürk.
11. Zaleznik, "Charismatic and Consensus Leaders."

10

1. B. Lewis, *Assassins: A Radical Sect in Islam*.
2. Reich, "Understanding Terrorist Behavior," p. 264.
3. Reported in Kramer, "Hizbullah: The Calculus of Jihad," p. 542.
4. "An Interview with the Secretary-General of Hezbollah Sheikh Hassan Nasrallah," *Middle East Insight* 12, no. 4–5 (May–August 1996), pp. 38–43, 84–85.
5. Ibid., p. 38.
6. Ibid., p. 39.
7. Kramer, "Moral Logic of Hizballah," p. 133.
8. Kramer, "Hizbullah: The Calculus of Jihad," p. 540.
9. Ibid.
10. Said Amir Arjomand, professor of sociology at the State University of New York at Stony Brook, has a concise description of Islamic fundamentalism:

> Unity in Islamic fundamentalism throughout history stems from its affirmation of the central tenets of Islam: belief in monotheism and the conviction of the possession of the final revelation in the Qur'an. This unity rests firmly on familiarity with the Qur'an, partaking of congregational worship, the five daily prayers, and fasting during the month of Ramadan, and is accompanied by the unquestioning acceptance (*bila kayf*) of the literal truth of the holy scripture. It produces a distinct type of God-fearing personality convinced of the possession of the truth of divine revelation and intolerant of alternative truths. ("Unity and Diversity in Islamic Fundamentalism," pp. 191–192)

Valerie J. Hoffmann, a religious studies scholar from the University of Illinois at Urbana-Champaign, adds:

> The perception of Islam as a comprehensive code for all aspects of life, and its intimate connection with both personal and national identity, grant the Islamic solution an authenticity no other ideology could have. ("Muslim Fundamentalists: Psychosocial Profiles," p. 225)

11. "Interview with Sheikh Hassan Nasrallah," p. 40.
12. Lomarsky, "Political Significance of Terrorism," p. 89.
13. Weinberg, "Terrorists and Terrorism," p. 81.
14. "Interview with Sheik Hassan Nasrallah," p. 42.
15. J. Knutson, unpublished notes, 1981.
16. CSMHI's Committee on Terrorism was composed of Maurice Apprey; Anatoly Golubovsky, from Russia; Max Harris; Ambassador W. Nathaniel Howell, retired; Katherine Kennedy; J. Anderson Thomson Jr.; Yuri Urbanovich, from Russia; Caroll A. Weinberg; and myself. The committee's findings are published. See Volkan and Harris, "The Psychodynamics of Ethnic Terrorism."
17. Joseph Montville, a former foreign service officer in Iraq, Lebanon, Libya, and Morocco who is now director of the Preventive Diplomacy Program at the Center for Strategic and International Studies, cities a number of terrorists from Israel and Northern Ireland whose "conversion" to terrorism can be dated to specific encounters with state-sanctioned violence. He wrote:

> Each of the original [IRA] hunger strikers of 1981 had what may have been a . . . conversation experience, from being "stopped and badly beaten at a check point operated by a unit from the Local Ulster Defense Regiment" at age seventeen (Francis Hughes), to being "shot in the foot by the British Army when he was twelve years old" (Patsy O'Hara). ("Psychological Roots of Ethnic and Sectarian Terrorism," pp. 176–177)

18. Malignant narcissism is an unusual and destructive version of habitually possessing excessive self-love (narcissistic personality organization). A person with enhanced narcissism behaves as if he were a special being entitled to the best things in the world. He acts as if he were the best looking, the most intelligent, and the most powerful. Narcissistic personality organization develops as a defensive adaptation to childhood hurts and humiliations as well as deficiencies in self-esteem. In a sense, an individual with excessive and habitual self-love says, "I am above being hurt," instead of saying, "Ouch!" Since life is full of many real cruelties, most narcissistic individuals' grandiosity is threatened now and then. At such times, they feel depressed and seek psychoanalysis or psychotherapy.

There are also successful narcissists. Those with high intelligence and leadership qualities may actualize being number one: they may become president of an organization, a company, or even a country.

Malignant narcissism, as a version of overall narcissistic personality organization, compels a person to damage or even kill the other to feel good. Using aggression pumps up not only his adrenal glands, but also his self-esteem. This makes him dangerous.

19. Stone, "Murder," p. 646.
20. Volkan and Ast, *Spectrum des Narzißmus*, p. 92.
21. Post, "Terrorist Psycho-Logic," pp. 37–38.
22. Ibid., p. 31. For radical ideological terrorists, it may be a matter of belonging to a small group whose very identity is bound up with being on the margins of society.
23. Clark, "Patterns in the Lives of ETA Members."
24. Kramer, "Moral Logic of Hizballah," p. 143.
25. C. Couglin, "Hamas, the Many," *The Sunday Telegraph* (London), 10 March 1996, p. 26.
26. Ibid.

11

1. Information for this chapter comes from a long dialogue Abdullah Öcalan had with a Turkish leftist writer, Yalçın Küçük. This dialogue has been published in Turkish in a 416-page book titled *Kürt Bahçesinde Sözleşi* in which Öcalan responds to questions put to him by Küçük. Öcalan, however, does more than simply answer. He wants to tell his life story; he returns again and again to his childhood memories, as if he wants to understand the internal motivations for his adult activities. There are enough descriptions of incidents during his childhood, his feelings about them, detectable symbols (such as snakes, representing his parents and his rage), and connections between childhood and adult activities that a psychoanalytic reconstruction of Apo's internal world is possible.
2. Öcalan and Küçük, *Kürt Bahçesinde Sözleşi*, p. 36.
3. Ibid., p. 37.
4. Ibid., p. 31.
5. Ibid., p. 59.
6. Ibid., p. 28.
7. Ibid., p. 28.
8. Ibid., p. 30.
9. Ibid., p. 62.
10. Ibid., p. 37.
11. Ibid., p. 32.
12. Ibid., p. 26.
13. Ibid., p. 56.

14. Ibid., p. 55.
15. Ibid., p. 55.
16. Ibid., p. 35.
17. Ibid., p. 63.
18. Ibid., p. 138.
19. Ibid., p. 136.
20. Ibid., p. 33.
21. Ibid., p. 33.
22. Ibid., p. 34.
23. Ibid., p. 35.
24. Blos, *Adolescent Passage*, p. 179.
25. Öcalan and Küçük, *Kürt Bahçesinde Sözleşi*, p. 98.
26. Ibid., p. 100.
27. Ibid., p. 44.
28. Ibid., p. 60.
29. Ibid., p. 146.
30. Ibid., p. 138.
31. Ibid., p. 60.
32. Ibid., p. 57.
33. Ibid., p. 57.
34. Ibid., p. 57.
35. Ibid., p. 400.
36. Ibid., p. 408.
37. Ibid., p. 64.
38. Ibid., p. 74.
39. Ibid., p. 75.

12

1. After joining, most of the patriots quickly became disillusioned in their hopes that opposition to the Soviet invasion would mean reforms at home. This information comes from personal communication with Ambassador Harry G. Barnes Jr., former U.S. ambassador to Ceauşescu's Romania and, as of 1995, director of the Conflict Resolution Program at The Carter Center in Atlanta, Georgia.
2. Because of this aggressive promotion of population growth and the extreme poverty of most families, orphanages were crowded with children from broken or dysfunctional families. Due to tainted needles and blood supplies used to treat them, more than three thousand of these children were early victims of pediatric AIDS. Today there are thousands of street children in Bucharest populating abandoned buildings and parks. Their sexual activity has spread the HIV virus, as well as hepatitis B, syphilis, and tuberculosis.
3. R. Cullen, "Report from Romania: Down with the Tyrant," *The New Yorker*, 2 April 1990, pp. 94–112.

4. Besides 2.2 million residing in Romania, there are 600,000 Hungarians in Slovakia and nearly 385,000 in Serbia. After the Serbs' ethnic cleansing activities started, more than 20,000 Hungarians took refuge in Hungary.

5. One of my informers, who was in Timişoara when the riot took place, told me that the people there could not phone to other cities. Cullen, however, reports on the story of a woman in Bucharest who was phoned by a friend in Timişoara during the event. Her friend, in a carefully veiled statement, said only: "There is a big storm, and the sky is red" (see Cullen, "Report from Romania," p. 96). Cullen also stated that the people in Bucharest learned about the events in Timişoara by listening to the BBC and Radio Free Europe. There are scholarly papers on this topic, but for my psychopolitical diagnosis, I was most interested in people's perception of events instead of the absolute truth. However, those with whom I spoke in Romania could not enlighten me on the matter. There was an aura of ambiguity regarding the first few days of the revolution.

6. Some observers in the United States, including a few in Congress, feared that the trauma caused by the fall of Ceauşescu, and Romania's subsequent search for a new identity and place in the world, would result in increased ethnic conflict or even open warfare between Romanians and Hungarians living in Romania. Accordingly, funds were made available for a team of Americans to study the situation in Romania. The team was headed by former diplomat Joseph Montville. The other members of the team were Merle Lefkoff, an expert in public dispute resolution, Jerome Delli Priscoli, of the U.S. Army Corps of Engineers' dispute resolution program, and myself.

7. See *Cuvîntul* (Bucharest), 28 March 1990, p. 1; and *Le Monde*, 26 April 1990.

8. In May 1990, free elections were held in Romania for the first time since 1937. Iliescu was elected by a landslide. Yet many Romanians spoke to me of their suspicions about the election results and of hearing reports of threats and even deaths at some polling places.

9. Nicu Ceauşescu died in September 1996 after an illness.

10. Gallager, "Vatra Româneasca," p. 594. The idea of Great Romania did not start with Ceauşescu. It was a rallying cry for Romanian nationalists in the period before and during World War I. It was a symbol of entitlement for recruiting all Romanians into one country—from Hungarian-, Russian-, or Bulgarian-held lands. Ceauşescu inflamed such sentiments but modified the scope of Great Romania. He was not asking for additional land but focusing on a kind of purification in Transylvania and sought to enhance the greatness of Romania through monumental building projects.

11. Shafir, "Best Selling Spy Novels Seek to Rehabilitate Romanian Securitate," p. 18. The origin of modern Romania goes back to 1859, when the Ottoman Empire, which still included the areas now part of Romania, was fast declining. That year, due to external pressure, the Ottomans consented to join the principalities of Moldavia and Walachia under one ruler. Thus, Romania was born, though it remained a suzerainty of Istanbul (Sugar, *Southeastern Europe under*

Ottoman Rule), and complete independence was not achieved until the Conference of Berlin in 1878. Transylvania, which is part of present-day Romania, had been given to the Hungarians by the Ottomans in 1699, long before the birth of modern Romania. Present-day Romania was consolidated in 1918 after World War I through the inclusion of Transylvania, the Banat of Temešvár, and other regions. In 1940, northern Transylvania and other areas were once again lost to Hungary only to be reacquired in 1944. The constant border shifting and the changing balances of power have left their impact on the region, as reflected in the ethnic conflict between Romanians and Hungarians living in Transylvania.

The roots of Romanian-Hungarian conflict over Transylvania go back more than a thousand years. According to traditional Romanian history, Roman legionnaires arriving in the first century B.C. intermarried with local Dacians (ancient Dacia is now known as Transylvania); those that remained behind after the Roman soldiers left established Romania's historical claim to the region. Hungarians trace their lineage to Magyars who settled in the reportedly uninhabited mountainous heart of Dacia many centuries later. Both groups claim the area as their ancestral homeland, and strong emotions abound on the subject. As an illustration: Hungarian and Romanian émigrés attending a conference at Columbia University in the early 1990s nearly came to blows when discussing "whether a few Latin words contained in a Hungarian chronicle written around AD 1200 prove or disprove the presence of Romanians in Transylvania well before the belated arrival, in the ninth century AD, of the Hungarians" (I. Deák, "Survivors," *New York Review of Books*, 5 March 1992, p. 41).

In the last decade of the Ceaușescu regime, possibly in order to deflect attention from deteriorating economic conditions, Romanian nationalistic sentiments were intensified. The government paid "relocation inducements" to ethnic Romanians for moving to Hungarian-populated regions and in turn curtailed cultural opportunities for Hungarians in Romania. Yet in juxtaposition to such times of ethnic conflict is the historic legacy of periods of ethnic harmony in Transylvania. In 1568, while wars of religious intolerance were raging elsewhere in Europe, an atmosphere of acceptance and understanding prevailed in Transylvania. At this time, Transylvania was a model for the coexistence of diverse nationalities and ethnic groups. But today, even without Ceaușescu to inflame ethnic tension, harmony and peaceful coexistence have not returned.

12. See *Adevarul* (Cluj), 27 December 1991.
13. During the 1993 trip to Romania, the U.S. team met with a senator and four congressmen from PUNR at the parliament building in Bucharest, but it soon became clear that they would answer none of our questions—instead they presented statements and exposition. Senator Adrian Mețiu reminded us repeatedly that, in considering ethnic conflicts, we could not put everything into

computers and trust their findings since computers do not reflect people's emotions (we had never mentioned computers to him and in fact did not use them in our study of Romania's ethnic problems). We were told that PUNR's policy for the solution to ethnic problems in Transylvania was the "natural way," which meant Romanians should not give in to any demand from the Hungarian minority since a response to one would have "a matrushka doll effect—you open one doll and there is another one under it, and when you open the second one, then you have to deal with a third, and so on." The senator gave us statistics to show how well the Hungarians were doing in Transylvania and how they were not discriminated against.

In reflecting on PUNR's position, Meţiu mentioned that when he was ten years old a mentally retarded Romanian gardener was viciously killed, "just for fun," by Hungarians in a park. He stated that the "occupiers" had come to Transylvania fully organized to settle forever and had even brought their own post office workers. Others joined the senator in giving us a list of historical grievances against Hungarians. They referred to the poor treatment Romanians received from Hungarians in the past and spoke of fears that if HUDR's demands were granted it would lead to the establishment of a Hungarian "zone of influence." According to them, Hungary wanted to expand its economic sphere into Transylvania.

14. Gallager, "Vatra Românesca," p. 576.
15. Gallager, "Ethnic Tension in Cluj," p. 28. In 1993 elections, Mayor Funar came in third in this presidential race, with only 10.8 percent of the vote, but he managed to increase the visibility of ultranationalism and generate nostalgia for the Ceauşescus.
16. Initially, ethnic tensions in Cluj-Napoca had flared over the Hungarian word *áruház* (shop), which had been hung over a store, prompting a ban on all Hungarian advertisements and posters—a form of language purification. The legislation, approved by Funar, made the prospects of bilingualism in Cluj-Napoca almost impossible. One tale told about Funar, while humorous, reflects his deep-seated fear of the Hungarian threat. When an ethnic Hungarian, Erno Jakap, applied to launch a private cable television service, he was not allowed to do so because the offerings included MTV. Funar apparently thought that MTV stood for Magyar Television instead of Music Television (see C. J. Williams, "Tempers Flaring in Transylvania City," *Los Angeles Times*, 27 October 1992, p. H2).
17. During my second trip to Romania, my friend greeted me with a book that contained Eminescu's poem *Luceafărul* (Lucifer), and she inscribed in it her ethnic pride by writing that Romania, a small country, has had, and would have in the future, great and beautiful peoples.
18. Abse and Jessner, "Psychodynamics of Leadership," p. 693.
19. Gilberg, "Religion and Nationalism in Romania," p. 181.
20. There were also signs of progress in Romania. During my first visit, Vasile

Popovici arranged for our team to observe a vote in the Romanian parliament that would allow Hungarians the right to buy businesses in Transylvania. Romanian ultranationalists had argued that such a move would pave the way for a Hungarian economic invasion of Romania, but the debate in parliament appeared more playful than serious; perhaps if they can debate such important ethnic issues with laughter, they can avoid the pitfalls of malignant xenophobia.

21. J. C. Scott, *Domination and the Arts of Resistance: Hidden Transcripts* (New Haven, Conn.: Yale University Press, 1990), as expanded upon by Harris, "Reading the Mask."

22. M. Jenkins, "After the Revolution," *Washington City Paper*, 16 January 1995, p. 33.

23. Reported by Ionescu, "Romania Admitted to the Council of Europe," p. 45.

24. During World War II, Romania initially participated in the extermination of Jews (approximately two hundred thousand to three hundred thousand were killed). After 1943, Romania protected the surviving Jews (about three hundred thousand) from Nazi Germany.

25. J. Perlez, "Romanians Vote Today, but Change Isn't Likely," *New York Times*, 3 November 1996, p. 19.

26. "Romanian Leader Takes Office," Associated Press report in *The Daily Progress*, 30 November 1996, p. A6.

13

1. The first song festival was made possible through reforms implemented by the Russian czar Alexander II (1855–1881), which included the abolition of serfdom. Between 1869 and 1896, six national song festivals were held with huge audiences.

2. Taagepera, *Estonia: Return to Independence*.

3. Conference on Security and Cooperation in Europe, "Human Rights and Democratization in Estonia," 1993, p. 9.

4. The song festivals continued to be held every five years during the Soviet period. Thirty thousand singers and two hundred thousand listeners typically attended.

5. Many Russian families immigrated to Estonia after 1945 and eventually made up nearly a third of the country's population. They are mostly concentrated in the northeast of Estonia around the border city of Narva.

6. Most Russians living in Estonia can meet the five-year residency requirement for citizenship. Knowledge of the Estonian language and constitutional and citizenship laws is also required.

There has been criticism in the West of Estonia's citizenship laws. In 1992, the Conference on Security and Cooperation in Europe (CSCE) created a new position, high commissioner on national minorities. The former Dutch foreign minister Max van der Stoel was named the first high commissioner. In 1993, after several visits to Estonia, he declared that charges of human rights abuses there were unfounded. Van der Stoel also put pressure on the Estonian government to enact more liberal laws.

My observation is that most Estonian decision makers do not regard the high commissioner as a friend of Estonia and perceive him as sympathetic to Russian complaints. Visiting the CSCE office in Tallinn in 1996, I got the impression that this organization's perceptions and activities were steeped in realpolitik, without taking into account either Estonians' or Russians' feelings of victimization. CSCE might be better received if it acknowledged the parties' emotional stake in issues of citizenship. Instead, CSCE is viewed as a voice of conscience (critical superego), particularly by Estonians, which taxes the working alliance between CSCE and the Estonian government.

In 1995, Manfred H. Weigandt, who was responsible for the Baltic states in the central European unit of Germany's Federal Ministry for Economic Cooperation in Bonn, came to the conclusion that, in general, Estonian laws do not violate international law ("Russian Minority in Estonia").

7. Since the language examinations for citizenship implemented by the Estonian government were at the center of controversy, it was necessary to learn as much as possible about their content and administration and also to investigate other citizenship and identity card policies. Joyce Neu, a socio-linguist at The Carter Center, observed numerous language examinations and met with the director of the National Language Board, the organization responsible for conducting citizenship exams under the Estonian Ministry of Culture and Education. The National Language Board staff received copies of Dr. Neu's suggestions, and she was later informed that the board had implemented several of them. She was also asked for information on linguistic integration policies in other countries.

8. The perception of threats was echoed in Estonia's physical environment, which was highly contaminated by pollution. Northeast Estonia was considered the most polluted area on the European continent, with dangerous toxins found in air, water, and soil. Industrial and human waste flowed untreated into drinking water supplies, people lived near radioactive waste piles, and pollution-related health problems were common. In addition, many houses and buildings were run-down or boarded up. It was estimated that $4 billion would be needed to rectify Estonia's most serious environmental problems. (Reported in "Them and Us," *Economist,* 17 August 1996, pp. 67–68.)

9. The Estonia project started after our team had gained considerable insight into the Baltic republics. Our team had two meetings, one in Kaunas, Lithuania (1992), and one in Riga, Latvia (1993), prior to the first meeting in Estonia. Influential representatives from all three Baltic countries as well as Russia were present (see Volkan and Harris, "Negotiating a Peaceful Separation" and "Vaccinating the Political Process").

10. During the Soviet period, direct expressions of anger toward the regime were dangerous. Thus the population "learned" and internalized methods of silent (psychosomatic) expressions of anger. After Estonia regained independence,

beginning in 1992, Swedish psychoanalyst Carl-Erik Brattemo began training a group of Estonian psychologists in the theory and techniques of psychoanalytic psychotherapy. In a communication to me in 1994, Brattemo shared his observations of how Estonians' minds, in general, functioned during the initial years of political transition. He wrote that Estonians were suspicious and cautious in dealing with others, whom they perceived as authoritarian. They were prone to judge and advise in terms of right and wrong. Estonian patients had a difficult time with free association in treatment, and therapists needed encouragement to listen to what spontaneously came to their minds. Meanwhile, Brattemo found Estonians hospitable, hungry for information, and full of a great love for songs, especially their national songs.

11. Tulviste, "History Discovered at Home," p. 124.

12. Ibid., p. 125.

13. According to Anatoly Golubovsky (formerly an international scholar at CSMHI who had served as a researcher at the All-Union Institute of Art Research of the Soviet Ministry of Culture), many young Russian scholars followed the work of Yury Lotman, a professor at Tartu who studied semiotics and structural analysis. Quoting Lotman's writings was common among those who sought to identify with the liberal minded.

14. On November 19, 1996, Russian and Estonian representatives agreed in Moscow to finalize terms for border sections of the Peipsi and Teploye lakes. Estonia backed off from its previous insistence on the border described in the 1920 Tartu Peace Treaty. This agreement brought out new anxieties. Russians believed that the willingness of Estonians to resolve controversial border issues was prompted by their wish to join NATO, since Estonia's inclusion was impossible as long as it had border problems. Russians were objecting vigorously to the inclusion of any Baltic republic in NATO, a potential development that they perceived as a danger to their security, and humiliating as well. In early 1997, the Estonian government officially agreed to accept the border, while the Russian government did not.

15. The following were key participants in the CSMHI/Carter Center dialogues in Estonia. Those with government responsibilities participated on an unofficial basis.

Estonians: Arnold Rüütel, former Estonian president and runner-up in the 1996 presidential elections; current or former parliamentarians Klara Hallik, Toomas Alatalu, Arvo Haug, Mati Hint, and Jaan Kaplinski; academicians Priit Järve, Peeter Vares, Mati Heidmets, and Mare Haab; psychiatrist Arno Aadamsoo; and psychologist Endel Talvik.

Estonian Russians (both citizens and noncitizens): Sergei Issakov, a professor at Tartu University and one of six Estonian Russians in the parliament; Alexei Semionov and Iliya Nikiforov, past and current chairman of the Russian Representatives Assembly, respectively; and Vladimir Homyakov and Sergei Gorokhov, both from Narva.

From Russia: Alexandre Trofimov, Russian ambassador to Estonia; Yuri Voevoda, until 1996, vice chairman of the Committee on CIS Affairs and Relations with Compatriots of the State Duma of the Russian Federation; Aivars Lezdinysh, then a member of the Russian Duma; Viacheslav Bakhmin, then director of the Department of International Humanitarian and Cultural Cooperation, Ministry of Foreign Affairs of the Russian Federation; Andrei A. Zakharov, first deputy director general of the Foundation for the Development of Parliamentarism in Russia; Valeriy Fadeev and Vera Gracheva, experts assigned to the Foreign Ministry; and academicians Alexander Obolonski, Zoya Zarubina, and Stanislav Roschin.

From Lithuania: Halina Kobeckaite, the Lithuanian ambassador to Estonia.

From CSMHI/Carter Center: Psychoanalysts Maurice Apprey and myself; psychiatrists Demetrios A. Julius, Gregory B. Saathoff, and J. Anderson Thomson Jr.; psychologist Carrie E. Schaffer; nurse/mediator Margie S. Howell; former diplomats Richard T. Arndt, Ambassador W. Nathaniel Howell, Joseph V. Montville, Harold H. Saunders, and Yuri V. Urbanovich; historian Norman Itzkowitz; socio-linguist Joyce Neu; environmental scientist George J. Moein; and CSMHI staff Joy R. Boissevain and Bruce A. Edwards.

16. The last active Russian military personnel pulled out of Estonia in September 1995, and the Paldiski base was finally closed. A month later, I visited Paldiski for a second time. Some Russians, all noncitizens, still lived there, and some Estonians had moved into empty barracks. Although some of Paldiski had been cleaned, it remained a hot spot for what it had represented and would represent in the future. The city council consisted of Estonians with a heightened sense of patriotism regarding Estonia's control of the base. A small detail of Estonian soldiers guarded the harbor, though it held no ships. Some Estonians envisioned Paldiski as an important NATO base if Estonia joined the treaty organization.

17. My understanding of small-group dynamics has roots in a teaching method called "the fieldwork method," which I developed in the late 1960s and early 1970s at the Department of Psychiatry in the University of Virginia's School of Medicine (see Volkan and Hawkins, "Field-work Case in Teaching Clinical Psychiatry," "Fieldwork Method of Teaching," and "Learning Group"). The teaching format consisted of a small group of about eight psychiatric residents who met regularly with me (the teacher/leader) and occasionally with my consultants for over 225 hours per year. The small groups observed (behind a one-way mirror) all the sessions of a patient's treatment conducted by one of the residents. This fieldwork involved simultaneous discussion with the leader, which helped the residents gain knowledge on the spot. The group's learning was a *process* and went through expected phases. I repeated this program for five consecutive classes of residents.

The experience of guiding the psychodynamics of these non-patient resident groups was essential to coordinating the dialogue groups in Estonia two decades later. As leader, I had developed techniques to deal with anxiety, made interpretations when residents became reservoirs of patients' projections, helped to combine intellectual understanding with emotional experience, dealt with resistances to learning, encouraged curiosity, and acted as a role model. In dealing with these learning groups, the aim was not to provide therapy for the participants, but to help them open new channels of conceptualizing what they were observing.

Other information about small-group dynamics comes from studies of patients in group therapy. Our team members, especially those in the psychological fields, have also benefited from the pioneering works of psychoanalysts such as Foulkes and Anthony, *Group Psychotherapy*; Bion, *Experiences in Groups*; and Abse, *Clinical Notes on Group Analytic Psychotherapy*.

Bion's studies, for example, of small working groups indicate that groups operate on a mature level whenever their members devote themselves to the performance of a specific task—they are then properly called a work group. However, when a small group cannot function in a mature way and regression occurs, it is prone to behave according to specific unconscious fantasies. The group members may, for example, increase their suspicions of others and perceive the leader as an omnipotent savior. Without a task that has been agreed on either tacitly or directly, a work group cannot be established, and the small group is no more than a collection of individuals. The leader of a work group must maintain effective contact with the real world, for without it he or she will contribute to the group members' fantasies.

While Bion's small-group dynamics are useful for therapy groups of eight to twelve people who meet to improve themselves with the help of a group leader, our Estonia meetings had a different purpose. They aimed to improve the members' understanding of their large-group conflicts. Unlike the learning or therapy groups, the Estonian dialogue groups were influenced by multiple leaders, which changed their psychodynamics. Each dialogue group contained opposing subsections (Estonians, Russians, and Russians living in Estonia), each with its own proclaimed or implicit leader. In addition, each small group was led by American facilitators. Group members also felt the influence of political leaders who were not present at the meetings.

Because the principal focus was on the psychology of large-group interaction as reenacted during the dialogues, small-group dynamics pertaining to the participants as individuals were only taken into consideration when they got in the way. To create a work group during the dialogues required attention to the way in which members wore their ethnic garments and the kinds of projections they made onto others' garments. When participants spoke about themselves, facilitators helped show how these personal stories reflected the history of the groups and helped illuminate the emotional investment in events and mental representations. When group history is thus taken to a personal level, it can be more intimately shared, which in turn helps loosen the rigidified positions of large groups.

In Estonia as elsewhere, when facilitators are involved in ongoing psychopolitical dialogues with opposing groups, they become targets of group members' projections. When this happens, facilitators who are also mental health professionals have an advantage because they are accustomed to receiving and dealing with their patients' projections (transference). Countertransference—irrational expectations on the part of the facilitators—may also surface. Rubbing elbows with politically important individuals, for example, may give the facilitators a sense of undeserved omnipotence. We are cognizant of this phenomenon and after decades of work in the field are less likely to succumb to countertransference responses.

18. Sandler, "Background of Safety."

19. This idea of mixing blood is reminiscent of the Armenians' refusing to accept Azerbaijani blood and the Serbs' denial of the existence of Muslim blood in the offspring of Muslim women they had raped. Large groups in conflict emphasize the purity of blood, and there is a psychological reason for doing so. During a child's developmental years, when his body image is evolving, he finds it more difficult to identify symbols for blood than for visible exterior aspects of the body (see Chasseguet-Smirgel, "Blood and Nation"). Through injuries that bleed, children become aware that there is something alive under their skin. As they develop their identities and recognize psychological borders and internal uniqueness, their sense of self, also alive within them, becomes symbolically intertwined with blood. Blood and identity become linked. I once knew a schizophrenic youngster who was told that he was adopted. In searching for where he came from, he had fantasies of various parents. He would repeatedly cut himself delicately and examine his blood under a microscope as if there he could find his true identity. The Estonians' concern about assimilation and their fear of mixed blood reflects a fear of diluting identity.

20. Kaplinski, *I Am Spring in Tartu*, p. 19.

21. See also Apprey, "Heuristic Steps for Negotiating Ethno-National Conflicts."

22. This situation is like using play in child psychoanalysis: the child and the psychoanalyst play with toys and symbolically re-create the child's mental conflicts, and then work to remove them.

23. Julius ("Practice of Track Two Diplomacy," pp. 203–204) described the evolving psychodynamics of the American Psychiatric Association–sponsored Arab-Israeli dialogue series.

24. Saunders and Slim, "Dialogue to Change Conflictual Relationships."

25. Problems between Estonia and Russia also surfaced in regard to religion. In 1993, the Estonian government designated the Estonian branch of the Orthodox Church as the legal successor to the pre-1940 Orthodox Church and hence the rightful owner of all church property. The Estonian branch also proclaimed its alliance to Constantinople (Istanbul) instead of Moscow. Russian congrega-

tions continued to attend their churches. In 1996, Boris Yeltsin sent a message to the Estonian president Lennart-Georg Meri demanding firm guarantees that parishes loyal to Moscow would retain their property. As of late 1996, Yeltsin's demand had not yet been responded to in a positive way.

26. In 1996, the non-Estonian (mostly Russian) population in Estonia could be divided into five categories: citizens through naturalization since 1991 (about 60,000); current applicants for citizenship in Estonia (about 80,000); current applicants for citizenship in countries other than Estonia (unknown number); citizens of other countries (about 80,000 Russians); and undecided (about 330,000 registered for temporary residence and 50,000 not registered). The most problematic categories were the last two.

27. The Estonian team carrying out CSMHI projects in Mustamäe, Klooga, and Mustvee is headed by Endel Talvik, a psychologist, and Gulnara Ishkuzina-Roll, an environmental policy specialist.

28. A society's internalization of a political system has not been discussed much in psychoanalytic literature, with the exception of some passages in Erik H. Erikson's work. Observing at close range how cultures, such as that created by the Soviets, have shaped people's behavior patterns and styles of thinking and communicating points to a need to study this phenomenon more closely.

29. Scientific methods to measure the effectiveness of unofficial diplomacy are rare. Psychologist Carrie Schaffer, a member of our team, is currently working on a test to demonstrate the perception of a group member's ethnic identity as well as that of members of an opposing ethnic group. This psychological test is being administered to participants in each of the three Estonian communities and a control group of Estonians and Russians living in Estonia. By measuring changes in ethnic identity perception, we hope quantitatively to illustrate changes in large-group relationships.

AFTERWORD

1. Petschauer, "Diplomacy of Vamık Volkan." Petschauer, who grew up in South Tirol, offered this example of ethnic tension reduction when he interviewed me for this article in 1995.

2. S. Ramphal, "Global Governance," the Second Global Security Lecture, Cambridge University, 5 June 1995, p. 11.

3. Ibid.

BIBLIOGRAPHY

Abse, D. W. *Clinical Notes on Group-Analytic Psychotherapy*. Charlottesville: University Press of Virginia, 1974.

Abse, D. W., and L. Jessner. "The Psychodynamics of Leadership." In *Excellence and Leadership in Democracy*, ed. S. Graubard and G. Holton, pp. 693–710. New York: Columbia University Press, 1961.

Adıvar, A. Adnan. *Osmanlı Türklerinde İlim* (Science among the Ottoman Turks). Istanbul: Remzi Kitabevi, 1970.

Ainslie, R. C. *No Dancin' in Anson: An American Story of Race and Social Change*. Northvale, N.J.: Jason Aronson, 1995.

Allcock, J. B. "Kosovo: The Heavenly and the Earthly Crown." In *Pilgrimage in Popular Culture*, ed. I. Reader and T. Walter, pp. 157–178. London: Macmillan Press, 1993.

Allen, B. *Rape Warfare: The Hidden Genocide in Bosnia-Herzegovina and Croatia*. Minneapolis: University of Minnesota Press, 1996.

Apprey, M. "The African-American Experience: Forced Immigration and Transgenerational Trauma." *Mind and Human Interaction* 4 (1993): 70–75.

———. "Broken Lines, Public Memory and Absent Memory: Jewish and African Americans Coming to Terms with Racism." *Mind and Human Interaction* 7 (1996): 139–149.

———. "Heuristic Steps for Negotiating Ethno-National Conflicts: Vignettes from Estonia." *New Literary History* 27 (1996): 199–212.

Arjomand, S. A. "Unity and Diversity in Islamic Fundamentalism." In *Fundamentalism Comprehended*, ed. Martin E. Marty and R. Scott Appleby, pp. 179–198. Chicago: University of Chicago Press, 1995.

Arndt, R. T. "New Diplomacy in the Post-Imperial World." *Mind and Human Interaction* 6 (1995): 144–148.

Auden, W. H. "The Sea and the Mirror." In *The Faber Book of Twentieth Century Verse*, ed. J. Heath-Stubbs and D. Wright, p. 36. Winchester, Mass.: Faber & Faber, 1947.

Baggally, J. W. *Greek Historical Folksongs*. Chicago: Argonaut, 1968.

Bauer, O. "Die Nationalitätenfrage und die sozialdemokratie." 1907. Reprint, Vienna: Europaverlag, 1975.

Bernard, V., P. Ottenberg, and F. Redl. "Dehumanization: A Composite Psychological Defense in Relation to Modern War." In *Sanctions for Evil: Sources of Social Destructiveness*, ed. N. Sanford and C. Comstock, pp. 102–124. San Francisco: Jossey-Bass, 1973.

Bion, W. R. *Experiences in Groups*. London: Tavistock Publications, 1961.

Blos, P. *The Adolescent Passage*. New York: International Universities Press, 1979.

Bodine, B. "Saddam's Siege of Embassy Kuwait: A Personal Journal, 1990." In *Embassies under Siege: Personal Accounts by Diplomats on the Front Line*, ed. J. G. Sullivan, pp. 113–131. Washington, D.C.: Brassey's, 1995.

Bohlen, C. E. *A Witness to History*. New York: Norton, 1973.

Boyer, L. B. "On Man's Need to Have Enemies: A Psychoanalytic Perspective." *Journal of Psychoanalytic Anthropology* 9 (1986): 101–120.

Brenner, C. *The Mind in Conflict*. New York: International Universities Press, 1983.

Burns, J. M. *Leadership*. New York: Harper Torchbooks, 1978.

Butler, T. "Yugoslavia Mon Amour." *Mind and Human Interaction* 4: (1993): 120–128.

Chasseguet-Smirgel, J. "Blood and Nation." *Mind and Human Interaction* 7 (1996): 31–36.

Cirić, A. "From Partisans to Security Service: The Short and Inglorious History of the Yugoslav People's Army." *Balkan War Report*, 17 November 1993, pp. 6–7.

Clark, R. "Patterns in the Lives of ETA Members." *Terrorism* 6 (1983): 423–454.

Cohen, L. J. *Broken Bonds: Yugoslavia's Disintegration and Balkan Politics in Transition*. Boulder, Colo.: Westview, 1995.

Cohen, R. "Ethnicity Problems and Focus on Anthropology." *Annual Review of Anthropology* 7 (1978): 374–403.

Cole, F-C. *The People of Malaysia*. New York: D. Van Nostrand, 1960.

Committee of International Relations, Group Advancement of Psychiatry. *Us and Them: The Psychology of Ethnonationalism*. New York: Brunner/Mazel, 1987.

Des Forges, A. "Burundi: Failed Coup or Creeping Coup." *Current History* 93 (1994): 203–207.

De Vos, G. "Ethnic Pluralism: Conflict and Accommodation." In *Ethnic Identity: Cultural Continuities and Change*, ed. G. De Vos and L. Komanucci-Ross, pp. 5–41. Palo Alto, Calif.: Mayfield, 1975.

Eissler, K. R. "Notes upon Defects of Ego Structure in Schizophrenia." *International Journal of Psycho-Analysis* 35 (1954): 141–146.

Emde, R. N. "Positive Emotions for Psychoanalytic Theory: Surprises from Infancy Research and New Directions." *Journal of American Psychoanalytic Association* (supplement) 39 (1991): 5–44.

Emde, R. N., and R. J. Harmon. "Endogenous and Exogenous Smiling Systems in Early Infancy." *Journal of the American Academy of Child Psychiatry* 11 (1972): 177–200.

Emmert, T. A. *Serbian Golgotha: Kosovo, 1389.* New York: Columbia University Press, 1990.

Erikson, E. H. "Ontogeny of Ritualization." In *Psychoanalysis: A General Psychology,* ed. R. M. Lowenstein, L. M. Newman, M. Schur, and A. J. Solnit, pp. 601–621. New York: International Universities Press, 1966.

———. "The Problem of Ego Identification." *Journal of the American Psychoanalytic Association* 4 (1956): 56–121.

Erikson, K. T. "Loss of Communality at Buffalo Creek." *American Journal of Psychiatry* 133 (1976): 302–325.

Evlambios, G. *The Amaranth: The Roses of Hellas Reborn: Folk Poems of the Modern Greeks* (in Russian and Greek). Saint Petersburg: Academy of Sciences, 1843; Athens: Notis Karavias, 1973.

Fine, J. "The Medieval and Ottoman Roots of Modern Bosnian Society." In *The Muslims of Bosnia-Herzegovina: Their Historic Development from Middle Ages to the Dissolution of Yugoslavia,* ed. M. Pinson, pp. 1–21. Cambridge, Mass.: Harvard University Press, 1994.

Fornari, F. *The Psychoanalysis of War.* Trans. A. Pfeifer. 1966. Bloomington: Indiana University Press, 1975.

Foulkes, S. H., and E. J. Anthony. *Group Psychotherapy.* London: Penguin Books, 1957.

Freud, A. "The Ego and the Mechanisms of Defense." In *The Writings of Anna Freud.* Vol. 2. 1936. Reprint, New York: International Universities Press, 1966.

Freud, S. *The Origins of Psychoanalysis: Letters to Wilhelm Fliess, Drafts and Notes: 1887–1902,* ed. M. Bonaparte, A. Freud, and E. Kris. 1887–1902. Reprint, New York: Basic Books, 1954.

———. "Address to the Society of B'nai B'rith." 1926. In vol. 20 of *Standard Edition.* London: Hogarth Press, 1964.

———. "Fetishism." 1927. In vol. 21 of *Standard Edition.* London: Hogarth Press, 1961.

———. "The Future of an Illusion." 1927. In vol. 21 of *Standard Edition.* London: Hogarth Press, 1964.

———. "Group Psychology and the Analysis of the Ego." 1921. In vol. 18 of *Standard Edition.* London: Hogarth Press, 1955.

———. "Mourning and Melancholia." 1917. In vol. 14 of *Standard Edition.* London: Hogarth Press, 1957.

———. "Taboo of Virginity." 1917. In vol. 13 of *Standard Edition.* London: Hogarth Press, 1961.

———. "Three Essays on the Theory of Sexuality." 1905. In vol. 7 of *Standard Edition*. London: Hogarth Press, 1961.

———. "Totem and Taboo." 1913. In vol. 13 of *Standard Edition*. London: Hogarth Press, 1961.

———. "Why War?" 1932. In vol. 22 of *Standard Edition*. London: Hogarth Press, 1964.

Gallager, T. "Ethnic Tension in Cluj." *RFE/RL Research Report* 2 (1993): 27–33.

———. "Vatra Româneasca and Resurgent Nationalism in Romania." *Ethnic and Racial Studies* 15 (1992): 570–598.

Gilberg, T. "Religion and Nationalism in Romania." In *Religion and Nationalism in Soviet and East European Politics*, ed. Pedro Ramet, pp. 170–186. Durham, N.C.: Duke University Press, 1984.

Gittler, J. B. "Toward Defining an Ethnic Minority." *International Journal of Group Tensions* 7 (1977): 4–19.

Glass, J. *Private Terror/Public Life: Psychosis and the Politics of Community*. Ithaca, N.Y.: Cornell University Press, 1989.

Grier, W. H., and P. M. Cobbs. *Black Rage*. New York: Basic Books, 1968.

Gutman, R. *A Witness to Genocide: The 1993 Pulitzer Prize–winning Dispatches on the "Ethnic Cleansing" of Bosnia*. New York: Maxwell MacMillian International, 1993.

Halman, T. H. "Istanbul." In *A Last Lullaby*, pp. 8–9. Merrick, N.Y.: Cross Cultural Communications, 1992.

Harris, M. "Reading the Mask: Hidden Transcripts and Human Interaction." *Mind and Human Interaction* 5 (1994): 155–164.

Hatiboğlu, M. T. *Bosna'ya farklı bir bakış* (A different look at Bosnia). Ankara, Turkey: Selvi Yayınları, 1996.

Herzfeld, M. *Ours Once More: Folklore, Ideology, and the Making of Modern Greece*. New York: Pella, 1986.

Hoffman, V. J. "Muslim Fundamentalists: Psychosocial Profiles." In *Fundamentalism Comprehended*, ed. Martin E. Marty and R. Scott Appleby, pp. 199–230. Chicago: University of Chicago Press, 1995.

Holden, M. "Bargaining and Command by Heads of U.S. Government Departments." *The Social Science Journal* 25 (1988): 255–276.

Horowitz, D. L. *Ethnic Groups in Conflict*. Berkeley: University of California Press, 1985.

Howell, W. N. "The Evil That Men Do . . . ': Societal Effects of the Iraqi Occupation of Kuwait." *Mind and Human Interaction* 6 (1995): 150–169.

———. "Tragedy, Trauma . . . and Triumph: Reclaiming Integrity and Initiative from Victimization." *Mind and Human Interaction* 4 (1993): 111–119.

Ionescu, D. "Romania Admitted to the Council of Europe." *RFE/RL Research Report* 2 (1993): 40–45.

Itzkowitz, N. "On the Ottomanization of the Soviet Union." *Mind and Human Interaction* 2 (1990):13–15.

———. *Ottoman Empire and Islamic Tradition*. New York: Alfred A. Knopf, 1972.

Jacobson, E. *The Self and the Object World.* New York: International Universities Press, 1964.

Julius, D. A. "The Practice of Track Two Diplomacy in the Arab-Israeli Conferences." In *Unofficial Diplomacy at Work.* Vol. 2 of *The Psychodynamics of International Relationships*, ed. V. D. Volkan, J. V. Montville, and D. A. Julius, pp. 193–205. Lexington, Mass.: Lexington Books, 1991.

Kakar, S. *The Colors of Violence: Cultural Identities, Religion, and Conflict.* Chicago: University of Chicago Press, 1996.

Kaplan, R. D. *Balkan Ghosts: A Journey Through History.* New York: Vintage Books, 1993.

Kaplinski, J. *I Am Spring in Tartu and Other Poems*, ed. L. P. A. Kitchen. Vancouver, B.C.: Laurel Press, 1991.

Kazantzakis, N. *Report to Greco.* Trans. P. A. Bien. New York: Simon & Schuster, 1965.

Kernberg, O. F. *Borderline Conditions and Pathological Narcissism.* New York: Jason Aronson, 1975.

Khrushchev, N. *Khrushchev Remembers.* Boston: Little, Brown, 1970.

Kinross, L. *The Ottoman Centuries: The Rise and Fall of the Turkish Empire.* New York: Morrow Quill Paperbacks, 1977.

Kohn, H. *Idea of Nationalism.* New York: Macmillan, 1944.

Kracke, W. H. *Force and Persuasion: Leadership in an Amazon Society.* Chicago: University of Chicago Press, 1978.

Kramer, M. "Hizbullah: The Calculus of Jihad." In *Fundamentalisms and the State: Remaking Politics, Economics, and Militance*, ed. Martin E. Marty and R. Scott Appleby, pp. 539–556. Chicago: University of Chicago Press, 1993.

———. "The Moral Logic of Hizballah." In *Origins of Terrorism*, ed. W. Reich, pp. 131–157. Cambridge: Cambridge University Press, 1990.

Kubie, L. S. "The Outgoing of Racial Prejudice." *Journal of Nervous and Mental Disease* 141 (1965): 265–273.

Lazarovich-Hrebelianovich, P., and E. Calhoun. *The Serbian People.* Vol. 1. New York: Scribner's, 1910.

Lebedeva, M. "Psychological Aspects of Ethnic Conflict and the Problem of Negotiation in the USSR." *Mind and Human Interaction* 3 (1991): 10–11.

Le Bon, G. *The Crowd.* 1895. Reprint, New York: Penguin, 1977.

Lewis, B. *The Assassins: A Radical Sect in Islam.* London: Weidenfeld and Nicholson, 1967.

Lewis, R. *Everyday Life in Ottoman Turkey.* London: B. T. Batsford, 1971.

Lifton, R. J., and E. Olson. "The Human Meaning of Total Disaster: The Buffalo Creek Experience." *Psychiatry* 39 (1976):1–18.

Lind, J. E. "The Dream as a Simple Wish-Fulfillment in the Negro." *Psychoanalytic Review* 1 (1914): 295–300.

Loewenberg, P. *Fantasy and Reality in History.* New York: Oxford University Press, 1995.

———. "The Psychological Reality of Nationalism: Between Community and Fantasy." *Mind and Human Interaction* 5 (1994): 6–18.

Lomarsky, L. E. "The Political Significance of Terrorism." In *Violence, Terrorism and Justice*, ed. R. G. Frey and C. W. Morris, pp. 86–115. Cambridge: Cambridge University Press, 1991.

MacFarlane, N. S., L. Minear, and S. D. Shenfield. *Armed Conflict in Georgia: A Case Study in Humanitarian Action and Peacekeeping*. Providence, R.I.: Thomas J. Watson Jr. Institute for International Studies, 1996.

Mahler, M. *On Human Symbiosis and the Vicissitudes of Individuation*. New York: International Universities Press, 1968.

Malkki, L. H. *Purity and Exile: Violence, Memory and National Cosmology among Hutu Refugees in Tanzania*. Chicago: University of Chicago Press, 1995.

Mango, A. "Greece and Turkey: Unfriendly Allies." *The World Today* 43 (1987): 144–147.

Manning, S. W. "Cultural and Value Factors Affecting the Negroes' Use of Agency Services." *Journal of Social Work* 5 (1960): 3–13.

Markides, K. C. *The Rise and Fall of the Cyprus Republic*. New Haven, Conn.: Yale University Press, 1977.

Marković, M. S. "The Secret of Kosovo." Trans. C. Kramer. In *Landmarks in Serbian Culture and History*, ed. V. D. Mihailovich, pp. 111–131. Pittsburgh, Pa.: Serb National Federation, 1983.

Mazumdar, S. "For Rama and Hindutva: Women and Right Wing Mobilization in Contemporary India." *Committee on South Asian Women Bulletin* 8 (1993): 2–8.

Millas, H. "Türk edebiyatında Yunan imajı: Yakup Kadri Karaosmanoğlu" (The Greek image in Turkish literature: Yakup Kadri Karaosmanoğlu). *Toplum ve Bilim* 51 and 52 (1991): 129–152.

Mitscherlich, A. "Psychoanalysis and Aggression of Large Groups." *International Journal of Psycho-Analysis* 52 (1971): 161–167.

Montville, J. "The Psychological Roots of Ethnic and Sectarian Terrorism." In *Concepts and Theories*. Vol. 1 of *The Psychodynamics of International Relationships*, ed. V. D. Volkan, D. A. Julius, and J. V. Montville, pp. 163–180. Lexington, Mass.: Lexington Books, 1990.

Moses, R., and Y. Cohen. "An Israeli View." In *Persistent Shadows of the Holocaust: The Meaning to Those Not Directly Affected*, ed. R. Moses, pp. 119–153. Madison, Conn.: International Universities Press, 1993.

Murphy, R. F. "Intergroup Hostility and Social Cohesion." *American Anthropologist* 59 (1957): 1018–1035.

Myers, H. J., and L. Yochelson. "Color Denial in the Negro." *Psychiatry* 11 (1948): 39–46.

Nnoli, O. *Ethnic Conflict in Africa*. Dakar, Senegal: Codesria, 1989.

Öcalan, Abdullah, and Yalçın Küçük. *Kürt Bahçesinde Sözleşi* (Dialogue in a Kurdish garden). Ankara, Turkey: Başak Yayınları, 1993.

Orwell, G. "Notes on Nationalism." *Collected Essays, Journalism and Letters of George Orwell*. Vol. 3, ed. S. Orwell and I. Angus, pp. 361–380. 1945. Reprint, New York: Harcourt Brace Jovanovich, 1971.

Parens, H. *The Development of Aggression in Early Life*. New York: Jason Aronson, 1979.

Parin, P. "Open Wounds: Ethnopsychoanalytic Reflections on the Wars in the Former Yugoslavia." In *Mass Rape: The War Against Women in Bosnia-Herzegovina*, ed. A. Stiglmayer, pp. 35–53. Lincoln: University of Nebraska Press, 1994.

Pennington, A., and P. Levi. *Marko the Prince: Serbo-Croat Heroic Songs*. London: Duckworth, 1984.

Peterson, W. "Concepts of Ethnicity." In *Harvard Encyclopedia of Ethnic Groups*, ed. S. Thermstrom, pp. 234–242. Cambridge, Mass.: Harvard University Press, 1980.

Peto, A. "On Affect Control." *International Journal of Psycho-Analysis* 49 (1968): 471–473.

Petschauer, P. "The Diplomacy of Vamık Volkan." *Clio's Psyche* 2, no.1 (1995): 34–39.

Pinderhughes, C. A. "The Origins of Racism." *International Journal of Psychiatry* 8 (1969): 934–941.

———. "Paired Differential Bonding in Biological, Psychological, and Social Systems." *American Journal of Psychiatry* 139 (1982): 5–14.

Politis, N. G. *Introductory Lecture for the Class in Hellenic Mythology* (in Greek). Athens: Aion, 1882.

———. "Khelidhonisma" (Swallow song). *Neoellinkia Analekta* 1 (1872): 354–368.

Pollock, G. H. *The Mourning-Liberation Process*. Vols. 1 and 2. Madison, Conn.: International Universities Press, 1989.

Post, J. M. "Terrorist Psycho-Logic: Terrorist Behavior as a Product of Psychological Forces." In *Origins of Terrorism: Psychologies, Ideologies, Theologies, States of Mind*, ed. W. Reich. Cambridge: Cambridge University Press, 1990.

Reich, W. "Understanding Terrorist Behavior: The Limits and Opportunities of Psychological Inquiry." In *Origins of Terrorism*, ed. W. Reich, pp. 261–284. Cambridge: Cambridge University Press, 1990.

Roberts, S. *Who We Are: A Portrait of America*. New York: Times Books, 1993.

Saathoff, G. B. "In the Halls of Mirrors: One Kuwaiti's Captive Memories." *Mind and Human Interaction* 6 (1995): 170–178.

———. "Kuwait's Children: Identity in the Shadow of the Storm." *Mind and Human Interaction* 7 (1996): 181–191.

Sandler, J. "The Background of Safety." *International Journal of Psycho-Analysis* 41 (1960): 352–356.

Sandler, J., and A. Freud. "Discussions in the Hampstead Index of the Ego and the Mechanisms of Defence." *Journal of American Psychoanalytic Association* (supplement) 31 (1983): 19–146.

Saunders, H., and R. Slim. "Dialogue to Change Conflictual Relationships." In *Higher Education Exchange*, pp. 43–56. Dayton, Ohio: Kettering Foundation, 1994.

Schwoebel, R. *The Shadow of the Crescent: The Renaissance Image of the Turk (1453–1517)*. New York: St. Martin's Press, 1967.

Scruggs, J. *To Heal a Nation*. New York: Harper & Row, 1985.

Seifert, R. "War and Rape, a Preliminary Analysis." In *Mass Rape: The War Against Women in Bosnia-Herzegovina*, ed. A. Stiglmayer, pp. 54–72. Lincoln: University of Nebraska Press, 1994.

Shafir, M. "Best Selling Spy Novels Seek to Rehabilitate Romanian Securitate." *RFE/RL Research Report* 2 (1993):15–18.

Shapiro, H. L. *The Jewish People: A Biological History*. Paris: UNESCO, 1960.

Sollenberg, M., and P. Wallensteen. "Major Armed Conflict." *SIPRI Yearbook 1996*. Oxford: Oxford University Press, 1996.

Spitz, R. *The First Year of Life*. New York: International Universities Press, 1965.

Stein, H. F. "The International and Group Milieu of Ethnicity: Identifying Generic Group Dynamic Issues." *Canadian Review of Studies in Nationalism* 17 (1990): 107–130.

———. "On Professional Allegiance in the Study of Political Psychology." *Political Psychology* 7 (1986): 245–253.

Stiglmayer, A. "The Rapes of Bosnia-Herzegovina." In *Mass Rape: The War Against Women in Bosnia-Herzegovina*, ed. A. Stiglmayer, pp. 82–169. Lincoln: University of Nebraska Press, 1994.

Stone, M. H. "Murder." In *Narcissistic Personality Disorder*, ed. O. F. Kernberg. The Psychiatric Clinics of North America, vol. 12, pp. 643–651. Philadelphia: W. B. Saunders Company, 1989.

Sugar, P. F. *Southeastern Europe under Ottoman Rule, 1354–1804*. Seattle: University of Washington Press, 1977.

Taagepera, R. *Estonia: Return to Independence*. Boulder, Colo.: Westview Press, 1993.

Tähkä, V. "Dealing with Object Loss." *Scandinavian Psychoanalytic Review* 7 (1984): 13–33.

Thomson, J. A., M. Harris, V. Volkan, and B. Edwards. "The Psychology of Western European Neo-Racism." *International Journal on Group Rights* 3 (1995): 1–30.

Tulviste, P. "History Taught at School Means History Discovered at Home: The Case of Estonia." *European Journal of Psychology and Education* 9 (1994): 121–126.

Vitols, M. M., H. G. Walters, and M. H. Keeler. "Hallucinations and Delusions in White and Negro Schizophrenics." *American Journal of Psychiatry* 120 (1963): 472–476.

Volkan, K. "The Vietnam War Memorial." *Mind and Human Interaction* 3 (1992): 73–77.

Volkan, V. D. *Cyprus—War and Adaptation: A Psychoanalytic History of Two Ethnic Groups in Conflict*. Charlottesville: University Press of Virginia, 1979.

———. *Linking Objects and Linking Phenomena: A Study of Forms, Symptoms, Metapsychology, and Therapy of Complicated Mourning*. New York: International Universities Press, 1981.

———. *The Need to Have Enemies and Allies: From Clinical Practice to International Relationships*. Northvale, N.J.: Jason Aronson, 1988.

———. *Primitive Internalized Object Relations*. New York: International Universities Press, 1976.

Volkan, V. D., and G. Ast. *Spectrum des Narziβmus*. Göttingen: Vanderhoeck & Ruprecht, 1994.

Volkan, V. D., and M. Harris. "Negotiating a Peaceful Separation: A Psychopolitical Analysis of Current Relationships between Russia and the Baltic Republics." *Mind and Human Interaction* 4 (1992): 20–39.

———. "The Psychodynamics of Ethnic Terrorism." *International Journal on Group Rights* 3 (1995): 145–159.

———. "Vaccinating the Political Process: A Second Psychopolitical Analysis of Relationships between Russia and the Baltic States." *Mind and Human Interaction* 4 (1993): 169–190.

Volkan, V. D., and D. R. Hawkins. "A Field-work Case in the Teaching of Clinical Psychiatry." *Psychiatry in Medicine* 2 (1971): 160–176.

———. "The 'Fieldwork' Method of Teaching and Learning Clinical Psychiatry." *Comprehensive Psychiatry* 12 (1971): 103–114.

———. "The Learning Group." *American Journal of Psychiatry* 128 (1972): 1121–1126.

Volkan, V. D., and N. Itzkowitz. *The Immortal Atatürk: A Psychobiography*. Chicago: University of Chicago Press, 1984.

———. " 'Istanbul, Not Constantinople': The Western View of 'the Turk.' " *Mind and Human Interaction* 4 (1993): 129–134.

———. *Turks and Greeks: Neighbours in Conflict*. Cambridgeshire, England: Eothen Press, 1994.

Volkan, V. D., and E. Zintl. *Life after Loss: The Lessons of Grief*. New York: Scribner's, 1993.

von Hammer-Purgstall, R. J. *Histoire de l'empire Ottoman*. 18 vols. Trans. J. J. Hellert. Paris: Ballitard Barthes, 1835–1843.

Vulliamy, E. *Season in Hell: Understanding Bosnia's War*. New York: St. Martin's Press, 1994.

Wallensteen, P., and K. Axell. "Major Armed Conflicts," *SIPRI Yearbook 1994*. Oxford: Oxford University Press, 1994.

Weber, M. *Wirtschaft und Gesellschaft* (Economy and society). 2 vols. Tübingen, Germany: J. C. B. Mohr, 1923.

Weigandt, M. H. "The Russian Minority in Estonia." *International Journal on Group Rights* 3 (1995): 109–143.

Weinberg C. "Terrorists and Terrorism: Have We Reached a Crossroad?" *Mind and Human Interaction* 3 (1992): 77–82.

Wilkerson, C. B. "Destructiveness of Myths." *American Journal of Psychiatry* 126 (1970): 1087–1092.

Williams, R. M., and C. M. Parkes. "Psychosocial Effects of Disaster: Birth Rate in Aberfan." *British Medical Journal* 2 (1975): 303–304.

Winnicott, D. W. "Transitional Objects and Transitional Phenomena." *International Journal of Psycho-Analysis* 34 (1953): 89–97.

Young, K. *The Greek Passion: A Study in People and Politics.* London: J. M. Dent and Sons, 1969.

Zaleznik, A. "Charismatic and Consensus Leaders: A Psychological Comparison." In *The Irrational Executive*, ed. M. F. R. Kets de Vries, pp. 112–132. New York: International Universities Press, 1984.

Zamblios, S. "Some Philosophical Researches on the Modern Greek Language" (in Greek). *Pandora* 7 (1856): 369–380, 484–494.

———. *Whence the Vulgar and Traghoudho? Thoughts Concerning Hellenic Poetry.* Athens: P. Soutsas and A. Ktenas, 1859.

Zimmerman, Z. D. *Serbian Folk Poetry: Ancient Legends, Romantic Songs.* Columbus, Ohio: Kosovo Publishing Co., 1986.

INDEX